3rd Edition

Pre-intermediate

MARKET LEADER

Business English Teacher's Resource Book

Bill Mascull

Introduction

Market Leader is an extensive business English course designed to bring the real world of international business into the language-teaching classroom. It has been developed in association with the *Financial Times*, one of the world's leading sources of professional information, to ensure the maximum range and authenticity of international business content.

1 Course aims

In addition to new authentic reading texts and listening material, the Third Edition features a number of exciting new resources:

- specially-filmed interviews with business practitioners for each unit
- *Case study commentaries* on DVD-ROM, with expert views on each case
- *Working across cultures* – regular input and tasks to develop students' intercultural awareness and skills
- four *Revision* units, one after every three main units
- an interactive *i-Glossary* on DVD-ROM
- additional photocopiable tasks in this Teacher's Resource Book
- *Active Teach* software to deliver the course digitally, through an interactive whiteboard or computer.

This course is intended for use either by students preparing for a career in business or by those already working who want to improve their English communication skills. *Market Leader* combines some of the most stimulating recent ideas from the world of business with a strongly task-based approach. Role plays and case studies are regular features of each unit. Throughout the course, students are encouraged to use their own experience and opinions in order to maximise involvement and learning.

2 The main course components

Course Book

This provides the main part of the teaching material, divided into 12 topic-based units. The topics have been chosen following research among teachers to establish which are the areas of widest possible interest to the majority of their students. The Course Book provides input in reading, speaking and listening, with guidance for writing tasks too. Every unit contains vocabulary development activities and a rapid review of essential grammar. There is a regular focus on key business functions and each unit ends with a motivating case study to allow students to practise language they have worked on during the unit. For more details on the Course Book units, see *Overview of a Course Book unit*.

After every three units is a spread called *Working across cultures*. Here students are introduced to key intercultural concepts, developing their awareness and skills in order to function effectively in international business situations. There are also four *Revision* units in the Course Book that revise and consolidate the work done in the main units and culture spreads.

Audio and DVD-ROM materials

All the listening material from the Course Book is available on the audio CDs. A number of these tracks provide students with exposure to non-native English accents which they may find challenging to understand, but which will help them build confidence in their own speaking. All of the audio files are also provided in fully-downloadable MP3 format on the DVD-ROM allowing transfer to personal computers and portable audio players.

The DVD-ROM is an integral part of the course. All 12 interviews from the Course Book can be viewed on the DVD-ROM with the option of subtitles, depending on the user's preference. The interviews are accompanied by 12 video commentaries on the *Case studies* delivered by experienced business consultants. The interviews (which form the main listening focus of each unit) and commentaries provide an opportunity for students to get expert perspectives on the latest business practice through English. None of the videos are scripted and, as such, expose students to authentic examples of natural speech.

In addition, the DVD-ROM provides the students with interactive, self-study practice activities. These allow them to revisit problem areas and reinforce work done in class in their own time. The activities provide further listening practice, opportunities for task repetition and instant, personalised feedback. The DVD-ROM also includes the *i-Glossary*, an interactive mini-dictionary which provides definitions and pronunciation of all the key vocabulary listed at the back of the Course Book and which encourages further self-study.

Vocabulary Trainer

This is an online, self-study tool that lets students take control of their own learning. Once students have created a personal account, the Vocabulary Trainer tests them on the meaning, spelling, collocation and use of vocabulary learnt in class. Their development is automatically recorded so they can chart their own progress outside the classroom.

Practice File

This gives extra practice in the areas of grammar and vocabulary, together with a complete syllabus in business writing. In each unit, students work with text models and useful language, then do a writing task to consolidate the learning. Additionally, the Practice File provides regular self-study pronunciation work (with an audio CD and exercises) and a valuable survival language section for students when travelling.

Teacher's Resource Book

This book provides teachers with an overview of the whole course, together with detailed teaching notes, background briefings on business content, the *Text bank* and the *Resource bank*.

The *Text bank* provides two extra *FT* reading texts per unit, followed up with comprehension and vocabulary exercises. The *Resource bank* provides photocopiable worksheet-based communication activities linked to particular sections of the Course Book units:

- *Listening bank*: extra activities based on each Course Book *Listening* interview
- *Speaking bank*: extra activities based on each *Skills* section
- *Writing bank*: a model answer to the Course Book *Writing* task, together with an additional writing exercise

Test File

Six photocopiable tests are available to teachers and course planners to monitor students' progress during the course. There is an *Entry test*, four *Progress tests*, which test both skills and language knowledge, and an *Exit test*, which reviews the work done throughout the course.

Test Master CD-ROM

Included in the Teacher's Resource Book, the Test Master CD-ROM is a useful assessment resource to accompany the course. It includes digital, editable versions of the Test File tests enabling valid, tailored assessment. It also contains the accompanying audio files and a further 12 unit tests. These tests assess students' progress in terms of the *Vocabulary, Language review* and *Skills* sections of their corresponding units. Full keys and audioscripts are also provided to make marking the tests as straightforward as possible.

Active Teach

The *Active Teach* software provides digital access to a range of course components via an interactive whiteboard or computer. Components include the Course Book, video and audio with printable scripts, the i-Glossary interactive activities based on the Course Book content, editable tests, the Teacher's Resource Book and the phonetic chart. It also includes the *Writing file*, which provides good models for writing work, and *Help* videos to make using the software as easy as possible.

Using *Active Teach* facilitates student engagement and enables clear giving of instructions and valuable feedback. It is ideal for use on a laptop in one-to-one classes.

3 Overview of a Course Book unit

A typical unit consists of the following sections:

Starting up

Students have the opportunity to think about the unit topic and to exchange ideas and opinions with each other and with the teacher. There is a variety of stimulating activities such as answering quiz questions, reflecting on difficult decisions, prioritising options and completing charts. Throughout, students are encouraged to draw upon their life and business experience as appropriate.

Vocabulary

Essential business vocabulary is presented and practised through a wide variety of creative and engaging exercises. Students learn new words, phrases and collocations and are given tasks which help to activate the vocabulary they already know or have just learnt. There is further vocabulary practice in the Practice File.

Reading

Students read interesting and relevant authentic texts from the *Financial Times* and other business sources. They develop their reading skills and acquire essential business vocabulary. The texts provide a context for language work and discussion later in the unit.

Listening

The authentic listening texts are based on interviews with businesspeople and experts in their field. Students develop listening skills such as prediction, listening for specific information and note-taking. They can, if they prefer, watch the interviews on the DVD-ROM.

Language review

These sections develop students' awareness of the common problem areas at pre-intermediate level. They focus on accuracy and knowledge of key areas of grammar. If students already know the grammar point, this section serves as a quick check for them and the teacher. If they need more explanation, they are referred to the *Grammar reference* at the back of the Course Book.

There is further grammar practice in the Practice File and in the *Essential Business Grammar and Usage* book (see *Extending the course*).

Skills

This section helps learners to develop their communication skills in the key business areas of presentations, meetings, negotiations, telephoning and social English. Each section contains a *Useful language* box which provides students with the phrases they need to carry out the business tasks in the regular role-play activities.

Case studies

Each unit ends with a case study linked to the unit's business topic. The case studies are based on realistic business problems or situations and are designed to motivate and actively engage students. Students use the language and communication skills which they have acquired while working through the unit. Typically, students will be involved in discussing business problems and recommending solutions through active group work.

Each case study ends with a realistic writing task. These tasks reflect the real world of business correspondence and will also help those students preparing for business English exams. Models of writing text types are given in the *Writing file* at the end of the Course Book.

After students have completed each case study they can watch the *Case study commentaries* on the DVD-ROM. Here, a consultant talks about the business issues raised by each case. This may in turn lead to further discussion of the case in class.

4 Using the course

Accessibility for teachers

Less-experienced teachers can sometimes find teaching business English a daunting experience. *Market Leader* sets out to provide the maximum support for teachers.

The *Business brief* section at the beginning of each unit in the Teacher's Resource Book gives an overview of the business topic, covering key terms (given in bold, and which can be checked in the *Longman Dictionary of Business English*) and suggesting a list of titles for further reading and information.

Authenticity of content

One of the principles of the course is that students should deal with as much authentic content as their language level allows. Authentic reading and listening texts are motivating for students and bring the real world of business into the classroom, increasing students' knowledge of business practice and concepts. Due to its international coverage, the *Financial Times* has been a rich source of text, video and business information for the course.

The case studies present realistic business situations and problems and the communication activities based on them – group discussions, simulations and role plays – serve to enhance the authenticity of the course.

Flexibility of use

An essential requirement of business English materials is that they cater for the wide range of needs which students have, including different areas of interest and specialisation, different skills needs and varying amounts of time available to study. *Market Leader* offers teachers and course planners a unique range of flexible materials to help meet these needs. There are suggestions in this book on how to use the unit material extensively or intensively, with fast-track routes through the units focusing mainly on speaking and listening skills. The lesson notes include suggestions on extending the classwork through the DVD-ROM and photocopiable materials in the *Text bank* and *Resource bank* sections of this book. In addition, this book gives suggestions on how to extend the course using components including the Practice File, the Business Grammar and Usage book, and the *Market Leader* specialist series, which develops vocabulary and reading skills (see *Extending the course*).

5 Case studies that work

The following teaching tips will help when using case studies:

1 Draw on the students' knowledge of business and the world.
2 Ensure that all students have understood the case and the key vocabulary.
3 Encourage the students to use the language and communication skills they have acquired in the rest of the unit. A short review of the key language will help.
4 Focus on communication and fluency during the case study activities. Language errors can be dealt with at the end. Make a record of important errors and give students feedback at the end in a sympathetic and constructive way.
5 Allow students to reach their own conclusions. Many students expect there to be a correct answer. The teacher can give their own opinion but should stress that there usually is no single 'right' answer.

6 Encourage creative and imaginative solutions to the problems.
7 Encourage students to use people-management skills such as working in teams, leading teams, delegating and interacting effectively with each other.
8 Students should identify the key issues of the case and discuss all the options before reaching a decision.

6 Extending the course

Some students will require more input or practice in certain areas, either in terms of subject matter or skills, than is provided in the Course Book. In order to meet their needs, *Market Leader* provides a wide range of optional extra materials and components to choose from.

Essential Business Grammar and Usage

For students needing more work on their grammar, this book provides reference and practice in all the most important areas of business English usage. It is organised into structural and functional sections. The book complements the *Language review* sections of the Course Book. Relevant chapters for further study are referenced throughout the lesson notes of this Teacher's Resource Book in the *At a glance* section at the start of each unit.

Market Leader specialist titles

Many students will need to learn the language of more specialised areas of business English. To provide them with authentic and engaging material, *Market Leader* includes a range of special-subject books which focus on reading skills and vocabulary development. Each book includes two tests and a glossary of specialised language.

Longman Dictionary of Business English New Edition

This is the most up-to-date source of reference in business English today. Compiled from a wide range of text sources, it allows students and teachers rapid access to clear, straightforward definitions of the latest international business terminology. The fully updated New Edition includes an interactive CD-ROM with 35,000 key words pronounced in both British and American English, together with practice material for both the BEC and BULATS exams, and is now available as an iPhone or iPod touch app to download from the Pearson website.

Market Leader website: www.market-leader.net

The *Market Leader* companion website provides up-to-date information about the Course Books and specialist titles and offers a wide range of materials teachers can use to supplement and enrich their lessons. In addition to tests for each level, the website provides links to websites relevant to units and topics in the Course Book and also downloadable glossaries of business terms.

The *Premier Lessons* subscription area of the website has a bank of ready-made lessons with authentic texts from the *Financial Times* that have student worksheets and answers. These lessons are regularly updated and can be searched in order to find relevant texts for the unit, topic and level that students are studying. *Premier Lessons* can be used in the classroom or for self-study.

Contents

Resource bank

Careers

AT A GLANCE

	Classwork – Course Book	Further work
Lesson 1 *Each lesson (excluding case studies) is about 45 to 60 minutes. This does not include time spent going through homework.*	<u>**Starting up**</u> Students talk about their level of ambition and say what makes for a successful career. **Vocabulary: Career moves** Students look at typical word combinations and verbs used with *career*.	**Practice File** Vocabulary (page 4) **Practice exercises:** **Vocabulary 1 & 2** (DVD-ROM) **i-Glossary** (DVD-ROM)
Lesson 2	**Reading: Be aware of your online image** Students read an article about how their social-networking profile could damage their employment prospects. **Listening: Changing jobs** Students listen to an interview with Melissa Foux, Finance Director of a UK television business.	**Text bank** (pages 116–119) **Resource bank: Listening** (page 189) **Practice exercises:** **Listening** (DVD-ROM)
Lesson 3	**Language review: Modals 1: ability, requests and offers** Students look at modals used for ability, requests and offers (*can*, *could* and *would*) and do exercises based around a job interview. <u>**Skills: Telephoning: making contact**</u> Students listen to some calls and learn how to get through to who they want to speak to, leave messages, etc.	**Practice File** Language review (page 5) **Practice exercises:** **Language review 1 & 2** (DVD-ROM) **ML Essential Business Grammar and Usage** (Unit 27) **Resource bank: Speaking** (page 177) **Practice exercises: Skills** (DVD-ROM)
Lesson 4 *Each case study is about 1 to 1½ hours.*	<u>**Case study: *YouJuice***</u> Students choose the right candidate for an internal promotion within an international drinks company.	**Case study commentary** (DVD-ROM) **Resource bank: Writing** (page 204) **Practice File** Writing (page 6)

For a fast route through the unit focusing mainly on speaking skills, just use the underlined sections.

For one-to-one situations, most parts of the unit lend themselves, with minimal adaptation, to use with individual students. Where this is not the case, alternative procedures are given.

BUSINESS BRIEF

Reports of the death of the traditional career have been greatly exaggerated. Despite the growth of **outsourcing** (buying in services that were previously performed by a company's employees from outside the organisation) and **teleworking** by freelancers working from home communicating via the Internet, most professional people still go to what is recognisably a job in a building that is recognisably an office. The average **tenure**, the length of time that people spend in a particular job, has remained unchanged (at about seven years) for two decades.

From the point of view of the **human resources (HR) department** of a large company, managing people's careers can still be seen in the traditional activities of **selection procedures** and **recruitment**, managing **remuneration** (how much people are paid), and working with department managers on **performance reviews**: annual or more frequent meetings with employees to tell them how well they are doing and how they may progress further on the career ladder. The HR department will also be involved with **training** and **professional development** of the company's staff.

A company's HR department may also be involved in making people **redundant**. Redundancies may be the result of an economic downturn with reduced demand for the company's goods or services, but they may follow a decision by a company to **de-layer** (to reduce the number of management levels) and **downsize**. It may offer **outplacement services**, advice to people on how they can find another job, perhaps after some **retraining**.

A manager made redundant in this way may become what Charles Handy calls a **portfolio worker**, offering their services to a number of clients. Some managers describe themselves as **consultants** but would prefer to be working in a salaried job in an organisation like the one they have been forced to leave.

Others may enjoy their new-found freedom and embrace the **flexibility** that it offers. (Companies too may talk about flexibility when they use the services of **freelancers** in this way, rather than relying on salaried employees.) Freelancers have to maintain their degree of **employability** by keeping up with the latest trends and skills in their profession or industry, for example by attending short courses. They may complain that working outside an organisation gives them fewer opportunities to learn these new skills. For many salaried employees, on the other hand, developing one's career in an (enlightened) organisation is a process of give-and-take – the environment they work in allows them to keep their skills up to speed.

Read on

The section on Careers, jobs and management on FT.com is a good up-to-date source of information on this area: http://www.exec-appointments.com/

Charles Handy: *The Elephant and the Flea*, Hutchinson, 2001

Fifty Lessons: *Managing your Career (Harvard Lessons Learned)*, Harvard Business Press, 2007

Jane Yarnall: *Strategic Career Management: Developing Your Talent (The HR Series)*, Butterworth-Heinemann, 2008

LESSON NOTES

Warmer

● Write the word *career* in big letters at the top of the board.

● Ask students to suggest different stages in a typical career using expressions such as: *go to school, go to university, get qualifications in …, get a job in a company, move to another company, retire,* etc. Do this as a quick-fire activity – don't spend too long on it.

Overview

● Ask the students to look at the Overview section on page 6. Tell them a little about the things you will be doing, using the table on page 8 of this book as a guide. Tell them which sections you will be covering in this lesson and which in later lessons.

Quotation

● Write the quotation on the board and ask students to discuss it briefly in pairs. Make sure students understand that in one sense, *work* has the same meaning as *a job*, but in another sense, *work* also means *making an effort*.

● With the whole class, ask pairs for their opinions. Can they think of examples (without naming names!) of people they have known who avoid work on the job? What about people who are hard-working on the job?

Starting up

Students talk about their level of ambition and say what makes for a successful career.

● If this is your first lesson with the group and they have done a needs analysis, this is a good opportunity to get more background information about people's jobs and their English-learning needs in relation to their future careers. You may have students whose careers depend on improving their level of English.

A

● Get students to discuss the points in groups of three or four. Circulate, monitor and assist if necessary, especially with career-related vocabulary.

● After the groups have discussed each point, get a spokesperson for each group to give the views of the group. Relate each group's points to those of other groups. Deal tactfully with the non-career-orientated students.

● Praise good language points and work on some areas that need it, especially in relation to career-related language.

B

● Get students to do this exercise in pairs.

---

1 e   2 c   3 a   4 g   5 b   6 d   7 f

C

● Get students to do the exercise in pairs or small groups. Circulate, monitor and assist if necessary.

One-to-one

If this is your first lesson with a one-to-one student, this will be a good opportunity to get to know them better and to supplement the information in the needs analysis, if there was one.

Vocabulary: Career moves

Students look at typical noun combinations (collocations) with *career*, verbs used with the word *career*, and verbs used with other career-related nouns (operating verbs).

● If it's the first lesson with the group, point out that memorising blocks of language – typical word combinations – is an important part of the learning process.

A

● Do this as a quick-fire activity with the whole class.

---

1 c   2 d   3 b   4 a   5 f   6 e

B ◀))) CD1.1–1.3

● Get students to look at question B and listen once or twice to the three speakers. Elicit their answers.

Person 1	middle
Person 2	beginning
Person 3	end

C ◀))) CD1.1–1.3

● Get students to look at question C and listen again to the three speakers. Elicit their answers.

Person 1	career break, career move
Person 2	career opportunities, career path
Person 3	career plan, career ladder

D

● Get students to do this exercise in pairs or small groups. Tell them they can use a good bilingual dictionary or a monolingual one such as the *Longman Active Study Dictionary*. Circulate, monitor and assist if necessary.

LESSON NOTES

1 have
2 take
3 make
4 offer
5 decide
6 climb

E

- Students do the exercise in pairs or small groups. Circulate, monitor and assist if necessary.

Odd items out:

1 a training course
2 progress
3 a part-time job
4 a mistake
5 a pension
6 an office job

F

- Ask students to do this exercise in pairs or small groups.

1 make a fortune
2 work flexitime
3 earn commission
4 get a promotion
5 do part-time work
6 take early retirement

◎ i-Glossary

Reading: Be aware of your online image

Students read an article about how their social-networking profile could damage their employment prospects.

A

- Pre-teach the following vocabulary: *Facebook profile* – the information about yourself that you share on Facebook; *online image* – your 'personality' on the Internet as shown by pictures of you, comments you write, and so on; *online reputation* – the opinion people have of you because of what they see on the Internet; *faux pas* – (from French) an embarrassing mistake; *personal brand* – the image you want people to have of you.

- You may prefer to discuss the first question with the whole group, writing answers on the board, before asking students to work on the second question in pairs.

- Bring the group together to compare students' answers.

B

- The idea behind this type of exercise is to get students to scan the article without trying to understand everything at the first attempt and to spot similar concepts, even if they are expressed differently. They can do this individually or in the same pairs as in Exercise A.

1 70%
2 Facebook, Twitter
3 Peter Cullen: Microsoft; Farhan Yasin: Careerbuilder.co.uk

C

- This requires an understanding of the main idea of the article, which is found in the first sentence. Students can work individually or in pairs.

b) Facebook profile 'could damage job prospects'

D

- This requires closer reading of the text to link the ideas. Get students to read through the article again and identify any words they don't understand. If you have time, encourage them to guess at the meaning by looking at the context or to look the words up themselves in a dictionary.

They can make your career because a strong online image could help you land your dream job. They can break your career because a huge number of employers take action against staff for writing negative comments on their social-networking page.

E

- Students work in pairs to write a list of things they should not do on their social-networking site. Follow up with a whole-group discussion to see if everyone had the same ideas.

F

- Students do the exercise in pairs or small groups. After the discussion, ask for a show of hands for and against using social-networking sites during work hours.

➡ Text bank (pages 116–119)

LESSON NOTES

Listening: Changing jobs

Students listen to an interview with Melissa Foux, Finance Director of CSC Media Limited.

A ◀)) CD1.4

- Before playing the first part of the interview, get students to read the three questions in this section.
- Play the first part of the interview through once.
- Once students have decided on their answers, play the track again, pausing after each answer.

> **1** CSC Media Ltd, part of the Chart Show Channels Group, is the largest independent television business in the UK. It has a mixture of 16 channels, including music, children's and movie channels.
>
> **2** She was the Finance Director for a chocolate-pudding business.
>
> **3** Because the basic skills you need are the same.

B ◀)) CD1.5

- Before playing the next part of the interview, get students to read the text.
- Play the second part of the interview through once and ask students to listen for the answers, but not write them. Elicit answers from the whole class and ask students to complete the text.
- Play the recording again and have students check their answers.

> **1** chemistry
>
> **2** different
>
> **3** internship
>
> **4** accountancy
>
> **5** understanding
>
> **6** experience

C ◀)) CD1.6

- Play the third part of the interview.
- Check answers quickly with the class.

> **1** c **2** a **3** b

D ◀)) CD1.7

- Play the final part of the interview. Elicit the answer from the class.

> **c)** How would you advise people who are starting their careers?

E

- Students do the exercise in small groups. Circulate, monitor and assist if necessary.
- Ask a few students to share with the class the answers of other members of their group.

➡ Resource bank: Listening (page 189)

Language review: Modals 1: ability, requests and offers

Students look at modals used for ability, requests and offers, and do exercises.

- Check that students know about modal verbs and their characteristics.
- Modals are verbs like *may, might, can, could,* etc. They don't change with different persons (for example, *I can, you can, he can*). The ones they will see here are *can, could* and *would.*
- Get students to match the functions with the examples in the Language review box.

> **1** c **2** a **3** b

A

- Get students to work in pairs to rearrange the words. Circulate, monitor and assist if necessary.
- Then get them to work out whether they are requests, offers or asking about ability.

> **1** Can I get you a drink? (b)
>
> **2** Could I confirm your e-mail address? (a)
>
> **3** Can you use spreadsheets? (c)
>
> **4** Can you speak any other languages? (c)
>
> **5** Could you tell us more about your present job? (a)
>
> **6** Could you tell me your current salary? (a)
>
> **7** Would you let us know your decision as soon as possible? (a)
>
> **8** When can you start? (a)
>
> **9** Would you like some more tea? (b)

- Discuss students' answers, clarifying any difficulties.

B

- Get students in pairs to match the questions and answers.
- Circulate, monitor and assist if necessary, for example by explaining *currently* and *notice period.*

LESSON NOTES

a 6	**b** 3	**c** 7	**d** 1	**e** 2	**f** 9	**g** 5	**h** 4	**i** 8

- Get students in pairs to practise reading the exchanges with good intonation. Circulate, monitor and assist if necessary.

- Point out that the politeness in the requests is in the intonation: none of them involve *please*.

- Then get one or two pairs to perform some of the exchanges for the whole class.

C

- Get students to role-play the situation in parallel pairs, following the instructions in the role play box. Circulate and monitor.

- When the students have done the exercise once, praise strong points and mention one or two things that students should pay attention to when they change roles.

- Get students to change roles and again to role-play the situation in parallel pairs. Circulate and monitor.

- Get one or two pairs to repeat their role play for the whole class.

Skills: Telephoning: making contact

Students discuss how they use the telephone in English. They then listen to three telephone calls, do exercises based on them and role-play a telephone call themselves.

A

- Point out that the focus of this section is on making contact and getting through.

- With the whole group, get students to discuss the calls they make and receive. Ask them what they find particularly difficult and bring their attention to points from the following activities that will help them.

- Write the telephone expressions students come up with on the board, preferably organising them into groups, such as *Getting through* or *Asking for someone*.

B 🔊 CD1.8–1.10

- Get students to listen to the calls once or twice, stopping after each call. Get them to describe the purpose of each call and say in complete sentences whether the callers know each other.

1 What is the purpose of the call?

Phone call 1: To ask about a job advert

Phone call 2: To tell Giovanna that he can't make the training course

Phone call 3: To ask for a phone number

2 Do the callers know each other?

Phone call 1: No

Phone call 2: No

Phone call 3: Yes

C 🔊 CD1.8

- Get students to listen again to the first call. Play it several times if necessary, stopping after each utterance to give them time to note it down. Circulate, monitor and assist if necessary.

1	like, speak
2	Hold on
3	put you through
4	Is that
5	Speaking
6	phoning about
7	Could you give me

- Go round the class and ask individual students to say these expressions with friendly, polite intonation.

D 🔊 CD1.9

- Before playing the recording, get students to read the conversation and try to remember the words and phrases that will go in the gaps.

- Play the second call again and get students to write the phrases, making sure that they get the exact words – *Could I speak to Giovanna …* rather than *Can*, etc.

1	Could I speak	**7**	tell
2	I'm afraid	**8**	make
3	take	**9**	call
4	message	**10**	back
5	This is	**11**	on
6	Could		

LESSON NOTES

E 🔊 CD1.10

- Play the third call again and get students to choose the correct alternatives.

1	you
2	word
3	let me have
4	engaged
5	here
6	catch
7	No problem

- Get students to read the conversation in pairs, using the underlined expressions. Then get one pair to read the conversation for the whole class.

- If time permits, get students to practise reading the conversation with the alternative expressions, those they did not underline, which are all correct usage. Then get another pair to read the conversation for the whole class.

F

- Ask your students to practise, in pairs, the expressions in the Useful language box. Circulate, monitor and assist with pronunciation and friendly intonation if necessary.

- Then move on to Role play 1. Get students to look at the job advert. Help with any difficulties of understanding and then explain the background to the role play.

- Allocate roles. Make sure that students are looking at the correct page for their role. Check that students with the A role understand that they will play two different people in the two parts of Role play 1: Jamie Vincent's colleague and then Jamie Vincent. Students with the B role card play themselves.

- Get your students to role-play the first call in pairs. Use telephone equipment if available; otherwise get students to sit back-to-back. Circulate, monitor and assist if necessary, especially with expressions relating to making telephone calls and applying for jobs.

- Bring the class to order. Praise strong language points and work on two or three points that require it, getting individual students to say the improved versions.

- Then get one of the pairs to do the role play for the whole class, integrating the improvements.

- Get students to role-play the second call in pairs. Circulate, monitor and assist if necessary.

- Again, praise strong language points and work on two or three points that require it, getting individual students to say the improved versions.

- Then get one of the pairs to do the role play for the whole class, integrating the improvements.

- Repeat the above steps for the second role play. Check that students with the B role understand that they will play two different people in the two parts of Role play 2: Alex Frantzen's colleague and then Alex Frantzen. Students with the A role card play themselves.

➡ Resource bank: Speaking (page 177)

CASE STUDY

YouJuice

Students choose a candidate for an internal promotion within an international drinks company.

Stage 1: Background

- Instruct the students to read silently the sections entitled 'Background' and 'A new appointment', including the extract of the job description giving the qualities required of the successful candidate. Circulate and answer any queries.

- While students are reading, write the headings from the left-hand column of the table below on the board. With the whole class, elicit information to complete the column on the right.

Company	YouJuice Inc.
Activity	Sells ready-to-drink juices all over the world
Based in	Monterrey, Mexico but owned by a large US corporation
Recent sales performance and reasons for this	Poor (35 per cent below target) because:
	Sales reps not motivated
	Strong competition
	Previous manager – no clear strategy
	Limited market research done, limited results from customer database
Nature of new sales position	Increasing sales and developing marketing strategies
	Managing sales team – more motivated and effective
	Carrying out market research
Number of candidates	3
Qualities required	Good academic background and relevant experience
	Good organizational and interpersonal skills
	Numeracy skills and analytical ability
	Good linguistic ability
	Must like travelling on business

- Without pre-empting the discussion to come in the task, clarify unfamiliar vocabulary and discuss some of the points above with the whole class. For example, ask students what it means to have *strong sales ability*.

Stage 2: Profiles of the candidates 🔊 CD1.11–1.16

- Divide the class into groups of three or four. Get each group to analyse the written information about *all* the candidates. Circulate, monitor and assist if necessary. Get each group to appoint a spokesperson who takes notes of the key points for each candidate, without getting into comparing the merits of the candidates.

- Play the recordings to the whole class, stopping at the end of the recording for each candidate and explaining any difficulties.

- Alternatively, if the room is big enough and if you have sufficient equipment, allocate one to each group and get the groups to specialise in a particular candidate, so, for example, one or two of the groups listen only to Juana Ramos's interview. Circulate, monitor and assist if necessary. Then ask a spokesperson for each group to summarise for the whole class the interview that they listened to.

Stage 3: Task

- The discussion in part 2 of the task does not, strictly speaking, need a chairperson, but if you think this would be useful to help structure the discussion, appoint a chair. If this is the first role play you have done with this class, choose a self-confident student to run the whole-class meeting. Do this while the group discussions below are still going on and brief the chair on what they should do – invite contributions, make sure everyone has a chance to speak, make sure that each candidate is given proper consideration, etc.

- Working in groups, students discuss the relative merits of each candidate for the job. Appoint a different spokesperson in each group (i.e. not the same person as in Stage 2 above) to note down the main points of the discussion and the reasons for the choice of candidate. Circulate, monitor and assist if necessary.

- Then get the whole class to discuss who should be chosen for the job, under the direction of the chair if you have decided to appoint one.

- While the discussion is going on, note down strong language points plus half a dozen points that need improvement. Come back to them when a candidate has been selected and the discussion is over. You may want to concentrate on the language used to:

  – describe people in the context of job interviews, such as *calm*, *relaxed*, *gets on well with others*.

  – make contrasts, for example: *X was rather aggressive at the interview **whereas** Y seemed nervous*.

CASE STUDY

One-to-one

Use the points above as the basis for discussion with your student. If there is time, you could go on to ask them how recruitment is done in their own organisation, whether internal promotion is favoured over looking for external candidates, etc.

◎ Students can watch the *Case study commentary* on the DVD-ROM.

Stage 4: Writing

● The students write up the decision of the meeting in e-mail form as if they were the head of the interviewing team. This can be done for homework. Make sure that each student knows that they have to say who was chosen and describe briefly the strengths of the candidate.

➡ Writing file, page 126

➡ Resource bank: Writing (page 204)

Companies

	Classwork – Course Book	Further work
Lesson 1 *Each lesson (excluding case studies) is about 45–60 minutes. This does not include administration and time spent going through homework.*	<u>**Starting up**</u> Students talk about the type of company they would most like to work for and the business sector they work in now. **Vocabulary: Describing companies** Students look at vocabulary used to describe companies and that used in company reports to describe performance.	**Practice File** Vocabulary (page 8) **Practice exercises: Vocabulary 1 & 2** (DVD-ROM) **i-Glossary** (DVD-ROM)
Lesson 2	**Listening: A successful company** Students listen to the Chief Executive Officer of Nature's Way Foods talk about the factors that make her company successful. **Reading: Two different organisations** Students read about and compare two companies.	**Resource bank: Listening** (page 190) **Practice exercises: Listening** (DVD-ROM) **Text bank** (pages 120–123)
Lesson 3	**Language review: Present simple and present continuous** The two tenses are compared and contrasted. Students then complete a job advertisement with the correct tenses. <u>**Skills: Presenting your company**</u> Students look at some advice for making presentations, listen to a presentation about a fashion company and then make a presentation about a company they invent.	**Practice File** Language review (page 9) **Practice exercises: Language review 1 & 2** (DVD-ROM) **ML Essential Business Grammar and Usage** (Units 5, 6 & 8) **Resource bank: Speaking** (page 178) **Practice exercises: Skills** (DVD-ROM)
Lesson 4 *Each case study is about 1 to 1½ hours.*	<u>**Case study: Dino Conti Ice Cream**</u> A maker of luxury ice cream is in difficulty. Students propose a strategy for revival and growth.	**Case study commentary** (DVD-ROM) **Resource bank: Writing** (page 205) **Practice File** Writing (page 10)

For a fast route through the unit focusing mainly on speaking skills, just use the underlined sections.

For one-to-one situations, most parts of the unit lend themselves, with minimal adaptation, to use with individual students. Where this is not the case, alternative procedures are given.

BUSINESS BRIEF

Multinationals are the most visible of companies. Their **local subsidiaries** can give them global reach, even if their **corporate culture**, the way they do things, depends largely on their country of origin. But the tissue of most national economies is made up of much smaller organisations. Many countries owe much of their prosperity to **SMEs** (small and medium-sized enterprises) with tens or hundreds of employees, rather than the tens of thousands employed by large **corporations**.

Small businesses with just a few employees are also important. Many governments hope that the small businesses of today will become the multinationals of tomorrow, but many owners of small companies choose to work that way because they find it more congenial and do not want to expand.

And then, of course, there are the **sole traders**, one-man or one-woman businesses. In the professional world, these **freelancers** are often people who have left (or been forced to leave) large organisations and who have set up on their own, taking the expertise they have gained with them.

But in every case the principle is the same: to survive – the money coming in has to be more than the money going out. Companies with **shareholders** are looking for more than survival – they want **return on investment**. **Shares** in the company rise and fall in relation to how investors see the future profitability of the company; they demand **shareholder value** in the way the company is run to maximise profitability for investors, in terms of increased **dividends** and a rising **share price**. **Publicly quoted companies**, with their shares **listed** or **quoted** on a **stock exchange**, come under a lot of scrutiny in this area. Some large companies (often family-owned or dominated) are **private**: they choose not to have their shares openly bought and sold, perhaps because they do not want this scrutiny. But they may have trouble raising the capital they need to grow and develop.

Profitability is key. Formulas for success are the subject of thousands of business courses and business books. Of course, what works for one person may not work for others. See below for books on two styles of running a company that might be hard to imitate!

Read on

Jack and Suzy Welch: *Winning: The Answers – Confronting 74 of the Toughest Questions in Business Today*, HarperBusiness, 2007

Lewis V. Gerstner Jr.: *Who Says Elephants Can't Dance? How I Turned Around IBM*, Collins, 2003

David Lester: *How They Started – How 30 Good Ideas Became Great Businesses*, Crimson Publishing, 2007

Richard Branson: *Losing My Virginity: How I've Survived, Had Fun, and Made a Fortune Doing Business My Way*, Virgin Books, 2000

LESSON NOTES

Warmer

- Write the word *company* on the right of the board.

- As a quick-fire activity, ask students to say which adjectives and verbs could come in front of the word *company*. You may end up with something like this, depending on their level. You could give the initial letters of the words on the left as clues.

family-owned multinational small medium-sized profitable failing bankrupt work for a stay with a change	company

Overview

- Ask the students to look at the Overview section on page 14. Tell them a little about the things you will be doing, using the table on page 17 of this book as a guide. Tell them which sections you will be covering in this lesson and which in later lessons.

Quotation

- Write the quotation on the board. Ask students to discuss briefly in pairs what they understand by it.

- With the whole class, ask pairs for their opinions.

Starting up

Students talk about the type of company they would most like to work for and, for those at work, the business sector they work in now.

A

- Get students to discuss the question in pairs. Obviously, in-work students will approach this differently to those not in work. Circulate, monitor and assist if necessary.

- Then ask each pair to present its ideas to the whole class.

- Alternatively, you could do the activity as a class discussion and provide a number of points for students to think about for each type of company by presenting a table like the one below.

- Write the headings from the left-hand column on the board. Then discuss what to put in the right-hand column. Of course, the ideas below are just

suggestions – people in different places will have different ideas about the merits of working for each type of company. The answer in many cases will be 'It depends'. Teach this expression, and then ask students to say what it depends on. Your students may mention other issues in addition to the headings given in the table.

Work environment	May be more friendly in a small family business. But some family-owned businesses are multinationals with thousands of employees, and the environment may not be that different to working in an ordinary multinational. Self-employed people working on their own sometimes complain about feeling isolated. You may feel more in control running your own company, but there again, if you have employees to look after, this can be a big responsibility.
Pay	Small family companies may or may not pay good wages and salaries. One issue here is that when multinationals come to an area with low unemployment, they may make it more expensive for firms in the area to employ people in office or factory jobs. On the other hand, some multinationals are well known for paying very low wages to people in places such as fast-food outlets. The pay of self-employed people, of course, varies enormously.
Promotion possibilities	There will be fewer opportunities for promotion in family companies, especially if family members are in key positions. Multinationals will probably offer more scope – the fast-food worker may become a branch manager and possibly go even further, but examples of top managers who have risen all the way from shop-floor level are rare.

LESSON NOTES

Job security (= probability that you will keep the job)	Family companies may hesitate longer before *laying people off* (explain this expression) out of a feeling of responsibility towards their employees. Multinationals have had different attitudes towards laying people off, but companies in general are probably quicker to lay people off than before.

B

- Before working on the activity itself, check that students know what the different industries are.

- Then practise stress and pronunciation of the names of the industries. Write them up on the board, putting the stressed syllable in capitals: *TelecommuniCAtions, EnginEERing, REtailing,* etc.

- Get students to repeat the names with the correct stress.

- Then get students to discuss the questions. Also ask them if there are any companies they would *not* like to work for. If you did the previous activity as a whole-class activity, do this one as pair work, and vice-versa.

- If doing this as pair work, circulate, monitor and assist if necessary. Students may need help with naming companies in each sector, especially if there are no well-known 'national champions' in their own country/countries.

- If there is interest and your students have access to the Internet, get them to look at the industries section on FT.com (click on 'Industries' on the FT.com home page) and see which companies are currently in the news in each industry. Students should not try to read the articles, just spot company names in the headlines. You could ask them to do this for homework.

Vocabulary: Describing companies

Students look at the vocabulary used to describe companies and that used in company reports to describe performance.

A

- Before doing the exercise, check comprehension and pronunciation of the words in the exercise, for example *pharmaceuticals*.

- Write the table from the Course Book on the board and get students to call out the answers to fill the gaps.

---

1 Toyota

2 Japanese

3 fashion/retail

4 American Express

5 pharmaceuticals

6 Korean

7 Nokia

8 Finnish

9 container-ship operator

10 oil and gas

- Go round the class and get students to talk about particular companies, following the model: *Cisco Systems is an American company which supplies Internet equipment.*

B

- Tell students to do the exercise in pairs. Circulate, monitor and assist if necessary.

---

1 turnover (Point out that this is only used in BrE. Americans just talk about 'sales'.)

2 net profit

3 parent company

4 workforce

5 market share

6 head office

7 share price

8 subsidiary

- Go through the exercise with the whole class, explaining any remaining difficulties.

C

- Get students to do the exercise in pairs. Circulate, monitor and assist if necessary. Make sure students read the whole extract before trying to complete it. Explain any difficult vocabulary, for example *loyal*.

---

1 parent company

2 Turnover

3 net profit

4 market share

5 share price

6 head office

7 subsidiary

8 workforce

LESSON NOTES

D 🔊 CD1.17

- Play the recording as students check their answers.

- Go through the exercise with the whole class, explaining any remaining difficulties.

E

- Ask students to work in pairs and to talk about either their own company or a company they know well. Write these example sentences on the board to help them:

  We have had excellent/poor/average performance.

  We have increased/decreased our ...

  Increased/Decreased production and strong/weak demand have ...

  We have successfully ...

  We are planning ...

- Circulate, monitor and assist if necessary.

- With the whole class, ask three or four students to say which companies they talked about.

 i-Glossary

Listening: A successful company

Students listen to the Chief Executive Officer of Nature's Way Foods, a fresh food preparation and packaging company. She talks about what makes the company so successful.

A 🔊 CD1.18

- Ask students to read the short text. Explain that some of the information in the text is incorrect.

- Play the recording, then ask students to identify which information in the text is incorrect. If necessary, play the recording again.

- Check answers with the class.

> Nature's Way Foods is a **food**-manufacturing company based on the **south** coast of **England**. They put chilled product, the majority of which is **lettuce** and **fruit**, into various types of packaging for the major retailers and various food-service companies in **the UK**.

B 🔊 CD1.19

- Get students to work in groups of three or four and discuss which factors they think contribute most to a company's success.

- Give the groups five minutes to reach agreement, then ask a spokesperson from each group to list the three factors they have chosen. If the groups have chosen different factors, have a short debate on the reasons for their choices. Can you reach a class consensus?

- Go through the eight bullet points to ensure that students understand them, focusing on difficult vocabulary, e.g. *convenience, sustainability, indulgence.*

- Have students read the notes and predict what words might fill the gaps.

- Play the recording for students to complete the notes, then check their answers. Play the recording a second time if necessary.

1	markets (in which they operate)
2	products
3	time
4	miles
5	run
6	volume
7	millions
8	efficient
9	systems

C 🔊 CD1.20

- Have students read the two questions and make sure they understand them.

- Play the recording for students to hear the answers. Play the recording a second time if necessary.

1	Achieving what you set out to achieve and creating a team ethic
2	The relentlessness of the role as a Chief Executive

D 🔊 CD1.21

- Have students read the text and predict what words might fill the gaps.

- Play the recording for students to complete the notes, then check their answers. Play the recording a second time if necessary.

1	people	**4**	direction
2	understanding	**5**	enthusiasm
3	achieve		

E

- Students do the exercise in pairs. Circulate, monitor and assist if necessary. Ask a few students to share their partner's answer with the class.

➡ Resource bank: Listening (page 190)

LESSON NOTES

Reading: Two different organisations

Students discuss the merits of employee ownership of companies, then read an article on either Tata or John Lewis and swap information. An employee-owned company is one where the company's employees are shareholders. In such companies, employees are often given shares in the company as part of their salary.

A

- Students do the exercise in small groups. Circulate, monitor and assist if necessary.

- Ask a few students to share with the class the answers of other members of their group.

B

- In pairs, students read one of the two articles on page 17 and make notes on the key information. Remind students that notes do not have to be complete sentences, and should not be lifted verbatim from the text.

C

- Students then expand on their notes to explain in their own words what they have learned about Tata and John Lewis, and make notes about their partner's company in the table.

- This practises the skills of talking from notes and taking notes from a talk, both of which are extremely useful in business.

> **Tata**
>
> India's biggest company
>
> CEO about to retire (for second time)
>
> Will consider candidates from outside to replace him
>
> Future of group important to national economy
>
> Has 100 subsidiaries (including India's biggest private-sector steel company, its biggest information-technology outsourcing company and its biggest automotive producer)
>
> 65% of its $71 billion revenue generated overseas
>
> **John Lewis**
>
> Owned by its employees
>
> Employs 69,000 people
>
> Has a 'bonus day'
>
> Has a reputation for trustworthy products and employees who know what they're talking about and are eager to help
>
> Each employee has a say in how the company is run and has a share of the profits
>
> Britain's largest example of a worker co-ownership
>
> Want their staff to be happy

D

- This is a speaking exercise. Students look at the information they have written and make comparisons and/or contrasts.

> **Sample answers**
>
> John Lewis is owned by its employees, but Tata isn't.
>
> Tata has got 100 subsidiaries, but John Lewis hasn't got any.
>
> John Lewis isn't family-owned, but Tata is.
>
> Both companies are successful.

E

- Students discuss the questions in small groups. Circulate, monitor and assist if necessary.

- Ask a few students to share with the class the answers of other members of their group.

➡️ Text bank (pages 120–123)

Language review: Present simple and present continuous

The two tenses are compared and contrasted. Students then complete a job advertisement with the correct tenses.

- Go through the examples with the whole class, then have students complete the rules with the phrases provided.

> **1** a **2** c **3** d **4** b

- The main thing to underline with the present simple is that it is for 'general truths': factual information about companies is one example of this. You could also give the example *Paris stands on the Seine.* Point out that *Paris is standing on the Seine* is very strange, implying perhaps that yesterday it was standing somewhere else, for example on the Loire.

- The present simple is also used for routine activities, with *always* as in the Course Book example, and also *never, sometimes, generally, often,* etc.

- The main thing to underline with the present continuous is that it is for temporary or changing situations, even if they are not taking place at the moment of speaking. A company marketing director can say 'We're constantly improving the way we sell our products' even when she is not at work.

- The present continuous can also be used for future arrangements, especially fixed plans (as in the third example in the Course Book).

LESSON NOTES

A

- Tell students to work on the sentences in pairs. Circulate, monitor and assist if necessary.

- Go through the exercise with the whole class, working on any difficulties.

> **1** hold; are holding
>
> **2** are using; use
>
> **3** works; is writing
>
> **4** deals; am dealing
>
> **5** come; am living
>
> **6** wants

B

- Tell students to work in pairs. Circulate, monitor and assist if necessary.

- Go through the exercise with the whole class, working on any difficulties.

> **1** are
>
> **2** offer
>
> **3** have
>
> **4** are growing
>
> **5** employ
>
> **6** are considering
>
> **7** are preparing
>
> **8** are looking
>
> **9** need
>
> **10** offer/are offering

C

- Explain that students are going to role-play a job interview. Point out that they will need to be careful about when they use the present simple and when they use the present continuous.

- Get students to role-play the situation in parallel pairs, following the instructions in the role play box. Circulate and monitor.

- When the students have done the role play once, praise strong points and mention one or two things that students should pay attention to when they change roles.

- Get students to change roles and to role-play the situation again in parallel pairs. Circulate and monitor.

- Get one or two pairs to perform the role play for the whole class.

Skills: Presenting your company

Students look at some advice for making presentations, listen to a presentation about a fashion company and then make a presentation about a company they invent.

A

- Ask students what experience they have of giving presentations both in their own language and in English. What did they find most difficult in each case? (Surveys show that speaking in front of an audience is the activity that most managers fear above all else, even in their own language. As a language trainer used to speaking in front of groups, don't lose sight of how difficult this is for most people.)

B 🔊 CD1.22

- Have students read the two questions and make sure they understand them.

- Play the recording for students to hear the answers. Play the recording a second time if necessary.

> **1** To talk about his company
>
> **2** A group of prospective employees

C 🔊 CD1.22

- Have students read the text and predict what words might fill the gaps.

- Play the recording for students to complete the notes, then check their answers. Play the recording a second time if necessary.

> **1** First
>
> **2** After that
>
> **3** Next
>
> **4** finally

D

- Get students to use the text in Exercise C as a model for this. Encourage them to make notes, but not to write out everything they're going to say.

- In pairs, have students practise giving their introduction. Circulate and monitor.

E 🔊 CD1.23

- Prepare students for what they are going to hear by getting them to look at the chart.

- Play the recording two or three times as necessary, stopping after key pieces of information, and get students to complete the chart.

LESSON NOTES

1 Florence

2 Clothing and fashion accessories

3 €300 million

4 €28 million

5 Talented team of designers, first-class distribution system, creative advertising and promotion

6 Advertises on all Italian TV networks and in other major European markets; sponsors fashion shows; products are endorsed by music and sport celebrities

F

- Ask students to number the phrases in the correct order. Elicit answers.

1 d   2 e   3 a   4 b   5 c

G

- Go through the phrases in the Useful language box with students. Have them read the phrases aloud and encourage them to think about the intonation.

- Give students a short time (e.g. five minutes) to prepare a few notes either on their company (or a company they know) or on MIFG (see Course Book page 133).

- Then ask them to make their presentation to their partner. Remind students that these can be very short – they only have to speak for a minute or two – but that what they say should be clear and well structured.

➡ Resource bank: Speaking (page 178)

CASE STUDY

Dino Conti Ice Cream

A maker of luxury ice cream is in difficulty. Students propose a strategy for revival and growth.

Stage 1: Background

- Tell students to look at the background information. Meanwhile, write up the headings on the left of the table below on the board, but don't put in the other information.

- Answer any questions from the students about vocabulary difficulties, etc.

- Then elicit information from the whole class to complete the table.

- Ask one student to summarise the table in their own words for the whole class.

Company	Dino Conti Ice Cream
Products	15 flavours of ice cream
Based in	Santa Barbara, California (USA)
Sold in	Supermarkets and company-owned stores
Most famous product	Supakool chocolate ice cream
Sales problems	Slow growth; falling profits

Stage 2: Listening 🔊 CD1.24

- Tell students that they will hear three people speaking.

- You may need to play the recording several times, as the information does not come in the same order as presented in the list in the Course Book.

- Copy the list onto the board while students are listening. After each playing of the recording, ask students if they can supply any more information. Continue until the list is complete.

Reasons for falling profits

Prices: Looking high, as two main competitors have cut theirs

Products: Not a very wide range of flavours; packaging not very exciting; need more new, exciting products; more health-conscious products (e.g. fat-free flavours, natural ingredients, no additives)

Equipment: Needs upgrading, especially fleet of trucks

Environment: Recycle containers; take fat out of waste products; give pure water to local communities

Outlets: Need more, in addition to supermarkets and ice-cream stores

---

Stage 3: The future

- Tell students to read the text about the future and the chart showing investment options (Chart 2) in pairs. Circulate, monitor and assist if necessary.

- With the whole class, get students to say what the options are, using different expressions, for example:

One option is to build a new factory. This would cost $2.4 million and it would increase production capacity and lower unit costs.

Dino Conti could export to China and Russia. This would cost $1.2 million, but they would reach new markets with great sales potential.

Stage 4: Task

- Put students in pairs again and tell them that they will weigh up the different options. Warn them that one member of each pair will have to present the findings of the pair, so one member of each pair should note down the main points from the discussion and what their final choice of options is.

- Circulate and monitor. Note down language points for praise and correction afterwards, especially those relating to planning and growth.

- When the pairs have drawn up their plans, call the whole class to order, praise some of the good language you heard and work on half a dozen points that need improving. Get individual students to say the correct forms.

- Get two or three pairs to present their investment plans. Try to choose pairs whose ideas are different in order to give variety and stimulate discussion. Note down language points for praise and correction afterwards, this time concentrating on presentations language.

- Praise some of the good presentations language you heard and work on half a dozen points that need improving. Get individual students to say the correct forms.

- Get students to discuss the different plans as one group. If the class is very large, divide it into two or three groups. Circulate and monitor. Note down language points for praise and correction afterwards, perhaps ones related to some you noted earlier.

- Bring the class to order. Work on half a dozen language points that require it.

- Rather than have another presentation of the final choice of investment options in this session, ask a representative of the group (or of each group) to prepare one for the following session. If you do this, don't forget to allow time for the presentation(s) in the next session. This will also allow you to recap key language that arose in the case study.

CASE STUDY

One-to-one

This case study can be done as a discussion between teacher and student and then as a basis for a presentation by the student. Don't forget to note language points for praise and correction afterwards. Also point out some of the key language you chose to use.

⦾ Students can watch the *Case study commentary* on the DVD-ROM.

Stage 5: Writing

● The students write up the final selection of investment options as a proposal document to the CEO of Dino Conti Ice Cream. Make it clear whether the memo should reflect the opinion of the group as a whole or the opinions of the student writing it. This proposal can be done for homework.

➡ Writing file, page 127

➡ Resource bank: Writing (page 205)

Selling

AT A GLANCE

	Classwork – Course Book	Further work
Lesson 1 *Each lesson (excluding case studies) is about 45–60 minutes. This does not include administration and time spent going through homework.*	**Starting up** Students talk about what they like and don't like about retail shopping. **Vocabulary: Making sales** Students work on words related to buying and selling.	**Practice File** Vocabulary (page 12) **Practice exercises:** **Vocabulary 1 & 2** (DVD-ROM) **i-Glossary** (DVD-ROM)
Lesson 2	**Listening: Selling on TV** Students listen to the Director of Marketing at QVC, the global shopping channel, talk about how to succeed in selling on TV. **Reading: Sales skills** Students read an article about qualities that make the best salespeople.	**Resource bank: Listening** (page 191) **Practice exercises:** **Listening** (DVD-ROM) **Text bank** (pages 124–127)
Lesson 3	**Language review: Modals 2: *must, need to, have to, should*** Students apply modals for obligation, necessity and prohibition (*must*, *need to*, *have to* and *should*) in the context of rules for a timeshare holiday accommodation club and in two texts about how to be a good salesperson. **Skills: Negotiating: reaching agreement** Students discuss tips for successful negotiating, listen to a negotiation and then role-play one themselves.	**Practice File** Language review (page 13) **Practice exercises:** **Language review 1 & 2** (DVD-ROM) **ML Essential Business Grammar and Usage** (Unit 28) **Resource bank: Speaking** (page 179) **Practice exercises: Skills** (DVD-ROM)
Lesson 4 *Each case study is about 1 to 1½ hours.*	**Case study: A partnership agreement** A business jet charter company wants to team up with a five-star hotel group. Students role-play negotiations between the two companies.	**Case study commentary** (DVD-ROM) **Resource bank: Writing** (page 206) **Practice File** Writing (page 14) **Test file: Progress test 1**

For a fast route through the unit focusing mainly on speaking skills, just use the underlined sections.

For one-to-one situations, most parts of the unit lend themselves, with minimal adaptation, to use with individual students. Where this is not the case, alternative procedures are given.

BUSINESS BRIEF

The world of selling can be a tough place to work. Though the rise of **e-commerce** has changed **retail sales**, the fact remains that at all levels, from **street markets** up to billion-dollar **business-to-government (B2G)** deals, most sales are still negotiated the old-fashioned way: by people talking to one another.

A company may produce a fantastic product or offer outstanding service, but without a successful sales team, the business will fail. But selling a product or a service goes beyond getting customers to part with their money. Everyone in business needs to do some selling: selling your own ideas to your co-workers; convincing potential business partners that you can deal with problems that may arise; keeping your team on side during hard times. Mastering the art of selling requires confidence, product knowledge, an ability to take rejection, and excellent **negotiation skills**.

Selling a product or services takes many forms. **Cold calling** is phoning or visiting someone you haven't had contact with before to convince them to buy something or do something. **Telesales** is cold calling using the telephone. **Business-to-business (B2B)** sales, for example distributors selling to retailers, tends to be relationship-based. The buyer and seller are doing business together rather than the seller trying to fill the buyer's emotional need for something. In B2G selling, which is highly formal, companies bid for government contracts.

E-commerce, mentioned earlier, is the increasing area of sales over the Internet. However, e-commerce courses in business schools are no longer oversubscribed and no longer preaching that 'everything has changed'. Companies look more at how e-commerce can be used in conjunction with other methods of selling: in retailing this means **clicks and mortar**, combining traditional retail outlets with online operations, rather than **pure e-tailing**. Some **old-economy** companies, like the UK supermarket company Tesco, have made a success of e-commerce by combining it with their existing operations, rather than investing in a whole new expensive **infrastructure**. Webvan, a pure online groceries company in the US, fell down on the hurdles of logistics: **warehousing** and **delivery**.

Read on

Tom Hopkins: *How to Master the Art of Selling*, HarperCollins, 2010

Stephan Schiffman: *The 25 Sales Habits of Highly Successful Salespeople*, Adams Media Corporation, 2008

Jeremy Cassell: *Brilliant Selling – What the Best Sales People Know, Do and Say*, Prentice Hall, 2009

Chet Holmes: *The Ultimate Sales Machine – Turbocharge Your Business with Relentless Focus on 12 Key Strategies*, Portfolio, 2007

LESSON NOTES

Warmer

- Write the word *selling* in big letters on the board.

- Ask the students to say what this means to them, if anything. Ask if anyone has bought anything online, but do not pre-empt the discussion in Starting up below.

Overview

- Ask the students to look at the Overview section on page 22. Tell them a little about the things you will be doing, using the table on page 27 of this book as a guide. Tell them which sections you will be covering in this lesson and which in later lessons.

Quotation

- Write the quotation on the board and ask students to discuss briefly in pairs what they understand by it.

- With the whole class, ask pairs for their understanding of the quote. Compare and contrast different pairs' views.

> The main point in this amusing quote is that it would be usual for a grandfather to give his grandson a gold pocket watch. However, Woody Allen's grandfather was such a good salesman that even on his deathbed he was able to sell a watch to his grandson.

Starting up

Students talk about what they like and dislike about shopping and about their recent shopping experiences.

A

- Get students to call out answers to the first two questions.

- Not all students may be familiar with the types of retail outlet on the list. Before putting them in pairs or small groups to answer the second two questions, elicit the following as you think necessary:

  – convenience store: open long hours selling a variety of food and drink and most household items, e.g. 7–11

  – department store: large store, often with many floors and divided into departments, each selling a different type of goods, e.g. Harrods, Selfridges (London); KaDeWe (Berlin), Macy's, Bloomingdales (New York), Karstadt (Germany), El Corte Inglés (Spain), Mitsukoshi, Sogo (Japan)

  – specialist retailer: individual store or part of a chain selling one type of goods, e.g. electrical goods, shoes, books, etc.

  – shopping centre/mall: large area with many different shops, usually under cover and where cars are not allowed

- Circulate, monitor and assist if necessary.

- Ask a few students to share the answers of the people they spoke with.

B 🔊 CD1.25–1.27

- Have students read the three questions and make sure they understand them.

- Before playing the recording, point out that one of the people doesn't say anything about dislikes (Person 3).

- Play the recording. Students note the likes and dislikes and then compare their answers in pairs.

- Elicit the answers. Play the recording a second time if necessary.

Person 1	Likes: shopping for things she's interested in (e.g. clothes)
	Dislikes: going to the supermarket
Person 2	Likes: shopping on the Internet, especially auction sites
	Dislikes: shopping malls
Person 3	Likes: the experience of shopping, specialist shops, trying to get discounts, shopping for shoes

- In pairs or small groups, students answer questions 2 and 3.

- Circulate, monitor and assist if necessary.

- Ask a few students to share the answers of the people they spoke with.

Vocabulary: Making sales

Students look at the vocabulary of buying, selling and payment.

A

- Go through the meanings of the words with the whole class.

- Get students to work on the exercise in pairs. Circulate, monitor and assist if necessary.

- Check the answers with the whole class.

> 1 c 2 a 3 b 4 c 5 b 6 a 7 c 8 b

B

- With the whole class, point out the principle of this matching exercise: there is sometimes more than one match, but you are looking for the matches that correspond to the definitions 1–8.

- Do the exercise as a quick-fire activity with the whole class. Explain any remaining difficulties.

LESSON NOTES

1 cooling-off period

2 credit-card details

3 method of payment

4 interest-free credit

5 out of stock

6 money-back guarantee

7 after-sales service

8 loyalty-card scheme

C

- Have students work in pairs. Circulate, monitor and assist if necessary.
- Ask a few students to share their answers with the class.

D

- Again have students work in pairs. Circulate, monitor and assist if necessary.
- Discuss the answers as a class.
- ◉ i-Glossary

Listening: Selling on TV

Sue Leeson, Director of Marketing at QVC, the global shopping channel, talks about how the company successfully sells products on television.

A ◀)) CD1.28

- Have students read the three questions and make sure they understand them.
- Play the recording and have students listen for the answers.
- Ask students to call out the answers as you list them on the board.

1 food, fashion, accessories, beauty, gardening, DIY

2 Germany, Japan, USA, UK, Italy

3 television and online

B ◀)) CD1.29

- Before playing the recording, get students to read the paragraph and try to guess the words that will go in the gaps.
- Play the recording and get students to fill the gaps.
- Ask students to check their answers with a partner, then check them with the whole class.

1 demonstrate

2 story

3 audience

4 benefits

5 clear

C ◀)) CD1.29

- Have students try to remember the words that go in the gaps.
- Play the recording and ask students to write the words.
- Check the answers with the whole class.

1 inside and out

2 do

3 suitable

D ◀)) CD1.30

- Have students read the questions.
- Play the recording. Ask students to say the answers. Play the recording again if necessary.

1 Because each beauty brand has a fantastic story behind it and each product is very easy to demonstrate.

2 Fragrance, because you can't communicate how it smells on TV.

E ◀)) CD1.31

- Play the recording and elicit the answers.

An image of the product; the product description; ratings and reviews of the product; a video demonstration

➡ Resource bank: Listening (page 191)

Reading: Sales skills

Students read an article about the qualities of the most successful salespeople.

A

- Get students to work in pairs. Circulate, monitor and assist if necessary.
- Elicit opinions from the whole class.

B

- Get students to check the answer (*honesty*) on page 136. Do students agree or disagree with this answer?

LESSON NOTES

C

- Divide the class into an A group and a B group. Then have each Student A find a Student B to form a pair.

- Student A reads the article on page 25 and Student B reads the article on page 137, each doing the relevant matching exercise. Circulate, monitor and assist if necessary.

- Check answers with the whole class.

> **Student A**
>
> **1** e **2** g **3** h **4** f **5** c **6** d **7** b **8** a
>
> **Student B**
>
> **1** g **2** c **3** a **4** b **5** e **6** h **7** f **8** d

D

- Students work in pairs. They may now need to read the article again in more detail before answering the questions.

> **Student A**
>
> **1** Show confidence on the outside.
>
> **2** Your product, your business and your industry
>
> **3** 30 seconds: The time you have to interact with someone before they form an opinion of you.
>
> 15 seconds: The initial period of a telephone call when you have a chance to make a good impression.
>
> **4** Don't take it personally.
>
> **5** Leads / Calling more people
>
> **6** Your starting point, the point which you won't drop below, and a mid-way point which you'll aim for
>
> **7** Not approaching selling with dread; seeing selling as a challenge; enjoy closing deals and making sales; seeing rejection as a result
>
> **Student B**
>
> **a)** The proportion of women who believe that women make the best salespeople.
>
> **b)** The proportion of men who believe that women make the best salespeople.
>
> **c)** The percentage of men who agreed that women make better salespeople.
>
> **d)** The percentage of women who agreed that women make better salespeople.
>
> **e)** The percentage of men who ranked *honesty* as most important.
>
> **f)** The percentage of women who ranked *personality* as most important.

> **g)** The ranking of *integrity* in the survey.
>
> **h)** The percentage of people who ranked *integrity* as important.
>
> **i)** The percentage of sales professionals who ranked *good looks* as important.
>
> **j)** The number of years over which the reputation of sales has improved.
>
> **k)** The percentage of men who believe that the reputation of sales has improved over the last 10 years.
>
> **l)** The percentage of women who believe that the reputation of sales has improved over the last 10 years.
>
> **m)** The percentage of men who agree that the top incentive for salespeople was money.
>
> **n)** The percentage of women who agree that the top incentive for salespeople was money.
>
> **o)** The salary (in thousands of pounds) that the average sales executive can expect to earn, including bonuses and commission, in their first year of work.

➡ Text bank (pages 124–127)

Language review: Modals 2: *must*, *need to*, *have to*, *should*

Students apply these modals in the context of the rules for a timeshare holiday accommodation club, and in relation to the interview that they listened to earlier.

- This is a difficult area. Go slowly and adjust the material to the level of the class. Go through the different examples and relate them to the article that students read and discussed in the Reading section.

- Point out that *need to*, *should* and *must* are of increasing 'strength' in the order mentioned. Point out the difference between *don't have to* and *mustn't*. Try to get students to see the 'logic' of the different modals in context rather than get bogged down in the terminology of *obligation*, *necessity*, etc.

A

- Get students to work on the activity in pairs. Circulate, monitor and assist if necessary.

- Check the answers with the whole class.

> **1** No **2** No **3** Yes **4** No **5** No **6** No **7** No

- Ask your students if any of them belong to any sort of club – an athletic club or music club, for example. Get them to explain what the rules are, using modals.

LESSON NOTES

B

- Get students to work on the activity in pairs. Circulate, monitor and assist if necessary.

- Check the answers with the whole class.

> **1** f **2** a **3** b **4** e **5** d **6** c

C

- Students work on the activity in pairs. Circulate, monitor and assist if necessary.

> **Possible answers**
>
> You must be honest.
>
> You must sound and appear confident.
>
> You need to know your product.
>
> You have to have a professional appearance.
>
> You shouldn't take rejection personally.
>
> You must know how far you will negotiate.
>
> You should approach selling with a positive mindset.

- Go through the exercise with the whole class, discussing the answers.

Skills: Negotiating: reaching agreement

Students discuss negotiating tips, listen to a negotiation between an electric-car salesman and a buyer who represents a city's government, and look at the language of agreement and disagreement. They then role-play the negotiation of the sale of the electric cars.

A

- Divide the class into two groups – A and B. (If there are more than about 10 students, divide the class into four groups – two group As and two Bs.)

- Get the groups to look at the negotiating tips for their group, choosing the five most important. Circulate, monitor and assist if necessary.

- When the groups have made their short lists, form new groups, consisting of A and B students.

- Get the new groups to make a short list of what they consider the five most important tips. Circulate, monitor and assist if necessary. The idea here is that deciding the most important tips is itself a negotiating process.

B 🔊 CD1.32

- Before you play the recording, establish the situation – a negotiation between the sales manager of an electric-car company (Martin) and an official from the Urban Transport Department of a Chinese city (Chen) who wants to buy ten electric cars. Ask students to say what they think they will hear in the recording. For example, Chen will probably want to lower the price, and Martin may want to increase the lead time.

- Play the first part of the negotiation for the whole class and get students to answer the questions.

- Go through the answers with the whole class.

> **1** So that people can rent them to do their shopping and go about their business – they are trying to reduce pollution.
>
> **2** quantity, price, discounts, delivery, warranty
>
> **3** after-sales service

C 🔊 CD1.32

- Before playing the recording, get students to read the conversation and try to remember the words and phrases that will go in the gaps.

- Play the recording again and ask students to complete the gaps in the script. Circulate, monitor and assist if necessary.

- Work on the points that have caused the most difficulty.

> **1** price list
>
> **2** discount
>
> **3** guarantee delivery
>
> **4** warranty
>
> **5** credit; policy; down payment

D

- As with all role plays, ensure that students understand the general situation: this is the continuation of Martin and Chen's negotiation about the delivery of electric cars.

- Before asking students to look at their role cards, get them to look at the Useful language and practise the expressions, asking individual students to read them after you with appropriate intonation. Insist on correct pronunciation of the contractions *We'd* and *I'll*.

- Allocate the roles. Give students plenty of time to assimilate the information and prepare their roles. Circulate, monitor and assist if necessary.

LESSON NOTES

- When the students are ready, get them to start the role play in pairs.

- Circulate and monitor. Note language points for praise and correction afterwards, especially negotiation language.

- When students have finished, ask one or two pairs to explain what happened in their negotiation and what the final outcome was.

- Praise strong language points that you heard and discuss half a dozen points that need improvement, getting individual students to say the correct forms.

- Ask individual pairs to re-enact short parts of their negotiation containing the forms you have worked on, getting them to put the correct forms into practice.

> **One-to-one**
>
> This role play can be done between teacher and student.
>
> Don't forget to note language points for praise and correction afterwards. Also point out some of the key language you chose to use. Ask the student about their negotiating plan, the tactics they were using, etc.

➡ Resource bank: Speaking (page 179)

CASE STUDY

A partnership agreement

A business jet charter company wants to team up with a five-star hotel group. Students study the background and role-play negotiations between the two companies.

Stage 1: Background and listening 🔊 CD1.33

- Ask students to look at the background information. Meanwhile, write up the headings on the left of the table below on the board, but don't put in the other information.

- Answer any questions about vocabulary or other difficulties.

- Then elicit information from the whole class to complete the table.

EPJS	
Type of service	Travel in private jets for top executives and VIPs
Existing customers	Mainly business executives
Aims	Offer an attractive package: good value prices, special assistance at airports, superb accommodation and service
State of business	Facing strong competition from other charter airlines

- Explain that students are going to listen to a conversation between a director of EPJS and a director of Megaluxe. Have them note down the agenda items.

Agenda

1 Length of agreement

2 Number and type of rooms

3 Services

4 Rates and discounts

5 Advertising

- Check answers as a class.

Stage 2: Task

- Divide the class into two groups, or if it is very large, into four or six groups for parallel negotiations. You could also appoint an observer for each negotiation. The observer does not take part but notes down key points from the negotiating process – how and when each side makes concessions, points they do not concede, etc.

- Make sure each group understands which side it will be negotiating for. You could also appoint a lead negotiator in each team if you think this will help.

- Circulate, monitor and assist students in preparing for the negotiation. Get them to write down key expressions they will use, like the ones in italics under 'Length of contract' on the role cards. Check that they look at the agenda for the meeting, as well as the information on their role cards.

- When the groups are ready, tell them to begin. Circulate and monitor. Note language points for praise and correction afterwards, especially negotiation language.

- Warn groups when they only have 10, then five, minutes left, hurrying them to reach an agreement.

- When groups have finished, ask a member of each group to describe the negotiating process and the final agreement. If you appointed an observer, get them to describe the process.

- Praise strong language points that you heard and discuss half a dozen points that need improvement, getting individual students to say the correct forms.

- If there is time, ask pairs of students to re-enact short parts of the negotiation containing the forms you have worked on, getting them to put the correct forms into practice.

One-to-one

Use the points above as the basis for discussion with your student. If there is time, you could go on to ask them how recruitment is done in their own organisation, whether internal promotion is favoured over looking for external candidates, etc.

◎ Students can watch the *Case study commentary* on the DVD-ROM.

Stage 3: Writing

- The students write up the outcome of the meeting in the form of a letter to a member of the other side. Point out that it should cover all five points on the agenda. This letter can be done for homework.

➡ Writing file, page 128

➡ Resource bank: Writing (page 206)

WORKING ACROSS CULTURES 1

Saying 'no' politely

As this is probably the first *Working across cultures* unit that you are doing with students, explain what cultural awareness is: the idea that people should be aware of different attitudes, ways of behaving, taking decisions, using time, etc. that other cultures may have, and how these must be taken into account when doing business in different cultures.

This unit focuses on different cultures' ways of saying 'no' politely.

A

- Get students to discuss the points in groups of three or four. Circulate, monitor and assist if necessary.

- Share answers and discuss as a class.

B 🔊 CD1.34

- Get students to read the five tips that they are going to complete.

- Play the recording while students complete the exercise.

- Play the recording a second time for students to check their answers.

- Check the answers with the whole class.

1	attention
2	alternatives
3	sympathy
4	(as) clear (as possible)
5	long reasons and excuses

C 🔊 CD1.35

- Have students read through the seven sentences.

- Play the recording while students complete the exercise.

- Play the recording a second time for students to check their answers.

- Check the answers with the whole class.

1	F (It is important to focus on non-verbal communication.)
2	T
3	T
4	F (They have 12 ways of saying 'no'.)
5	T
6	F (Silence in the Arab world is quite common and does not necessarily mean 'no'.)
7	F (It is not considered rude in America, but it could be in Saudi Arabia.)

D – **E** 🔊 CD1.36

- Have students do the exercise individually, then check their answers in pairs.

- Play the recording and check the answers with the whole class.

1 b	2 c	3 d	4 e	5 a

- In pairs, have students practise reading the invitations and responses. Encourage them first to read the sentences silently to themselves, then to look up from their book and say the sentences with feeling. Let them practise several times, changing roles. Encourage them to perform the exchanges from memory rather than by reading.

Task

- With the whole class, have a different student read each role card aloud. Briefly explain each situation and answer any questions students may have.

- Students work in pairs. Circulate, monitor and assist if necessary.

- When the students have done the activity once, praise strong points and mention one or two things that students should pay attention to when they change roles.

- Get students to change roles and again to role-play the situations. Circulate and monitor.

- Get one or two pairs to perform each role play for the class.

Revision

This unit revises and reinforces some of the key language points from Units 1–3 and from Working across cultures 1. (Course Book page numbers are given below.)

1 Careers

Vocabulary (page 7)

1	plan	**8**	her best
2	living	**9**	break
3	opportunities	**10**	early retirement
4	bonus	**11**	path
5	ladder	**12**	overtime
6	commission	**13**	€60K per year
7	move	**14**	the sack

Modals (page 10)

1 Can	**2** Would	**3** could	**4** could	**5** can
6 would	**7** Would	**8** Can	**9** could	

Skills (page 11)

Part A

1 d **2** f **3** g **4** a **5** c **6** h **7** b **8** e

Part B

1 f **2** b **3** e **4** g **5** d **6** c **7** h **8** i **9** a

2 Companies

Vocabulary (pages 14–15)

1	pharmaceutical	**5**	share price
2	turnover	**6**	Spanish subsidiary
3	net profit	**7**	parent company
4	workforce		

Present simple and present continuous (page 18)

1	'm	**6**	'm looking
2	love	**7**	feel
3	work	**8**	'm starting
4	're developing	**9**	's
5	're trying	**10**	think

Skills (page 19)

1 a **2** c **3** b **4** a **5** c **6** a **7** b **8** a

3 Selling

Vocabulary (page 23)

1	offer	**4**	sale
2	return	**5**	manufacture
3	purchase	**6**	out of stock

Modals (page 26)

1 b **2** a **3** a **4** b **5** b **6** a

Writing

● This exercise is similar to the writing exercise for the case study on page 29.

Sample answer

Dear Mr Ulrich,

Following our meeting last week, I'm pleased to say that we're ready to move ahead with a distribution agreement. I enclose a draft contract for your approval. Please could you read through it and let me know if you would like to make any changes or additions.

I look forward to doing business with you.

Yours sincerely,

Cultures 1: Saying 'no' politely

A

1 I wish I could, but I really have to go.

2 Thanks for the invitation, but I'm not feeling very well. Maybe some other time.

3 Nothing more for me, thanks. It was delicious.

4 I'm afraid you've come to the wrong person. You'll have to ask Keith.

5 I'm sorry. I'd love to, but I have other plans that day.

B

a 3 **b** 5 **c** 1 **d** 2 **e** 4

AT A GLANCE

	Classwork – Course Book	Further work
Lesson 1 *Each lesson (excluding case studies) is about 45–60 minutes. This does not include administration and time spent going through homework.*	**Starting up** Students talk about how new ideas are found and nurtured. **Vocabulary: Verb and noun combinations** Students look at and use typical verb and noun combinations in relation to new ideas, opportunities, etc., and hear them used in context.	**Practice File** Vocabulary (page 16) **Practice exercises: Vocabulary 1 & 2** (DVD-ROM) **i-Glossary** (DVD-ROM)
Lesson 2	**Listening: Great business ideas** Students listen to an Oxford University researcher talk about the best business ideas of the past 15 years. **Reading: Three great ideas** Students read about three good business ideas and exchange information about them.	**Resource bank: Listening** (page 192) **Practice exercises: Listening** (DVD-ROM) **Text bank** (pages 128–131)
Lesson 3	**Language review: Past simple and past continuous** The two tenses are compared and contrasted. Students then use them in the context of an article about the inventor of Post-it notes. **Skills: Successful meetings** Students look at what makes for successful meetings and listen to a meeting in progress. They then study meetings language.	**Practice File** Language review (page 17) **Practice exercises: Language review 1 & 2** (DVD-ROM) **ML Essential Business Grammar and Usage** (Units 10, 11 & 13) **Resource bank: Speaking** (page 180) **Practice exercises: Skills** (DVD-ROM)
Lesson 4 *Each case study is about 1 to 1½ hours.*	**Case study: The new attraction** A rich man has set up a competition that will encourage great ideas for a new visitor attraction. Students brainstorm ideas for a new attraction in their own area/country.	**Case study commentary** (DVD-ROM) **Resource bank: Writing** (page 207) **Practice File** Writing (page 18)

For a fast route through the unit focusing mainly on speaking skills, just use the underlined sections.

For one-to-one situations, most parts of the unit lend themselves, with minimal adaptation, to use with individual students. Where this is not the case, alternative procedures are given.

BUSINESS BRIEF

Resistance to new ideas is well known. In organisations, the best way of killing an idea may well be to take it to a meeting. The very things that make companies successful in one area may prevent them from developing success in new activities. Early work on personal computers at Xerox was dismissed by its senior managers because they considered that the company's business was copying, not computing. Company leaders talk about **corporate venturing** and **intrapreneurship**, where employees are encouraged to develop **entrepreneurial** activities within the organisation. Companies may try to set up structures in such a way that they do not stifle new ideas. They may put groups of talented people together in **skunk works** to work on **innovations** – development of the PC at IBM is the most famous example. Skunk works are outside the usual company structures and are less likely to be hampered by bureaucracy, in-fighting, and so on.

When innovators go to large companies with new designs for their products, they face similar problems. The inventor of the small-wheeled Moulton bicycle could not persuade Raleigh to produce it, so he set up his own company. But a single innovative **breakthrough** is not enough. There has to be **continuous improvement** and **market response**. The current winners in bicycle innovation are producers of mountain bikes, who have taken the original bicycle design and eliminated its irritations, revolutionising an old concept by providing relative comfort, easy gear changes, a 'fun' ride, and so on.

The initial idea for a car will be turned into a series of **prototypes** and tested. In software development, the final 'prototype' is the **beta version**, which is **beta-tested**. Pharmaceuticals go through a series of **trials**. Even the most brilliant entrepreneurs will not have the resources to go it alone in industries like these, as the investment and experience required are enormous. Cars, software and pharmaceuticals are examples of industries dominated by giants. The 'rules of the game' are well established, and newcomers are rare, unless they can find a small **niche** unexploited by the giants. There may be more opportunity for innovation where the rules of the game are not yet established. This may involve selling and delivering existing products in new ways: think, for example, of selling books and airline tickets on the Internet.

One thing is certain: business will continue to benefit from the creativity of individuals and organisations who can develop great ideas and bring them to market.

Read on

Jeff Dyer: *The Innovator's DNA – Mastering the Five Skills of Disruptive Innovators*, Harvard University Press, 2011

Carmine Gallo: *The Innovation Secrets of Steve Jobs – Insanely Different Principles for Breakthrough Success*, McGraw-Hill Professional, 2010

Luke Williams: *Disrupt – Think the Unthinkable to Spark Transformation in Your Business*, Financial Times/Prentice Hall, 2010

Professor Pervaiz Ahmed and Dr Charlie Shepherd: *Innovation Management – Context, Strategies, Systems and Processes*, Financial Times Press/Prentice Hall, 2010

LESSON NOTES

Warmer

- Write the words *an idea* in big letters on the right of the board. Work on the pronunciation of *idea* if necessary.

- Ask students to suggest verbs that can come in front of it. Some possibilities are given below.

have	
suggest	
think of	an idea
like	
develop	

- Then, without pre-empting the material in the unit too much, get students to make complete sentences using these combinations.

Overview

- Ask students to look at the Overview section on page 36. Tell them a little about the things you will be doing, using the table on page 37 of this book as a guide. Tell them which sections you will be covering in this lesson and which in later lessons.

Quotation

- Write the quotation on the board. Ask students if anyone can explain *controversial* (= causing a lot of disagreement because people have different opinions).

- Ask students if they can think of examples of good ideas from the past that were controversial at first. A few ideas:

  – Early critics of railways believed the human body couldn't withstand the speed of train travel.

  – The proposal that the planets orbit the sun was initially rejected.

  – Many believed that home video would destroy the cinema business.

- Ask students to think of ideas that are controversial now. Which ones do they think will become more accepted over time?

Starting up

Students talk about how new ideas are found and nurtured.

A

- Tell students to discuss the statements in pairs. Circulate, monitor and assist if necessary.

- With the whole class, ask different pairs to say what their findings were.

B

- Discuss the questions with the whole class.

Vocabulary: Verb and noun combinations

Students look at typical verb and noun combinations in relation to new ideas, opportunities, etc. and use them to complete an extract from a talk by the head of a research and development department.

A

- Match the verb/noun combinations and their meanings as a quick-fire activity with the whole class and clarify meanings where necessary.

> **1** c   **2** f   **3** e   **4** a   **5** b   **6** d

B

- Explain the context: students will later hear an extract from a talk by the head of a research and development department. The text in the Course Book is the audio script with gaps.

- Get students to work on the exercise in pairs, using the phrases from Exercise A. Circulate, monitor and assist if necessary.

> **1** takes advantage of an opportunity
>
> **2** extend its product range
>
> **3** enter a market
>
> **4** make a breakthrough
>
> **5** meet a need
>
> **6** raises their status

C ◀)) CD1.37

- Play the recording and tell students to check their answers. Assist with any remaining difficulties.

- Play the recording again for students to complete the remaining gaps in the text.

D ◀)) CD1.38

- Have students read the paragraph and try to predict the words that will go in the gaps.

- Play the recording and have students write the answers.

- When they have finished, check their answers and get them to make a note of the featured collocations (e.g. *to reduce waste*).

> **1** reduces   **2** protects   **3** fills   **4** win

LESSON NOTES

E

- Students work in pairs. Circulate, monitor and assist if necessary.

◎ i-Glossary

Listening: Great business ideas

Students listen to an Oxford University researcher talk about the best business ideas of the past 15 years.

A

- Explain that Oxford is a city in southern England and that Oxford University is considered to be one of the world's top universities.

- Discuss this question with the whole class.

B ◀)) CD1.39

- Play the recording. Students do the exercise individually.

- Check answers with the class.

> eBay, because it provides individuals and small businesses with a channel to market that didn't exist before.
>
> The USB stick, because it enables data and pictures to be easily transportable.
>
> The digital camera, because it's revolutionised photography and is incorporated into many other devices.

C ◀)) CD1.40

- Get students to work in pairs to discuss the first question.

- Play the recording.

- Go through the answers with the whole class.

> 1 Product-based companies, like pharmaceuticals and high-tech companies
>
> 2 Ericsson (The interviewee refers to the company as Finnish, but in fact it is Swedish.)

D ◀)) CD1.40

- Have students read the extract and try to predict the words that will go in the gaps.

- Play the recording and have students write the answers.

- When they have finished, check their answers.

> | **1** information | **2** relationships | **3** products |
> | **4** innovation | **5** different | **6** increase |
> | **7** extending | **8** time | |

E

- Help differentiate the two questions by pointing out that the best business idea of the next 15 years will be something that's actually possible and could succeed as a business. The second question is one of imagination. What sort of dream invention would you like to see?

- Discuss the questions in small groups, then as a class.

➡ Resource bank: Listening (page 192)

Reading: Three great ideas

Students read about three good business ideas and exchange information about them.

A

- Get students to work in small groups to discuss this question.

- Give them five minutes or so, then have a spokesperson from each group present their ideas to the class. Encourage students who don't normally say much to act as spokesperson.

B

- Divide the class into groups of three and ensure that each student knows if they are Student A, B or C.

- Ask students to read the correct article. Circulate, monitor and assist if necessary.

- Get students to complete the relevant box with the answers to the questions relating to the article they have just read.

> **Who needs translators?**
>
> 1 Phone software that can translate foreign languages almost instantly
>
> 2 People of different languages talking to each other on the phone
>
> 3 phone users
>
> 4 Should be ready in a couple of years
>
> **Safer cycling**
>
> 1 Cycling 'collar' with an airbag inside
>
> 2 Protecting cyclists in case of accidents
>
> 3 cyclists
>
> 4 Will be on sale early next year
>
> **Going for gold**
>
> 1 Vending machine for gold bullion
>
> 2 People wanting a quick and easy way to buy gold
>
> 3 global, fitness centres, cruise ships
>
> 4 20 machines already in place, new machines opening in the US next month

LESSON NOTES

C

- Get students to work in their groups of three to exchange information about their articles and take notes on the two articles they didn't read.

D

- Students work in pairs. Circulate, monitor and assist if necessary.

- Have a brief class discussion on one or all of the questions to bring students' ideas together.

➡ Text bank (pages 128–131)

Language review: Past simple and past continuous

The two tenses are compared and contrasted. Students then use them in context.

- Focus students' attention on how the two tenses are used in the examples in the Language review box.

- Get students to read the three rules and ensure that they understand them.

A

- Tell students to work on the story in pairs. Circulate, monitor and assist if necessary.

- Go through the answers with the whole class.

> 1 were writing
>
> 2 invented
>
> 3 was working
>
> 4 noticed
>
> 5 developed
>
> 6 died

B

- Point out that the next exercise is a role-playing game. Be aware that some of the language here may sound very accusatory, and that some students may not be comfortable with that. Keep the exercise light by encouraging the students to smile, have fun, and inject as much drama and acting into the exercise as possible.

- In pairs, students do the exercise. Circulate, monitor and assist as necessary.

- Praise strong language points that you hear and discuss half a dozen points that need improvement, getting individual students to say the correct forms.

Skills: Successful meetings

Students look at what makes for successful meetings and listen to a meeting in progress. They then study meetings language.

A

- Ask students to discuss the points in pairs or groups of three.

- Circulate, monitor and assist if necessary. Note down language points for praise and correction, especially those relating to the language of meetings.

- Discuss the statements with the whole class.

- The following ideas may help to stimulate discussion. Be tactful about meetings in the students' own organisation(s) and culture(s).

> 1 It probably depends on the type of meeting. It's probably good to have at the meeting only those who really need to be there and to limit this number as far as possible. However, large meetings can be successful if they are well chaired.
>
> 2 Different companies and cultures deal with this in different ways. Coffee and water may be freely available, but snacks between meals are unknown in some places. The working lunch is a possibility in some places, with perhaps sandwiches in the meeting room or lunch in a restaurant.
>
> 3 Again, different cultures have different ideas about this. In some places, starting a 2 o'clock meeting at 2.20 may count as starting 'on time'.
>
> 4 Some companies are well known for having all their meetings standing up, in order to encourage quick decisions. (You could also discuss the shape of the table – for example whether round tables make for more 'democratic' meetings.)
>
> 5 Again, it probably depends on the type of meeting. This is a good opportunity to teach *chair* in the sense of *chairman* or *chairwoman*.
>
> 6 Organised turn-taking can be very clear in some cultures, with long pauses to show that consideration is being given to what has just been said, but overlapping is the norm elsewhere. Perhaps this is a good opportunity to teach *Please let me finish*.

LESSON NOTES

B ◀)) CD1.41

- Explain the situation to students before they listen to the meeting.

- Then play the recording once or twice and explain any difficulties, without pre-empting the questions, of course.

- Ask the whole class for the answers.

> 1 To decide the launch date for the DM 2000 and the recommended retail price
>
> 2 September

C ◀)) CD1.41

- Play the recording again and get students to tick the expressions they hear.

> 1, 2, 5, 6

D ◀)) CD1.41

- Play the recording again and get students to write in the words and expressions.

> 1 in favour
>
> 2 competitors
>
> 3 campaign
>
> 4 Hold on
>
> 5 launch
>
> 6 point
>
> 7 target
>
> 8 department
>
> 9 channels

E

- Go through the expressions in the Useful language box, working on intonation. Tell students to be careful with *I don't agree,* which has to be said with 'softening' intonation.

- Explain the situation about the launch of a new wallet.

- Divide the class into groups of three to five. Nominate a chair (Student A) and allocate the other roles.

- Circulate, monitor and assist if necessary with preparation of the roles. Make sure the chair is ready to use the chairing language and the participants are ready to use their language.

- When the groups are ready, they can begin to role-play the meeting. Circulate and monitor. Note language, especially meetings-related language, for praise and correction afterwards.

- When the discussions have reached some sort of conclusion, bring the class to order and ask some of the groups what their decision was and how the discussion went.

- Praise strong language points and work on half a dozen points that need improving, getting students to say the correct forms.

➡ Resource bank: Speaking (page 180)

CASE STUDY

The new attraction

A rich man has set up a competition that will encourage great ideas for a new visitor attraction. Students brainstorm ideas for a new attraction in their own area/country.

Stage 1: Background and listening 🔊 CD1.42

- With the whole class, quickly read the introductory text to establish the context.

- Explain to students that they are going to hear a conversation between Dilip Singh and his personal assistant, Jane Ferguson.

- Explain that they need to listen for the three key points Dilip makes about the new attraction.

- Play the recording for students to note their answers. Play it again if necessary, then go through the answers.

> **Key points**
>
> 1 Great idea, something different/unusual, linked to culture of community/country
>
> 2 Provide an enjoyable experience for visitors
>
> 3 Must make money / be self-financing / be a commercial proposition

- Ask students to look at the three attractions that have impressed Dilip. Work on difficult vocabulary and write up notes about the three attractions on the board.

> **Shakespeare's Globe Theatre – London, England**
>
> Opened 1997, reconstruction of 1599 original
>
> Open-air playhouse and exhibition
>
> Popular London attraction
>
> **The Vulcan Tourism and Trek Station – Alberta, Canada**
>
> In Vulcan, Alberta
>
> Based on *Star Trek*
>
> Includes replica of *Enterprise*
>
> **The Sunken Ship Museum – Yangjiang, South China**
>
> Underwater museum opened 2010
>
> 800-year-old ship 24 metres under water
>
> Visitors view ship and treasures from it

- As a class, discuss the two questions.

Stage 2: Task

- Divide the class into groups of four or five and appoint a chair for each. Tell the groups that their ideas must be *creative*, *exciting* and *innovative*. They should remember that marketing considerations are very important for any tourist attraction.

- Make sure the chair is ready to use the chairing language and the participants are ready to use their language.

- When the groups are ready, tell them to start. Circulate and monitor. You may have to assist less imaginative groups with ideas. Note down language points for praise and correction afterwards, especially meetings-related language from the Useful language box on page 41.

- When each group has come up with a number of ideas, tell them to move on to choose the best idea to propose to Dilip's committee.

- When the groups have done this, bring the class to order. Ask a member of each group to say what its chosen attraction is. Note them on the board.

- Each group presents its idea to the rest of the class. Presenters should be prepared to respond to questions from the class.

- As a whole class, students meet to choose the best idea of all.

- Concentrating on meetings language, praise strong language points that you heard in the group discussions and work on half a dozen that need improving, getting individual students to say the correct forms.

> **One-to-one**
>
> This case study can be done as a discussion between teacher and student followed by a presentation by the student. Don't forget to note language points for praise and correction afterwards. Also point out some of the key language you chose to use.

◎ Students can watch the *Case study commentary* on the DVD-ROM.

Stage 3: Writing

- Students should write a short report to Dilip in their capacity as a member of his committee. They should recommend *one* of the attractions chosen by the class, outline its key features and say why it represents a commercial opportunity. This report can be done for homework.

⇨ Writing file, page 129

⇨ Resource bank: Writing (page 207)

AT A GLANCE

	Classwork – Course Book	Further work
Lesson 1 *Each lesson (excluding case studies) is about 45–60 minutes. This does not include administration and time spent going through homework.*	<u>**Starting up**</u> Students discuss stressful situations and ways of relaxing. **Vocabulary: Stress in the workplace** Students look at stress-related vocabulary. Then they compare stress levels in different jobs and in their own job.	**Practice File** Vocabulary (page 20) **Practice exercises:** **Vocabulary 1 & 2** (DVD-ROM) **i-Glossary** (DVD-ROM)
Lesson 2	**Listening: Dealing with stress** Students listen to a director of a health-at-work consultancy talking about stress. **Reading: Business owners feeling stressed** Students read about business owners feeling a recent increase in stress levels.	**Resource bank: Listening** (page 193) **Practice exercises:** **Listening** (DVD-ROM) **Text bank** (pages 132–135)
Lesson 3	**Language review: Past simple and present perfect** The tenses are compared and contrasted. Students then do exercises to find the correct tense and use the correct tense with time expressions. <u>**Skills: Participating in discussions**</u> Students listen to members of a human resources department talking about ways of improving the staff's health and then use these expressions in another context.	**Practice File** Language review (page 21) **Practice exercises:** **Language review 1 & 2** (DVD-ROM) **ML Essential Business Grammar and Usage** (Units 14, 15 & 16) **Resource bank: Speaking** (page 181) **Practice exercises: Skills** (DVD-ROM)
Lesson 4 *Each case study is about 1 to 1½ hours.*	<u>**Case study: Davies–Miller Advertising**</u> Students analyse and tackle problems of stress and low morale in an advertising agency that has recently lost two major accounts.	**Case study commentary** (DVD-ROM) **Resource bank: Writing** (page 208) **Practice File** Writing (page 22)

For a fast route through the unit focusing mainly on speaking skills, just use the underlined sections.

For one-to-one situations, most parts of the unit lend themselves, with minimal adaptation, to use with individual students. Where this is not the case, alternative procedures are given.

BUSINESS BRIEF

People like work that is **rewarding** and gives them **satisfaction**. For this, a reasonable amount of pressure may be necessary: many employees want work that **stretches** them, to have the feeling that it can sometimes be difficult, but that it is also **stimulating** and **challenging**. This is necessary if one is to have pleasant feelings of **achievement**.

But when **pressure** builds up, it's easy to feel **overwhelmed** by work, and this can produce feelings of **stress**. It is possible to become **stressed out** through **overwork** or other problems. People can **burn out**, become so stressed and tired that they may never be able to work again. The general consensus is that most jobs have become more demanding, with longer hours and greater pressures.

More and more people want to get away from what they call the **rat race** or the **treadmill**, the feeling that work is too competitive, and are looking for **lifestyles** that are less **stressful** or completely **unstressful**. They are looking for more relaxed ways of living and working, perhaps in the country. Some people choose to work from home so as to be nearer their families. People are looking for a better **quality of life**, a healthier **work–life balance**. Perhaps they are looking for more **quality time** with their partners and children. Choosing to work in less stressful ways is known as **downshifting** or **rebalancing**.

A whole **stress industry** has grown up, with its **stress counsellors** and **stress therapists** giving advice on how to avoid stress and on how to lessen its effects. However, other experts say that stress levels today are lower than they used to be. They point to the difficult working conditions and long hours of our great-grandparents. Perhaps the answer is that the material advantages of modern times give us the illusion that we should have more control over our lives. Like lottery winners who quickly become accustomed to the idea of being rich, we become 'spoilt' by material comforts and start to worry when we think we are losing even a little control over events.

Whatever the truth, people love to talk about the stress of their work. In the language classroom there should be no shortage of students willing to talk at length about the stress they are under. This stress might even be part of their **job satisfaction**.

Read on

P.K. Jha: *Time Management: The Art of Stress-Free Productivity*, Global India Publications, 2008

Martha Davis et al.: *The Relaxation and Stress Reduction Workbook*, 6th edition, New Harbinger, 2008

Fergus O'Connell: *Work Less, Achieve More – Great Ideas to Get Your Life Back*, Business Plus, 2009

Aljona Shchuka: *Stress at Work – Stress Management*, LAP Lambert Academic Publishing, 2010

Professor David A Buchanan and Dr Andrzej A Huczynski: *Organizational Behaviour,* Financial Times Press/Prentice Hall, 2010

LESSON NOTES

Warmer

- Write the following expressions related to *stress* on the board.

- Ask students for examples of each, without pre-empting the content of the unit too much.

> a **stressed** person
>
> a **stress-free** job
>
> a **stressful** experience

Overview

- Ask students to look at the Overview section on page 44. Tell them a little about the things you will be doing, using the table on page 44 of this book as a guide. Tell them which sections you will be covering in this lesson and which in later lessons.

Quotation

- Write the quotation on the board and ask the students if they agree with it. Ask if any students *always* think rest is boring.

Starting up

Students discuss stressful situations and ways of relaxing.

A

- Before they do this exercise, brainstorm with students situations that they find stressful in everyday life.

- Then get them to complete the phrases describing stressful situations.

- Go through the list. Do students consider all these situations to be stressful? (For example, not all students may consider going to the dentist to be stressful.)

- If you have time, encourage students to rank the list from most to least stressful and ask them to explain why. Insist on the correct use of *stress*, *stressful*, etc. Do not accept *stressing*.

- Ask students for other stressful situations they can think of that aren't listed and ensure they have the correct verbs to describe them.

1 going	**2** waiting	**3** being
4 finding	**5** shopping	**6** moving
7 having	**8** making	**9** travelling
10 taking		

B

- Get students in pairs to discuss the activities and the ways of relaxing. Circulate, monitor and assist if necessary.

C

- Here, you could get the students to work individually to rank the situations. While they are doing this, write the 10 situations up on the board, as below.

- Then ask for their scores and do an overall ranking for the whole class as shown in the first line of the chart below. If there are more than 10 students, get them to do the ranking in pairs or threes and complete the table with scores given by each pair or three. (Of course, your students may not have experience of these situations. If that is the case, ask them to imagine how stressful it would be if they did have to do them.)

	S1	S2	S3	S4	S5	S6	Total
Making a presentation to senior executives	5	8	3	4	4	6	30
Leading a formal meeting							
Telephoning in English							
Writing a report with a tight deadline							
Negotiating a very valuable contract							
Meeting important visitors from abroad for the first time							
Asking your boss for a pay rise							
Dealing with a customer who has a major complaint							
Covering for a colleague who is away							
Taking part in a conference call							

LESSON NOTES

Vocabulary: Stress in the workplace

Students look at stress-related vocabulary. Then they compare stress levels in different jobs and in their own job.

A – B

- Go through the pronunciation of the words 1–8. Point out the connection between *workaholic* and *alcoholic*. You could also mention *shopaholic*. (*Flexitime* is *flextime* in AmE, but don't raise this unless someone mentions it.)

- Ask students to do the two exercises. Circulate, monitor and assist if necessary.

- With the whole class, elicit the answers and clear up any difficulties.

Exercise A

1 h **2** d **3** f **4** b **5** a **6** e **7** c **8** g

Exercise B

1 deadline   **2** workaholic   **3** workload
4 lifestyle   **5** flexitime   **6** work–life balance
7 quality of life   **8** working environment

C

- Students write sentences on their own. Circulate, monitor and assist if necessary.

- Ask a few students to share their sentences with the whole class.

D

- Go through the list of jobs and the table with the whole class, explaining the different jobs.

- Explain that they have to place the seven professions – advertising executive, architect, etc. – in the correct position in the stress league.

- Get your students to complete the table in pairs. Circulate, monitor and assist if necessary. Note down language points for praise and correction afterwards, especially those relating to stress.

- Praise strong language points and work on half a dozen points that need improving, getting students to say the correct forms.

- Ask pairs for their findings. Then have them turn to page 132 for the answers.

E

- Discuss with the whole class the kind of stress each job has and what might cause it. For example, the stress felt by many actors might be related to finding work in the first place, teachers from aggressive students, etc.

F

- Continue the discussion and ask students where their own jobs should go in the table.

G

- Get the whole class to discuss these points. Some will be very willing to say how much stress they are under (see Business brief for this unit). Get them to talk about specific problems, for example deadlines. For question 3, you could say that some people are workaholics because they want to be seen to be working hard in order to get promotion, or because of insecurity. Get your students to suggest other ideas.

 i-Glossary

Listening: Dealing with stress

Students listen to a director of a health-at-work consultancy talking about stress. She discusses how she helps companies deal with stress and different causes of stress in men and women.

A

- Do this as a quick-fire activity with the whole class. Write students' ideas quickly on the board, for example long hours, deadlines, endless meetings, competition and conflict with colleagues. If your students are pre-work, ask them what is most stressful about being a student, for example essays and exams.

B ◀)) CD1.43

- Before playing the interview, ask students what they think Jessica Colling will mention.

- Then play the first part of the interview two or three times, explaining any difficulties. Ask students to make notes.

- Go through the answers.

---

1 Having too much to do, not feeling in control, and not having good relationships with the people that they work with.

2 *Resilience to stress* is helping people to respond differently to stressful situations, so that they actually feel calmer when they're put in situations that they previously found stressful.

C ◀)) CD1.44

- Play the second part of the interview two or three times and get students to note key words. Check the answers with the whole class.

LESSON NOTES

A high level of continued pressure can sometimes spill over into feelings of stress. So, although you might be doing quite well at managing stress for a long period of time, if it continues without any break, then people sometimes tip over into feeling very stressed.

D 🔊 CD1.44

● Before playing the recording again, ask students to read the extract and try to predict the words they might hear.

● Then play this part of the interview again and get students to write the correct answers.

1 normal   **2** motivating   **3** stressful   **4** pressure

E 🔊 CD1.45

● Read the question. Play the recording. Check the answers with the whole class.

1 If somebody doesn't like travelling in rush hour, they could come in a little bit early and leave a little bit early.

2 Making sure that people don't feel that they have to stay late, just because their boss is working late.

F 🔊 CD1.46

● Read the question. Play the recording. Check the answers with the whole class.

1 Because women tend to have more responsibility in the home (e.g. managing the home, looking after children), so they have many more sources of pressure in their life and therefore are more likely to feel stressed because of that.

2 Women are more open about their feelings and therefore feel more comfortable in reporting feeling under pressure or feeling stressed.

G

● Tell students to discuss the two questions in pairs or threes. Encourage them to give specific examples, if possible.

● Circulate, monitor and assist if necessary. Note down language points for praise and correction afterwards, especially relating to the language of stress.

● Bring the class to order. Praise good language you heard and work on half a dozen points that need improving, getting individual students to say the correct forms.

● With the whole class, get the groups to give their opinions. Encourage discussion, especially on points where opinions differ.

➡ Resource bank: Listening (page 193)

Reading: Business owners feeling stressed

Students read about a survey that found that business owners all over the world are feeling more stressed than ever.

A

● Students quickly rank the countries on their own.

● Ask students to call out their choices for most stressed and least stressed country.

B

● Get students to read the article and compare the results of the survey to their own ideas from Exercise A.

● With the whole class, elicit the answers and explain any common difficulties.

1 China	**2** Mexico	**3** Turkey
4 Vietnam	**5** Greece	**6** Australia
7 Finland	**8** Denmark	**9** Sweden

C – D

● Students answer the questions in pairs. Check answers with the whole class.

Exercise C

1 Group a) are all countries where high growth is expected; Group b) are countries where the economy is shrinking.

2 In China, the pressure is on to keep up with the speed of expansion, while in Ireland, the economy is shrinking, and business owners are worried about how they will keep their business alive.

3 The economic climate, pressure on cashflow, competitor activities and heavy workload

4 Economic, business and personal

Exercise D

1 China, Mexico, Vietnam

2 Sweden, Denmark, Finland

E

● Get your students to discuss these questions in pairs.

● With the whole class, compare answers.

➡ Text bank (pages 132–135)

LESSON NOTES

Language review: Past simple and present perfect

The tenses are compared and contrasted. Students then do exercises to find the correct tense and use the correct tense with time expressions.

- This area is very difficult, and further complicated by the fact that the rules are different in AmE – the ones here are for BrE. Take things slowly and don't expect students to get things right first time.

- Go through the examples and elicit answers to the questions.

> These two examples are with time expressions: *for five years* and *for three years* respectively.
>
> **1** Yes, she does. (present perfect)
>
> **2** No, she doesn't. (past simple)
>
> Sentence 2 uses the past simple; sentence 1 uses the present perfect.

- Go through the rules for the past simple. When you have a time expression referring entirely to the past ('finished time') – *last weekend, on Monday,* etc. – you must use the past simple.

- Go through the rules for the present perfect. When you have a time expression referring to 'time up to now' (*just, so far,* etc.), you must use the present perfect.

A

- Go through the exercise with the whole class, eliminating the incorrect sentences and discussing with your students why they are wrong. Note: item 5b may be heard in AmE.

> **Incorrect sentences: 1** b **2** a **3** b **4** b **5** b

B

- Get your students to work on the time expressions in pairs. Before they start, make sure they have understood the distinction between 'finished time' and 'time up to now'.

- Circulate, monitor and assist if necessary.

- With the whole class, ask pairs for their answers and discuss how they arrived at them.

- Encourage students to discuss events in their lives using the expressions. They can invent things if they wish.

Past simple	Present perfect
two years ago, in 2009, yesterday, last Friday, during the 1990s, when I was at university	so far, ever, yet, just, for the past two weeks, already, never, in the last few days, since 2005

C

- Get students to work in pairs to invent the mini dialogues. Circulate, monitor and assist if necessary.

- Bring the class to order and get pairs to perform particular dialogues for the whole class, for example:

A: *Have you ever travelled abroad on business?*

B: *Yes, I have.*

A: *Where did you go?*

B: *(I went to) New York.*

Skills: Participating in discussions

Students listen to members of a human resources department talking about ways of improving the staff's health and then use these expressions in another context.

A

- Have students brainstorm ideas in pairs.

- Then compare answers with the whole class.

B ◀)) CD1.47

- Explain the situation and play the recording two or three times. Explain any difficulties (e.g. *counselling*) and get students to write down the suggestions in note form.

- Go through the answers with the whole class.

> They mention: paying a gym subscription, hiring more staff, stopping weekend work, introducing flexitime, allowing employees to work from home, setting up a counselling service, changing staff duties and roles

C ◀)) CD1.47

- With the whole class, get students to predict the words they might hear.

- Play the recording again and get the students to complete the expressions.

> **1** we should
>
> **2** Why don't; How about
>
> **3** could hire
>
> **4** good idea
>
> **5** Let's

- Go through the answers and explain any difficulties.

LESSON NOTES

D 🔊 CD1.48

- Play the recording of the second meeting once or twice and ask students to tick the expressions they hear.

- Play the recording again and get students to say if the speakers are agreeing or disagreeing. Also get them to say whether the expressions they don't hear are agreeing or disagreeing.

---

1 (D), **2** (D), **3** (A), **5** (A), **7** (D)

- Point out the tendency in British English to 'hedge' (without using this word). For example, *Mm, I don't know* is a way of disagreeing politely.

E

- Go through the expressions in the Useful language box with the whole class. Work on intonation and try to eliminate any tendency for students to say *I am agree* or *I am not agree*.

- Point out that the purpose of the exercise is to put into action the language in the Useful language box. Put students into pairs and tell them that they should treat the three points as an agenda for the discussion.

- Start the activity. Circulate, monitor and assist if necessary. Note down language points for praise and correction afterwards, especially language used for discussions.

- Bring the class to order and ask the pairs what conclusions they came to on each point. Praise correct use of the expressions in the Useful language box and work on points for improvement, getting individual students to say the correct forms.

➡ Resource bank: Speaking (page 181)

CASE STUDY

Davies–Miller Advertising

Students analyse and tackle problems of stress and low morale in an advertising agency that has recently lost two major accounts.

Stage 1: Background

- Tell students to read the background information. Circulate, monitor and assist if necessary, clarifying any difficulties.

- Go round the class and elicit key points from the information, writing them on the board.

Suggested key points

Rapid expansion

Strong competition

Good pay, but long hours

Worries about job security

Recent loss of two major accounts

65% feel highly stressed

Stage 2: Listening and reading 🔊 CD1.49

- Tell students that they are going to hear a phone call between two members of the Davies–Miller team and read information about three other team members.

- Play the recording once or twice for students to make notes.

- Then give them time to read the three texts and to make notes.

Suggested key points

1 James has disappeared in the middle of the negotiation after getting drunk in front of the clients; Jessica thinks he has had a breakdown; Sheila promises to help.

2 Brigitte is stressed and unhappy at work, thinks there is too much gossip, thinks her supervisor favours others, has poor work–life balance.

3 Juliana is stressed about deadlines, thinks the company is competing for too many contracts, thinks she is being pushed out because of her age.

4 Jolanta doesn't feel appreciated or that she has the chance to get on or contribute.

Stage 3: Task parts 1–2

- Keep the points from Stage 2 above on the board for students to focus on while they do the task.

- Put students into groups of three or four and appoint a chair for each group.

- Point out that all the points are related, but that students have to come up with answers to the

two questions in part 1 of the task. Write the two questions on the board to focus students' attention on them:

1 What are the main reasons why the staff mentioned above are highly stressed or demotivated?

2 What action(s) should the HR department take in each case?

- Circulate and monitor the discussions. Remind students that they should try to use expressions from the Useful language box on page 49. Note down language points for praise and correction, especially those relating to stress and language used in discussions.

- When the groups have finished, bring the class to order and praise strong language points. Work on half a dozen points that need improving, getting students to say the correct forms.

Stage 4: Task part 3

- If the class is very large have two or three groups rather than just one. Appoint a chair for the group and get them to start the discussion.

- Circulate and monitor. Note down language points for praise and correction afterwards.

- When the group has produced its list of recommendations, bring the class to order. Praise strong language points and work on those points that need improving, getting students to say the correct forms.

- Ask for the recommendations, getting one member of the group to write key points on the board. If there is more than one group, do the same with the others.

- Point out that the subsequent writing task follows on from the recommendations in the discussion and give your students time to write them down.

One-to-one

This case study can be done as a discussion between teacher and student followed by a presentation by the student. Don't forget to note language points for praise and correction afterwards. Also point out some of the key language you chose to use.

◉ Students can watch the *Case study commentary* on the DVD-ROM.

Stage 5: Writing

- Students should write the final section of the report as if they were Head of Human Resources, giving recommendations for reducing stress in the company. This can be done for homework.

➡ Writing file, page 129

➡ Resource bank: Writing (page 208)

Entertaining

AT A GLANCE

	Classwork – Course Book	Further work
Lesson 1 *Each lesson (excluding case studies) is about 45–60 minutes. This does not include administration and time spent going through homework.*	<u>**Starting up**</u> Students look at different options for entertaining businesspeople. **Vocabulary: Eating and drinking** Students look at the language of food and describing restaurants.	**Practice File** Vocabulary (page 24) **Practice exercises:** **Vocabulary 1 & 2** (DVD-ROM) **i-Glossary** (DVD-ROM)
Lesson 2	**Listening: Corporate events** The Chief Executive of a corporate entertainment company talks about successful corporate entertainment. **Reading: Corporate entertainment** Students read three entertainment experts' answers to questions about corporate hospitality.	**Resource bank: Listening** (page 194) **Practice exercises:** **Listening** (DVD-ROM) **Text bank** (pages 136–139)
Lesson 3	**Language review: Multiword verbs** Students look at the behaviour of multiword verbs in the context of entertaining. <u>**Skills: Socialising: greetings and small talk**</u> Students look at what to say in different situations, listen to people socialising and apply the language in a number of contexts, including a role play.	**Practice File** Language review (page 25) **Practice exercises:** **Language review 1 & 2** (DVD-ROM) **ML Essential Business Grammar and Usage** (Units 25 & 26) **Resource bank: Speaking** (page 182) **Practice exercises: Skills** (DVD-ROM)
Lesson 4 *Each case study is about 1 to 1½ hours.*	<u>**Case study: Organising a conference**</u> Students analyse the different possible venues for a company conference and choose the most suitable one.	**Case study commentary** (DVD-ROM) **Resource bank: Writing** (page 209) **Practice File** Writing (page 26) **Test file: Progress test 2**

For a fast route through the unit focusing mainly on speaking skills, just use the underlined sections.

For one-to-one situations, most parts of the unit lend themselves, with minimal adaptation, to use with individual students. Where this is not the case, alternative procedures are given.

BUSINESS BRIEF

It has been said that when two American or European businesspeople meet, they are there **to do a deal**, but in Asia they are there **to establish a relationship**. Entertaining in Asia is often used to 'size up' a potential **business partner** – partner in the sense of future supplier or joint venture associate. Asians will want to know more about their guest, their background and their contacts before going ahead and doing business. This is an essential part of the business process, not just polite **etiquette**.

Relationship building takes different forms in different places – invitations to karaoke evenings in Japan or the yacht on the French Riviera are not to be refused. The demand for **corporate hospitality** in the UK has been criticised for making events such as Grand Prix racing or Wimbledon more expensive for ordinary people. But **corporate sponsorship** of sport and culture brings in large amounts of money, and many such events benefit from this overall.

Entertaining in the form of invitations to your host's home exists in some cultures but not others, where work and private life are kept entirely separate.

Cultural awareness of **norms** in these and other areas can lead to better communication and avoidance of misunderstandings. Companies are spending more time and money these days on **cross-cultural training**, often but not always in tandem with language training, in order to facilitate better **social interaction**.

Socialising in another language is not easy. There is more focus on the language itself than in business discussions. Students, rightly, demand formulaic expressions for particular situations. This is often called **small talk**. But to refer to it as 'small' undervalues its importance. Language learners see it as a minefield of potential problems and, inevitably, **gaffes**. People have their favourite stories about such mistakes, perhaps ones they made themselves. Telling these stories can be a useful form of ice-breaking activity in the classroom when working on this much-demanded **social English**.

Read on

Judy Allen: *Event Planning: The Ultimate Guide to Successful Meetings, Corporate Events, Fundraising Galas, Conferences, Conventions, Incentives and Other Special Events*, Wiley, 2009

Judy Allen: *The Executive's Guide to Corporate Events and Business Entertaining – How to Choose and Use Corporate Functions to Increase Brand Awareness, Develop New Business, Nurture Customer Loyalty and Drive Growth*, Wiley, 2007

Kathy Schmidt and Marish Rogers: *Small Talk – The Art of Socialising*, New Holland Publishers, 2008

Warmer

- Write the word *entertainment* in big letters on the board. Ask students to suggest different forms of entertainment in general, rather than in a corporate context. Some examples are given below.

entertainment	shows – e.g. plays, musicals, films
	concerts – e.g. classical, rock, jazz
	(night) clubbing
	sports – e.g. football, tennis, rugby

- Ask if any of these would be suitable for corporate entertaining.

Overview

- Tell your students that they will be looking at the subject of corporate entertaining and the language that goes with it, including small talk.

- Ask the students to look at the Overview section on page 52. Tell them a little about the things you will be doing, using the table on page 52 of this book as a guide. Tell them which sections you will be covering in this lesson and which in later lessons.

Quotation

- Write the quotation on the board.

- Ask your students if they agree with the quotation, in a business context.

Starting up

Students look at different options for entertaining businesspeople.

A

- Get students in pairs to discuss the activities. Circulate, monitor and assist if necessary.

- With the whole class, ask different pairs to say what their findings were, why they chose the things that they did and whether they thought of any new activities.

B

- Discuss this question with the whole class. You could ask what the purpose of these events is – to obtain immediate sales or to *generate goodwill* (teach this expression) in the longer run? You could point out that a company may not just invite clients and potential clients but other contacts as well.

- Ask students how they feel about spending time outside of normal working hours entertaining customers or socialising with business partners.

Vocabulary: Eating and drinking

Students look at the language of food and describing restaurants.

A

- This exercise tests common collocations used when describing restaurants.

- Tell students to complete the collocations using the words from the box.

- Go through the answers quickly. You may want to ask students to copy each collocation into their vocabulary notebooks for future reference.

> 1 cosy/exciting atmosphere
>
> 2 local/regional food
>
> 3 convenient/exciting location
>
> 4 reasonable prices
>
> 5 efficient/reasonable service
>
> 6 exciting/local/regional entertainment

- Students discuss the question in pairs.

- With the whole class, ask different pairs what their findings were.

B

- Go through the words in the box to make sure students understand them.

- Work with the whole class to complete the exercise.

> 1 beef, lamb, pork, veal, venison
>
> 2 chicken, duck, turkey
>
> 3 crab, lobster, prawns/shrimp, salmon, tuna
>
> 4 broccoli, cabbage, cucumber, mushroom, onion, spinach

C

- Go through the words in the box to make sure students understand them.

- Students work in pairs to complete the exercise.

- Go through the answers with the whole class.

> 1 alcohol-free/dry/house/medium/red/rosé/ sparkling/sweet/vintage/white wine
>
> 2 alcohol-free/bottled/draught beer
>
> 3 bottled/mineral/sparkling/still/tap water

LESSON NOTES

D

- Have a quick brainstorming session to list four or five typical dishes. If students are from different countries, choose one dish from each country.

- Ask students to try to describe each dish. With strong classes, you may wish to do this first without reference to the phrases given in the book.

- Be prepared to supply additional vocabulary if students are having trouble describing their dishes, e.g. *It's made with ... , The ingredients are ... .*

- If you have time, ask one or two students to describe a dish for the others to guess.

E

- Look at the stages and assist with any difficulties, for example the pronunciation of *dessert* and the meaning of *aperitif* (a drink before the meal).

- Ask students to put the stages into the correct order as a quick-fire activity with the whole class.

> **a** 3 **b** 7 **c** 1 **d** 8 **e** 5 **f** 6 **g** 4 **h** 2
>
> (This is the 'standard' order. Your students may point out that it is possible to have an aperitif before you look at the menu or ask for the bill before you have the dessert, for example if you are in a hurry.)

F ◀)) CD1.50

- Students listen and check their answers.

G

- Students do steps 1 and 2 in pairs, then join with another pair for step 3. Circulate, monitor and assist if necessary.

- Ask a few pairs to share their ideas with the whole group.

 i-Glossary

Listening: Corporate events
The Chief Executive of a corporate entertainment company talks about successful corporate entertainment.

A ◀)) CD1.51

- Ask students to read the three questions to see what information they will be listening for.

- Play the recording once for students to try to answer the questions.

- Check their answers quickly. If they are having difficulty, play the recording again.

> **1** horse racing, football/soccer, motor racing
>
> **2** Cricket – because the rules are complicated
>
> **3** *Phantom of the Opera*

B ◀)) CD1.52

- Ask students to read the question to see what information they will be listening for.

- Play the recording once for students to try to answer the question.

- Check their answer, playing the recording again if necessary.

> Fewer people are doing corporate hospitality, but they are taking the more expensive products.

C ◀)) CD1.53

- Tell students to read the notes.

- Play the recording and ask students to complete the notes.

- Go through the answers with the class.

> **1** aim/purpose **2** back-ups **3** food; drink
> **4** quality, training **5** follow

D ◀)) CD1.54

- Ask students to read the three questions to see what information they will be listening for.

- Play the recording once for students to try to answer the questions.

- Check their answers quickly. If they are having difficulty, play the recording again.

> **1** British Grand Prix and Soccer World Cup Final
>
> **2** helicopter
>
> **3** Concorde/supersonic jet

E

- Students discuss the questions in groups. Circulate, monitor and assist if necessary.

- Discuss answers with the entire class. For question 2, point out that entertaining is on the one hand an opportunity to build relationships and to establish a company as a 'serious player', and possibly to get attention in the media. On the other hand, if entertaining is seen as a form of bribery, the effect on image could be negative.

➡ Resource bank: Listening (page 194)

Reading: Corporate entertainment

Students read three entertainment experts' answers to four questions about corporate hospitality.

A

- If your students are from different countries, ask them to work in same-country groups to discuss these questions. If they are all from the same country, ask them to work in pairs or small groups.

- If your students are not working, for question 2, you could ask them if they have ever been invited to a corporate event and if so, whether they enjoyed it.

B

- Go through the questions and check that students understand them.

- Get students to work in pairs to match the questions with the four sets of answers in the text.

- Check answers as a whole class.

> **1** b   **2** e   **3** d   **4** c

C

- Give students five minutes to discuss the question in pairs. Circulate, monitor and assist if necessary.

- With the whole class, ask different pairs to say what they thought and why.

D

- Students work in pairs to answer the question. This could be done very quickly if you want to keep it simple, or could be expanded into a mini-project.

- After students have worked in pairs, have them explain their package to another pair. Circulate, monitor and assist if necessary.

- Then ask different pairs to present their package to the whole class.

➡ Text bank (pages 136–139)

Language review: Multiword verbs

Students look at the behaviour of multiword verbs in the context of entertaining.

- Students are often interested in, but confused by, these verbs, also known as phrasal verbs. Go through the examples with your students.

- With multiword verbs that can be separated from their particles, point out that if the object is a pronoun, they cannot be separated. For example, you say *I turned it down* not *I turned down it*.

- Optionally, you could get your students in pairs to look up these multiword verbs in a general ELT dictionary such as the *Longman Active Study Dictionary*.

A

- Tell students to read the sentences, then match the multiword verbs in bold with the definitions.

- Students check their answers in pairs. Then check answers with the whole class.

> **1** d   **2** a   **3** f   **4** g   **5** c   **6** e   **7** b   **8** h

B

- Students read the e-mail extract and choose the correct options.

- Students check their answers in pairs. Then check answers with the whole class.

> **1** part in   **2** around   **3** after   **4** turn down
> **5** take up   **6** forward to

C

- Students work in pairs to ask and answer the questions.

- Have a few students share their partner's answers to the questions with the whole class.

Skills: Socialising: greetings and small talk

Students look at what to say in different situations, listen to people socialising and apply the language in a number of contexts, including a role play.

A

- Ask two confident students to come to the front of the class and demonstrate how they would introduce themselves to each other if they did not know each other. Insist on the correct use of *Hello, I'm … /My name is … .*

> **Example**
>
> A: Hello, I'm Patricio Montenegro. I'm with AEG.
>
> B: Hi. My name is Agatha Ellis. I work for Telefónica.
>
> People who first meet usually talk about where they work, their job, the weather, and so on.

- Then get a third student, C, to come up. A introduces C to B. Point out that *How do you do* is quite old-fashioned now. Say that *Hello, pleased to meet you* or even just *Hello* are adequate responses.

LESSON NOTES

B 🔊 CD1.55–1.59

- Explain the exercise.

- Then play the recording once or twice and get students to match the people and say if they know each other.

- Go through the answers.

> **1** d (Yes) **2** e (No) **3** b (Yes) **4** c (No) **5** a (No)

C 🔊 CD1.56, 1.58

- Play conversations 2 and 4 again and get students to complete the gaps.

> **1** met **2** Good; you **3** know
> **4** worked **5** Give; regards **6** Pleased
> **7** hear **8** great **9** love
> **10** forward

- As an optional extra activity, get students to read the conversations in pairs. Circulate, monitor and assist if necessary, especially with natural intonation.

- Then get particular pairs to read the conversations for the whole class.

- As a further step, get students to do conversation 4 again, substituting names of other people, other places for Amsterdam, and other adjectives for *great*.

D – **E**

- Go through the expressions and ask students to say who says what. Then get them to match the utterances.

> **Exercise D**
>
> **1** H **2** H **3** G **4** H **5** H **6** G **7** H **8** G
> **9** G **10** G
>
> **Exercise E**
>
> 1+6 9+2 5+3 4+8 7+10

- Practise intonation with the whole class and get pairs to read the different exchanges with feeling.

F

- Go through the Useful language box as consolidation, again practising intonation.

- Explain the situation, allocate roles and get students to prepare their roles. Circulate and assist if necessary.

- When pairs are ready, ask them to start the role play. Circulate and monitor. Note down language points for praise and correction afterwards, concentrating particularly on socialising expressions.

- When the students have finished, bring the class to order, praise strong language points and work on half a dozen points that need improving, getting students to say the correct forms.

- If there is time, ask one of the pairs to give a performance of their conversation for the whole class, integrating the improvements you have made.

➡ Resource bank: Speaking (page 182)

CASE STUDY

Organising a conference

Students analyse the different possible venues for a company conference and choose the most suitable one.

Stage 1: Background

- Give the general topic of the case study and ask students to read through the background information. Meanwhile, write the headings on the left of the table below on the board.

- Elicit information from your students to complete the column on the right.

Company and its base	GFDC, Dubai
Activity	Food and drink
Aims of the conference	1 Discuss improvements to products and services 2 Thank managers for hard work 3 Allow managers to get to know each other – stronger team
Who will attend?	CEO, senior managers from head office, 100 managers from overseas
Dates/ duration	July; Thursday evening – Monday a.m.
Budget	$4,000 per person

Stage 2: Listening and reading 🔊))) CD1.60

- Do a quick brainstorm with students on the type of features that might be mentioned, e.g. size, facilities, location.

- Play the recording for students as many times as is necessary for them to list the five features.

- Check the answers with the whole class.

> The venue must:
>
> be good value for money
>
> have one large conference room, for 100 people
>
> have preferably four or more meeting rooms
>
> have reasonable access to an international airport
>
> have good leisure facilities.

- Ask students to read the descriptions of the four hotels.

- Then go round the class and ask individual students to use the notes on each hotel to give a full description of it in their own words, for example:

The Seagreen Hotel in Miami is on the sea. Guest reviews say that it has excellent service but, unfortunately, the business centre has got limited hours …

- However, don't allow students to pre-empt the task by commenting on the hotels they describe. Just get them to talk about the advantages and disadvantages in different ways, for example:

The good thing about the Seagreen Hotel is its very attractive beach. However, the food in the restaurant is mainly Mexican, and that may not appeal to everyone.

- Ask students to look at the results of the questionnaire and ask them which is the preferred location (rural area).

Stage 3: Task

- Divide the class into groups of four or five. Make sure that each group understands the task it must perform: as members of GFDC's marketing department, choose the hotel that best meets the requirements of the conference.

- When the situation is clear, the discussion can begin. Circulate and monitor. Note down language points for praise and correction afterwards, concentrating on the language of advantages and disadvantages.

- When each group has come to a conclusion, bring the class to order.

- Praise strong language points that you heard and point out half a dozen that need improving. Ask individual students to repeat the correct forms.

- Then get students to pool their findings in one group or, if the class is very large, in two groups, and discuss the final choice of venue. Circulate and monitor the language of advantages and disadvantages.

- Ask the group(s) for their final choice and why they chose it.

- Praise strong language points and work again on points that need improvement, getting individual students to say the correct forms.

> **One-to-one**
>
> This case study can be done as a discussion between teacher and student and then as a basis for a presentation by the student. Don't forget to note language points for praise and correction afterwards. Also point out some of the key language you chose to use.

◉ Students can watch the *Case study commentary* on the DVD-ROM.

Stage 4: Writing

- Students should write an e-mail in their capacity as CEO of GFDC, inviting the overseas sales managers to the conference and giving details of its purpose and the location. This e-mail can be done for homework.

⇨ Writing file, page 126

⇨ Resource bank: Writing (page 209)

WORKING ACROSS CULTURES 2

Doing business internationally

This unit deals with a UK businessperson having a business meeting in Morocco, an American businessperson posted in Mexico, and four businesspeople talking about their experiences of doing business in South Korea.

A

- Students do the quiz in pairs, then check their answers on page 134 of the Course Book.

> See Activity file, page 134

Task 1 🔊 CD1.61

- Explain that the recording is a conversation between a British businessman and an Arab businessman.

- Have students read the three questions. Then play the recording.

- Play the recording again for students to check their answers.

- Check the answers with the whole class.

> 1 His company wants to sell its products in Morocco.
>
> 2 Through department stores
>
> 3 Distributors for his company

- Play the recording again while students make notes.

- Have students check their answers in pairs, comparing their answers to those on page 135 of the Course Book.

- Go through the answers with the whole class.

> See Activity file, page 135

B

- Briefly explain the situation: an American woman is working in Mexico, but she's having trouble adjusting to Mexican culture.

- Students work in groups of three. Each student reads one text and summarises it for the others. Circulate, monitor and assist if necessary.

Task 2

- Get students to work in small groups to discuss these questions. Circulate, monitor and assist if necessary.

- Give them five minutes or so, then have a spokesperson from each group present their ideas to the class. Encourage students who don't normally say much to act as spokesperson.

> 1 She does not have a sufficient command of Spanish, so she cannot answer questions about her country.
>
> She is not used to having business breakfasts, and lunches seem to go on too long.
>
> She thinks that colleagues are not interested in her ideas. Instead, they are trying to decide if they like her.
>
> There is less eye contact than she is used to, and people stand too close to her when they talk to her.
>
> 2 She has tried to overcome some of her difficulties by:
>
> - attending classes to improve her Spanish;
>
> - asking a lot of questions about Mexican culture when she is invited to dinners.
>
> 3 Possible answers: Joanna should make as much effort as possible to improve her Spanish. She should observe how things are done in Mexico and do her best to adapt.
>
> 4 This is open to debate. Because she doesn't speak Spanish well and doesn't seem comfortable in Mexican business culture, she isn't very well suited to being there. However, the fact that she's aware that there are cultural differences and that she's trying to improve her Spanish may mean that she can find creative solutions to the challenges.

C

- Explain that the recording is a radio programme and that they will listen to four people talking about their experiences of doing business in South Korea.

- Explain that students will need to make a list of dos and don'ts for business travel in Korea.

Task 3 🔊)) CD1.62–1.65

● Play the recordings while students make notes.

● Play the recordings a second time for students to check their notes.

● Check the answers with the whole class.

Sample answers

Do

Get information about people you're going to do business with.

Have your business card printed in Korean.

Present your business card with both hands.

Prepare for a lot of red tape.

Be patient.

Build up a network of contacts.

Don't

Forget that the oldest person is often the most senior in a group of Korean executives.

Forget that ideas come from the top in Korean business, but there needs to be consensus.

D

● Get students to work in small groups to discuss these questions. Circulate, monitor and assist if necessary.

● When the students have completed their discussion, praise strong points and mention one or two things that students should pay attention to.

● With the whole class, go through the questions one at a time and ask some students to share their group's answers.

Revision

This unit revises and reinforces some of the key language points from Units 4–6 and from Working across cultures 2. (Course Book page numbers are given below.)

4 Great ideas
Vocabulary (pages 36–37)

1 made	**2** take	**3** fill	**4** meet
5 reduce	**6** protect	**7** extend	**8** enter

Past simple and past continuous (page 40)

1	was listening	**8** began
2	had	**9** made
3	didn't have	**10** was trying
4	was	**11** had
5	were receiving	**12** appeared
6	weren't getting	**13** was watching
7	went	**14** became

Skills (pages 40–41)

- Explain that Ben, Lisa, Anna and Tom are in a meeting to discuss a job application.

a) 4 **b)** 5 **c)** 2 **d)** 7 **e)** 8 **f)** 1 **g)** 3 **h)** 6

5 Stress
Vocabulary (page 45)

1	working environment	**5** quality of life
2	lifestyle	**6** work–life balance
3	deadline	**7** workload
4	flexitime	**8** workaholic

Skills (page 49)

1 f **2** h **3** a **4** g **5** i **6** b **7** j **8** d **9** e **10** c

Writing

> **Sample answer**
>
> Hello Mike,
>
> We had a project meeting this morning. The project's going well. It's running on time because everyone is working hard. We all love our work, but we're feeling very stressed out. We're working late every night, but even when we do that, we have to start work the next day at 8.30. Would you consider starting a flexitime system to reduce stress and overwork?
>
> Best wishes,

6 Entertaining
Vocabulary (pages 52–53)

1 convenient	**2** cosy	**3** efficient
4 prawns	**5** cabbage	**6** reasonable
7 wines	**8** non-alcoholic	

Multiword verbs (page 56)

1 part	**2** down	**3** out	**4** up
5 around	**6** up	**7** to	**8** after

Skills (pages 56–57)

1 d **2** h **3** a **4** g **5** b **6** f **7** c **8** e

Cultures 2: Doing business internationally

1	the oldest person	**6** business culture
2	trust and respect	**7** red tape
3	business card	**8** food
4	local language	**9** eye contact
5	business breakfasts and business lunches	**10** personal space

New business

AT A GLANCE

	Classwork – Course Book	Further work
Lesson 1 *Each lesson (excluding case studies) is about 45–60 minutes. This does not include administration and time spent going through homework.*	<u>**Starting up**</u> Students discuss some ideas to encourage people to start new businesses and give examples of companies in different sectors. **Vocabulary: Economic terms** Students look at words used to describe an economy and put them into practice.	Practice File Vocabulary (page 28) Practice exercises: Vocabulary 1 & 2 (DVD-ROM) i-Glossary (DVD-ROM)
Lesson 2	**Listening: New business** Students listen to two CEOs talk about new businesses. **Reading: New business ideas** Students read two articles about people who started their own business.	Resource bank: Listening (page 195) Practice exercises: Listening (DVD-ROM) Text bank (pages 140–143)
Lesson 3	**Language review: Time clauses** Students look at clauses with *when*, *while*, *before*, *after*, *until* and *as soon as*. <u>**Skills: Dealing with numbers**</u> Students practise using numbers, fractions, decimals and amounts of money.	Practice File Language review (page 29) Practice exercises: Language review 1 & 2 (DVD-ROM) ML Essential Business Grammar and Usage (Unit 66) Resource bank: Speaking (page 183) Practice exercises: Skills (DVD-ROM)
Lesson 4 *Each case study is about 1 to 1½ hours.*	<u>**Case study: Taka Shimizu Cycles**</u> A Japanese bicycle maker wants to expand in Europe and South-East Asia. Students analyse the economies of four countries and propose the best place to build the factory.	Case study commentary (DVD-ROM) Resource bank: Writing (page 210) Practice File Writing (page 30)

For a fast route through the unit focusing mainly on speaking skills, just use the underlined sections.

For one-to-one situations, most parts of the unit lend themselves, with minimal adaptation, to use with individual students. Where this is not the case, alternative procedures are given.

BUSINESS BRIEF

A recent TV advert for an airline shows an executive receiving an e-mailed presentation from a potential supplier and then quickly forgetting about it when another potential partner walks into the room and gives his presentation in person. The advert is trying to persuade businesspeople of the merits of **face-to-face contact** in drumming up new business. Flying to meetings is still the preferred way of doing things: companies worldwide spend $3 billion on video-conferencing equipment every year, but US companies alone spend $410 billion a year on business travel. **Road warriors** (even if they often travel by plane) will probably be necessary to gain new business for some time to come.

Clients and suppliers refer to each other as partners to underline the fact that they are in a **relationship** with mutual benefits: the supplier is making money out of helping the client to make money by providing products or services to customers. Some cultures give great importance to getting to know potential partners before working with them. There is some truth in the idea that Americans walk into a room expecting to reach a deal immediately; Asians, to build a relationship that may later lead to a deal. (See also the Business brief for Unit 6.)

In the past, companies often worked with large numbers of suppliers. Car manufacturers, for example, worked with numerous component suppliers, perhaps playing them off against each other to demand lower and lower prices. The tendency now is to work more closely with fewer suppliers. This is a necessary part of **just-in-time (JIT) delivery** and **total quality management (TQM)**. It is much easier to make improvements in these areas when dealing with fewer organisations. This means that it is difficult for new suppliers to break into the privileged circle and get new business.

Another form of new business is **start-ups**. At one end of the scale, there are one-person operations, often started by people who have gained expertise as salaried employees in organisations and then struck out (or been forced to strike out) on their own. At the other end, there are **serial entrepreneurs**, who are gifted at transforming ideas into businesses, and who found a number of start-ups, moving on when each business becomes viable. Their talent lies in combining ideas with people and finance, and they may be less interested in the more mundane activity of running established operations.

Breaking into new markets is another form of new business. A company may try to break into **e-commerce** and may often spend large amounts of money before making any. Likewise, a company trying to establish itself in a country where it has not been present before can make large losses before seeing any **return on investment**. It may be necessary to have local partners who are already familiar with the market and are willing to invest in a **joint venture**.

Read on

Michael Miller and PayPal Press: *The PayPal Official Insider Guide to Growing your Business – Make Money the Easy Way*, New Riders, 2011

Alexander Osterwalder: *Business Model Generation – A Handbook for Visionaries, Game Changers, and Challengers*, Wiley, 2010

David Ford et al.: *Managing Business Relationships,* 3rd edition, Wiley, 2011

Bruce R Barringer and Duane Ireland: *Entrepreneurship – Successfully Launching New Ventures,* 4th edition, Prentice Hall, 2012

Warmer

- Write the words *new business* in big letters on the board.
- Ask students to suggest different types of new business.

> The most obvious type of new business is when there is a new *start-up*, but get students to think also about *existing* companies.
>
> With their existing products, companies can:
>
> - get new customers similar to the ones they have already.
> - find different types of new customers.
> - sell in new areas or countries.
>
> Companies can also develop new products for:
>
> - existing customers.
> - existing sales areas or countries.
> - new customers.
> - new sales areas or countries.

Overview

- Ask the students to look at the Overview section on page 66. Tell them a little about the things you will be doing, using the table on page 62 of this book as a guide. Tell them which sections you will be doing in this lesson and which in later lessons.

Quotation

- Write the quotation on the board and ask students to discuss it briefly in pairs.
- With the whole class, ask pairs for their opinions. You could point out that the most obvious meaning of *resources* is money, but that it can also refer to personal qualities or relationships or other factors that can contribute to making a business successful.

Starting up

Students discuss some ideas to encourage people to start new businesses and give examples of companies in different sectors.

A

- Go through the list of conditions, explaining any difficulties.
- Tell your students to work in pairs. Make the activity concrete for the students by asking them which conditions would be most important if they were starting a company.

- Bring the class to order and ask the pairs what conclusions they came to. Ask them what sorts of businesses they had in mind when discussing the points. Encourage general discussion.

Low taxes: Students may talk about a **flexible labour market,** where there are not only low taxes on companies but also low **social costs** (low payments from companies and employees for benefits such as health care and unemployment benefit), where it is easy to fire people when activity decreases, and where people quickly find new jobs when activity increases again.

Good transport links are important for your employees to get to work and for salespeople to get to customers, but also for distribution of goods if your business does this.

Skilled staff: Students might mention the requirement for a good national education system and good company training of employees.

Training courses provided or funded by the government can be helpful in developing the skills of budding entrepreneurs.

Low interest rates mean that it is cheap to borrow money to develop new business activities.

High unemployment may mean that the wages you can pay are lower, but you may not be able to find the people with the skills you want if you set up your business in an area with a high level of joblessness.

Cheap rents for office and factory space are of course more attractive than expensive ones, but having your office in the right place at a higher rent may be more attractive than having it in the wrong place at a lower one.

In manufacturing, a **strong currency** means that imported raw materials are cheaper but that your exports will be more expensive than those from some competing countries. But if your products offer more benefits, they may justify a higher price.

A **healthy economy** is beneficial because business people are able to plan better when there is less uncertainty about future inflation, taxes, etc.

Government grants may be used to try to persuade companies to set up in areas with high unemployment but if the area is unsuitable for other reasons (such as unskilled staff, distance from markets, etc.), these grants will not be enough.

A **stable political situation** is important for a business to plan for the future. Sudden changes in the political environment can lead to unexpected economic results that could very quickly make doing business virtually impossible.

LESSON NOTES

Easy access to credit makes financing a business and dealing with unexpected shortfalls simpler.

Other conditions: Students may talk about the importance of language in setting up abroad. For example, countries such as India, where English is widely spoken in business, may be attractive for this reason – see, for example, the growth of India's software businesses.

B – C

- Work on the language, for example companies that were *publicly owned* or *state-owned*, that have now been *sold off*, *privatised* or *denationalised*.

- With the whole class, get students to talk about the companies they know, probably ones in their own country/countries.

- You could ask whether some industries such as rail will or should always be publicly owned because of their national importance, safety issues, uncertain return on investment for investors, etc. (Some students might refer to the unhappy UK experience in this area.) However, avoid getting into ideological debates about the relative merits of public and private ownership.

Vocabulary: Economic terms

Students look at words used to describe an economy and put them into practice.

A

- Go through the pronunciation of the economic terms without explaining their meanings.

- Then ask your students to work on the matching exercise in pairs. Circulate, monitor and assist if necessary.

- With the whole class, go through the answers, explaining and recapping pronunciation where necessary.

1 c	**2** d	**3** b	**4** f	**5** g	**6** i	**7** a	**8** e	**9** h	**10** j

B – C ◀)) CD2.1

- Ask your students to do the exercise in pairs. Circulate and assist if necessary.

---

1 inflation rate

2 interest rate

3 exchange rate

4 GDP

5 balance of trade

6 unemployment rate

7 foreign investment

8 tax incentives

9 government bureaucracy

10 labour force

- Play the recording and ask pairs to check their answers.

- Clarify any difficulties.

D – E

- Get your students to work in pairs again. Circulate, monitor and assist if necessary.

F

- Get your students to continue working in pairs. Continue circulating, monitoring and assisting if necessary.

- Alternatively, this activity could be done as homework, to give your students a chance to gather the necessary information.

- You could advise students to consult the information for particular economies in *Financial Times World Desk Reference* published by Dorling Kindersley. There is also a regularly updated website: www.dk.com/world-desk-reference

 i-Glossary

Listening: New business

Students listen to two CEOs talk about new businesses.

A ◀)) CD2.2

- Ask students what they think a global money-transfer company does (a company that sends money from one country to another for individuals and businesses).

- Play the recording and ask students to answer the questions.

---

1 nearly 144

2 Students, business organisations, international organisations (like the World Bank and United Nations), migrant workers (in Europe or other parts of the world who want to send money back home to their family)

LESSON NOTES

- Play the recording again, or encourage students to read the transcript to check.

B ◀)) CD2.3

- Explain to students that they are going to hear Abdirashid Duale answering a question about what successful new businesses have in common.

- Have them read the eight points, then play the recording once.

- Give them a minute to complete the notes, then play the recording again for them to check that their chosen answers make sense.

- Check their answers.

> **1** plan **2** vision **3** reach **4** staff **5** loyal
> **6** relationship **7** services **8** expenditure

C ◀)) CD2.4

- Allow students a minute to read the text, then play the recording.

- Students write the words in the gaps as they listen.

- Play the recording again for them to check, then check with the whole class.

> **1** energy **2** work **3** marketplace **4** competitors
> **5** product **6** value **7** customer **8** cash

D

- Students discuss the questions in small groups. Each group should appoint a spokesperson. Circulate, monitor and assist if necessary.

- Have the spokespeople from the groups share their group's ideas with the whole class.

➡ Resource bank: Listening (page 195)

Reading: New business ideas

Students read two articles about people who started their own business.

A

- Students discuss the question first in pairs, then as a class.

B

- Divide the class into As and Bs. Students read their assigned article and complete the chart with notes.

	Article A	Article B
name of new business	Groupon	Dinka
name of founder	Andrew Mason	Sandra Felsenstein
age of founder	29	27
age of business at time of writing	two years old	just over one year old
location of new business (city and country)	Chicago, USA	Buenos Aires, Argentina
number of employees	about 1,000	four
what the new business is / what it does	offers discounts on a wide range of products and services	links 'micro-manufacturers' of craft items to retail outlets and distributors

C

- Ask students to note down two additional pieces of interesting information, then to compare their answers with a partner who read the same article.

D

- Students now work in pairs of Student A and Student B. While one partner summarises the article, the other partner makes notes. Circulate, monitor and assist if necessary.

- Go through the answers for both articles with the whole class.

E

- The mix of individuals in each group for this activity will obviously greatly influence the discussion, so you may want to choose which students work with which. If students do not have much experience, encourage them to focus on hobbies or areas of interest for their company.

- Control the progress of discussion by allowing a limited time for each stage – this will ensure that students cover each element of the discussion and don't spend all the time on one stage.

- Circulate, monitor and assist if necessary.

LESSON NOTES

- At the end, ask each group to give a brief presentation, describing their business, presenting their team and summarising their strengths and weaknesses in a mini-SWOT analysis.

➡ Text bank (pages 140–143)

Language review: Time clauses

Students look at clauses with *when, while, before, after, until* and *as soon as*.

- Go through the examples, pointing out the verb tenses used. Ask students if the tenses would be the same in their own language(s).

- Many Latin-based languages are different in their treatment of this – for example *When I'll be in Geneva, I'll review all the start-up costs* could be the French 'translation' for future uses.

- In 3, point out that *As soon as we've finished the report, we'll e-mail it to you* is also possible.

A – B

- Ask your students to do the exercises in pairs. Point out that in Exercise A they should look at overall sense before deciding on the matches. Circulate, monitor and assist if necessary.

- With the whole class, go through the answers to both exercises.

> **Exercise A**
>
> **1** g **2** h **3** a **4** b **5** f **6** c **7** d **8** e
>
> **Exercise B**
>
> **1** until   **2** as soon as/when/after
> **3** while/when   **4** as soon as/when   **5** before

C – D 🔊 CD2.5

- Ask your students to do Exercise C in pairs.

- Play the recording so students can check their answers.

> **1** when   **2** before   **3** as soon as   **4** while
> **5** while   **6** until   **7** as soon as

Skills: Dealing with numbers

Students practise using numbers, fractions, decimals and amounts of money.

A 🔊 CD2.6

- Go round the class and ask individual students to say a number each. Then play the recording.

- Refer your students to the Useful language box and go through the notes below.

1 Point out the difference between BrE (*Three hundred and sixty-two, One thousand eight hundred and forty-one, Thirty-six thousand five hundred and three*, and so on) and AmE (*Three hundred sixty-two, One thousand eight hundred forty-one, Thirty-six thousand five hundred three*, and so on).

2 With decimals, tell your students that the figures after the decimal point are said individually, for example *Nine point eight seven five*.

3 Point out that you read 3/4 as *three-quarters* in BrE and AmE, but that you can also say *three-fourths* in AmE. Work on the pronunciation of *-th* and *-ths* in *one-eighth* and *six-sevenths*.

4 Point out that you can write % as *percent* or *per cent*.

5 Work on the pronunciation of *euros*.

B

- Before getting your students to answer the questions, teach or remind them about the words *about* and *roughly*. (Tell them that, in spoken English, these words are better than *approximately*, which sounds rather formal.)

- Ask your students to ask and answer the questions in pairs. If they come from different organisations, pair students from different places.

- Circulate, monitor and assist if necessary. Note down language points for praise and correction later, especially in relation to figures.

- With the whole class, get some of the students to talk about the figures given to them by their partner.

- Praise strong language points and work on half a dozen points that need improving, getting students to say the correct forms.

C 🔊 CD2.7–2.10

- Tell students what they should do in the exercise and then play the recordings once or twice, explaining any difficulties.

- With the whole class, go through the answers.

> **1** a) 1.2%   b) 1,258,000
>
> **2** a) $1.8 billion   b) 18%
>
> **3** a) 1/3 [fraction]   b) 5,000
>
> **4** a) 0.5%   b) 2.8%

LESSON NOTES

D

- Explain the idea behind the exercise to your students. Then divide the class into pairs, allocating the roles A and B.

- Circulate and monitor. Note down language points for praise and correction afterwards, concentrating on the use of numbers.

- When the pairs have finished exchanging information, bring the class to order. Praise strong language points and work on half a dozen points that need improving, getting students to say the correct forms.

- Quickly ask students for the information and write it up on the board.

- With the whole class, discuss which markets would be best for the launch of the new range of mobile phones. Discuss, for example, whether the fact that there are a lot of people with an Internet connection is a good indicator of technical sophistication and therefore willingness to buy mobiles, or if the relative age or youth of the population is a factor, etc.

➡ Resource bank: Speaking (page 183)

Biggest cities (population in millions)		
1	Tokyo, Japan	36.7
2	Delhi, India	22.1
3	São Paulo, Brazil	20.3
4	Mumbai, India	20.0
5	Mexico City, Mexico	19.5
6	New York, US	19.4

% of households with Internet (2008)		
1	South Korea	94.3
2	Iceland	87.7
3	Netherlands	86.1
4	Sweden	84.4
5	Norway	84.0
6	Denmark	81.9

Oldest populations (% aged over 65)		
1	Japan	30.5
2	Italy	26.7
3	Germany	26.0
4	Sweden	25.0
5	Finland	24.7
6	Bulgaria	24.5

Cars per 1,000 people		
1	Iceland	669
2	Luxembourg	664
3	New Zealand	656
4	Italy	609
5	Brunei	608
6	Malta	559

CASE STUDY

Taka Shimizu Cycles

A Japanese bicycle maker, well known in Japan and the US, wants to expand production in Europe and South-East Asia. Students analyse the economies of four countries and propose the best place to build the factory.

Stage 1: Background

● Get your students to silently read the background information. Meanwhile, write the headings on the left of the table opposite on the board.

● Ask students for key points to complete the column on the right of the table. Encourage them to suggest notes like the ones here, rather than longer sentences.

Company	Taka Shimizu Cycles
Based in	Nagoya, Japan
Models	Road, touring, racing, mountain
Segment(s)	Non-enthusiasts, serious cyclists, professional cyclists, adventurous cyclists
Main sources of sales revenue	Road bicycles and mountain bicycles
Wants to expand into	Europe and South-East Asia
New factory – no. of workers	2,000
Source of frames	Made locally
Source of components	Imported
New factory – location	To be decided among countries A, B, C, D

Stage 2: Task part 1: Pairwork

● Explain to your students that they should work in pairs to compare the advantages and disadvantages of each country. Suggest that they draw a chart interpreting the information in the Course Book with headings like the following.

	Country A	Country B	Country C	Country D
Economy				
Growth	low	low	high	average
Inflation	average	very low	average	average
Interest rates	average	very low	average	high
Unemployment	very high	low	high	high
Taxes				
Business	high	average	average	very high
Import	low	high	very high	low
Transport	good rail but poor roads and seaports, new airport	good road and rail, airport, two seaports (expensive)	good near ports, good airport, bad roads	good airports, road and rail not so good, entire system improving
Labour				
Skilled workforce	no	no	yes	no, but used to long hours
Wages	rising	high	low but rising	average
Other comments				
Business	good government grants	strict pollution laws, tax incentives	strong protest movement against foreign business	lot of paperwork, pollution problems, tax-free profits for first three years
General	political problems	stable government	majority of people in cities under 30	—

CASE STUDY

- With the whole class, complete the chart with notes about Country A to give students the idea. Point out that *high*, *average*, *low* are used in relation to the other three countries. Then get students in pairs to complete the rest of the chart. Circulate, monitor and assist if necessary.

Stage 3: Task part 2: Small group discussion

- Divide the class into groups of three or four and get them to discuss the relative merits of each place for Taka Shimizu's new factory and to rank them in order.

- Circulate and monitor. Note down language points for praise and correction afterwards, especially in relation to numbers.

- When the groups have come to a conclusion, bring the class to order. Praise strong language points and work on half a dozen points that need improving, getting students to say the correct forms.

Stage 4: Task part 3: Large group discussion

- If the class is very large, the discussion can be run in two or more parallel groups.

- Appoint a chair for the group, or a chair for each group if there is more than one. Get each of the small groups from stage 3 to contribute to the decision on the most suitable location for the new factory.

- Circulate and monitor. Note down language points for praise and correction afterwards, especially in relation to numbers.

- When the group(s) has/have come to some sort of conclusion, bring the class to order. Praise strong language points and work on half a dozen points that need improving, getting students to say the correct forms.

- Ask the group(s) what conclusions were reached and how they made their choice.

- To prepare for the writing task, get students to write down key points from the discussion that led to the choice that they made.

One-to-one

This case study can be done as a discussion between teacher and student and then as a basis for a presentation by the student. Don't forget to note language points for praise and correction afterwards. Also point out some of the key language you chose to use.

◉ You can also refer to the *Case study commentary* section of the DVD-ROM, where students can watch an interview with a consultant discussing the key issues raised by the case study.

Stage 5: Writing

- Make sure that your students understand what they have to do: write an e-mail to the Head of the Chamber of Commerce in the country the group has chosen, asking for a meeting. You may want to ask your students to include in the e-mail some of the positive points about the country that led them to their choice. This can be done for homework.

⊒ Writing file, page 126

⊒ Resource bank: Writing (page 210)

Marketing

AT A GLANCE

	Classwork – Course Book	Further work
Lesson 1 *Each lesson (excluding case studies) is about 45–60 minutes. This does not include administration and time spent going through homework.*	**Starting up** Students look at the four Ps – product, price, promotion and place – and talk about impressive marketing campaigns. **Vocabulary: Word partnerships** Students look at combinations of words to do with marketing, and then use them to talk about particular products.	Practice File Vocabulary (page 32) **Practice exercises:** **Vocabulary 1 & 2** (DVD-ROM) **i-Glossary** (DVD-ROM)
Lesson 2	**Listening: Marketing pharmaceuticals** Students listen to a marketing manager talking about marketing pharmaceuticals. **Reading: Adidas and the Chinese market** Students read an article about the expansion of Adidas in China.	Resource bank: Listening (page 196) **Practice exercises:** **Listening** (DVD-ROM) **Text bank** (pages 144–147)
Lesson 3	**Language review: Questions** Students look at how questions are formed in the context of a consumer questionnaire. **Skills: Telephoning: exchanging information** Students listen to calls and note down specific information relating to numbers, names, etc.	Practice File Language review (page 33) **Practice exercises:** **Language review 1 & 2** (DVD-ROM) **ML Essential Business Grammar and Usage** (Units 2 & 7) Resource bank: Speaking (page 184) Practice exercises: Skills (DVD-ROM)
Lesson 4 *Each case study is about 1 to 1½ hours.*	**Case study: Wincote International** Students analyse the reasons for the underachievement of an outdoor-clothing company's key product range, and propose corrective action.	Case study commentary (DVD-ROM) Resource bank: Writing (page 211) Practice File Writing (page 34)

For a fast route through the unit focusing mainly on speaking skills, just use the underlined sections.

For one-to-one situations, most parts of the unit lend themselves, with minimal adaptation, to use with individual students. Where this is not the case, alternative procedures are given.

BUSINESS BRIEF

'We must be smarter at devising packages of services that our customers want and pricing them attractively. Set the marketing department free to shape new packages. Don't confine it to coming up with cute names for offerings designed by engineers and accountants.'*

This sums up the position of marketing in many companies, where it is often seen as a fancy name for selling or advertising. But, as the quote shows, marketing people should be involved not just in promoting sales but in all aspects of the marketing mix:

- **product**: deciding what products or services to sell in the first place;

- **prices**: setting prices that are attractive to particular groups of customers (**segments**) and that are profitable for the company;

- **place**: finding suitable **distribution channels** to reach these customer groups;

- **promotion**: all the activities, not just advertising, used to support the product – everything from pre-sales information to after-sales service.

These are the **four Ps** of the marketing mix, the 'levers' of a company's marketing machine, levers that it can adjust in different ways for different products and different buyers.

Another way of looking at this is from the point of view of customers, with the **four Cs**. From this perspective, the marketing mix is expressed in terms of:

- **customer solution**: offering the right product to satisfy particular **customer needs**;

- **customer cost**: the price paid directly by the customer to buy the product, including the 'price' involved in not buying another product of the same or another type;

- **convenience**: distributing the product in the way most suitable for each type of customer;

- **communication**: exchanging information with the customer. Customers are informed about products through advertising, sales literature and so on, but customers also communicate with the seller, for example through **customer helplines**. This is a good way for sellers to find out more about customers and their requirements and to change or improve their **offer**.

Thinking of the marketing mix in these terms helps sellers maintain a **customer orientation** – a focus on customer needs.

*Peter Martin, 'A second chance for telecoms', *Financial Times*, 18th December 2001

Read on

Richard Hall: *Brilliant Marketing – What the Best Marketers Know, Do and Say*, Prentice Hall, 2009

David Jobber: *Principles and Practice of Marketing*, McGraw-Hill Higher Education, 2009

David Meerman Scott: *The New Rules of Marketing & PR – How to Use Social Media, Blogs, News Releases, Online Video, and Viral Marketing to Reach Buyers Directly*, Wiley, 2010

LESSON NOTES

Warmer

- Write the word *marketing* in big letters on the board.

- Ask students for the things that they think of when they see the word. They will probably come up with things like *selling*, *salesperson*, *advertising*. If they have trouble coming up with words, put hints on the board, for example for *selling*, you could write *s e l l _ _ _*, for *salesperson*, write *s a l e s p _ _ _ _ _*, and give definitions of the words you are looking for, for example *This is what you call someone who sells things*.

Overview

- Ask students to look at the Overview section on page 74. Tell them a little about the things you will be doing, using the table on page 71 of this book as a guide. Tell them which sections you will be covering in this lesson and which in later lessons.

Quotation

- Write the quotation on the board and ask students to discuss it briefly in pairs.

- With the whole class, ask pairs for their opinions. (They may feel that it's unfair to suggest that marketing always makes products seem better than they really are.)

Starting up

Students look at the four Ps – product, price, promotion and place – and talk about marketing campaigns that have impressed them.

A

- Do this as a quick-fire activity with the whole class. (Refer to the Business brief for background on the four Ps.)

> 1 d 2 a 3 b 4 c

B 🔊 CD2.11–2.14

- Tell students the general subject of what they are going to hear and play the recordings right through once or twice and then again, stopping after each speaker in order to give students time to answer.

> 1 place   2 promotion   3 price   4 product

C

- To give students the idea, tell them about something you bought recently. Make up a story if necessary. For example:

Sample answer

I bought some cosmetics in a discount store near where I live. I'd seen some advertising in a women's magazine for a new luxury shampoo. There was a free sample sachet and I tried it and liked it. Of course, it's not as pleasant as buying in a department store, but I saved at least 30 per cent on the usual price. Anyway, parking near the department store in my town is impossible and the discount store is just round the corner, so place was an important factor.

- Ask students to work in pairs. They think of a product that they have bought recently and talk about the factors that influenced them in the buying process. Circulate, monitor and assist if necessary.

- With the whole class, get pairs to talk about some of their products.

D

- With the whole class, talk about a marketing campaign that has been on TV, on *hoardings/billboards* (teach these words) or in the press recently. Then get students to suggest other campaigns and talk about them in pairs.

Vocabulary: Word partnerships

Students look at combinations of words to do with marketing and then use them to talk about particular products.

A

- Get students to work in pairs on the exercise. Circulate, monitor and assist if necessary.

1	market	research – b
		segment – c
		share – a
2	consumer	behaviour – b
		profile – a
		goods – c
3	product	launch – a
		lifecycle – b
		range – c
4	sales	forecast – b
		figures – c
		target – a
5	advertising	campaign – c
		budget – b
		agency – a

- Work on the pronunciation of difficult words such as *behaviour, campaign*.

B 🔊 CD2.15

- Show students the example and if necessary, revise the concept of stress. Get students to do the exercise.

- Play the recording for students to check their answers.

'market re'search	'product 'range
'market 'segment	'sales 'forecast
'market 'share	'sales 'figures
con'sumer be'haviour	'sales 'target
con'sumer 'profile	'advertising cam'paign
con'sumer 'goods	'advertising 'budget
'product 'launch	'advertising 'agency
'product 'lifecycle	

C

- With the whole class, ask your students to suggest brands that they will then work on in pairs. (If they are short of ideas, suggest some for them.) Try to get a good range so that they do not all work on luxury products.

- It's probably easier to get students to think of typical individual users, rather than groups of users. Go through the Mercedes example below to give them the idea.

Typical consumer profile for Mercedes

Age : 25+

Gender: male

Job: executive

Income level: €70,000+

Interests/hobbies: diving, holidays in the Seychelles

Other products: Hugo Boss suits, Rolex watches

- Then start the pair work. Circulate, monitor and assist if necessary. Note down language points for praise and correction afterwards.

- Praise strong language points and work on half a dozen points that need improving, getting students to say the correct forms.

- With the whole class, ask for some of the products and typical users that the pairs came up with.

D – E

- This may be difficult for students, as they will be competing with some of the best marketing minds around! Start by asking students to think of existing advertising campaigns for these brands (or their competitors), and discuss the pros and cons of them.

Encourage them to think of things that would appeal to the typical consumer that they identified.

- Ask students what other marketing techniques could be used to increase sales (e.g. special promotions).

- Pairs join with other pairs and compare ideas. Then ask a few students to share their ideas with the whole class.

◎ i-Glossary

Listening: Marketing pharmaceuticals

Students listen to a marketing manager talking about marketing pharmaceuticals.

A 🔊 CD2.16

- Explain to students that they are going to hear an interview with Richard Turner, who is a marketing manager for a pharmaceutical company. Make sure that they understand that a pharmaceutical company manufactures medicines.

- Read the four questions as a class. Then play the recording.

- Have students check their answers in pairs. Then check as a class.

---

1 Spending quality time face-to-face with them

2 Five or 10 minutes

3 Why doctors should use this product compared to the ones they've been using in the past

4 The benefits of the product for doctors' patients, and how it will make them have easier lives

---

B 🔊 CD2.17

- Ask students to read the text and ask them to guess what the missing words might be. (Even if they aren't sure, they should be able to work out whether they are nouns, verbs, etc.) You may want to tell students that all the gaps are single words.

- Play the recording and give students a few minutes to try to complete the text.

- Play it again for them to check their answers.

---

1 challenge   2 strict   3 patients   4 fair
5 products   6 campaigns

C 🔊 CD2.18

- Ask students to read the three sentences.

- Play the recording. Students decide their answers.

LESSON NOTES

- Check the answers with the class.

> **1 F** (They are not allowed to promote products directly to patients.)
>
> **2 F** (Although they would love to use all the benefits and opportunities that the Internet and the new communication methods offer, they are not able to use them as much as they would like.)
>
> **3 T**

D 🔊 CD2.19

- Play the recording and ask students to put the stages in the correct order.

- Check the answers with the whole class.

> d)   b)   c)   a)

E

- Students work in small groups to discuss the different products.

> **Sample answers**
>
> **Pharmaceutical drugs:** A long time required for development and testing; may have a long product life, too. Patents may only last ten years.
>
> **Computer software:** Relatively quick to develop and launch; product life can be extended by new versions of programs.
>
> **Cars:** 'Classic' cars such as the original VWs and Minis can last for generations, but most models will be replaced by car companies every five years or so.
>
> **English-language textbooks:** Again, some classics have been around for over 30 years now. Development time for a multi-level series can be four to five years. A recent trend has been for bestsellers to be relaunched in new editions, with technological extras.
>
> **Rubik's cubes:** A classic toy product which has remained popular with both children and adults. It created its own niche.
>
> **Skateboards:** Again a classic type of product which has become popular with consumers beyond its original target market – e.g. adults commuting to work, sports people.
>
> **Famous team football shirts:** Notoriously these are often redesigned every few years (sometimes after one season), in order to force fans to buy new designs. This can create a lot of resentment and damage a club's reputation.

➡️ Resource bank: Listening (page 196)

Reading: Adidas and the Chinese market

Students read an article about the expansion of Adidas in China.

A

- Read the two questions together as a class.

- Give students a minute or two to discuss the questions in pairs.

- Ask two or three pairs to tell the class what they discussed.

B

- Ask students to quickly do the matching exercise without reading the article. (The idea is that students use language clues to match the questions and answers.)

- Check the answers with the class.

> **1** f **2** a **3** d **4** e **5** b **6** c

C

- Tell students that the facts in the answers of Exercise B were all wrong and that they need to read the article to find the correct answers.

- Give them a few minutes to scan the article, then ask them to find the correct information. If necessary, tell students that the correct answers are similar to the incorrect ones in structure, e.g. that a) is still a number, c) is still a shoe manufacturer, etc.

- Go through the answers with the class.

> **a)** 5,600
>
> **b)** It is hoping to take its brand upmarket.
>
> **c)** Nike
>
> **d)** He is Adidas's Managing Director for Greater China.
>
> **e)** It comes from the Olympic gymnast who lit the flame at the opening ceremony of the 2008 Beijing Olympics.
>
> **f)** Because it wants to regain market share lost to foreign and domestic competitors.

LESSON NOTES

D – E

- Students work individually to do the exercise then check their answers in pairs.

- Go through the answers with the class.

Exercise D

1 g **2** c **3** a **4** e **5** f **6** d **7** b

Exercise E

1 penetrate **2** disposable income **3** saturated
4 upmarket **5** rebrand

➡ Text bank (pages 144–147)

Language review: Questions

Students look at how questions are formed in the context of a consumer questionnaire.

- Remind students about how to form questions with *do*, *does* and *did*. Write the examples on the board:

  I trust this market-research survey.

  ➡ *Do you trust this market-research survey?*

  ➡ *Does he/she trust this market-research survey?*

- Remind them about forming questions with parts of the verb *to be*, by inverting the order of the subject and the verb.

  The price is competitive.

  ➡ *Is the price competitive?*

- Remind them about forming questions in the present perfect with *has* or *have* and inverting the order of the subject and the auxiliary verb.

  They have agreed to the credit terms.

  ➡ *Have they agreed to the credit terms?*

- Point out how you put the question word in front of the auxiliary verb to form questions with words like *what*, *why*, *where*, *when* and *how*. Explain the steps like this:

  I want the sales figures.

  ➡ *Do you want the sales figures?*

  ➡ *When do you want the sales figures?*

A

- Ask students in pairs to correct the grammatical mistakes and then go through them with the whole class, relating the questions to the above explanations.

---

1 **What does** *market position* mean?

2 How much **does** it cost?

3 Why **don't you** sell it on eBay?

4 When **must the cars** be recalled?

5 Did you **go** to the farmers' market last week?

6 Is **your boss coming** tomorrow?

B

- Do the first couple of questions with the whole class as examples.

- Then get students to work individually and reorder the questions, and then answer them. Circulate, monitor and assist if necessary.

- Go through the questions with the class, clarifying any difficulties relating to the structures and vocabulary.

---

1   Which group do you belong to?

2   How old are you?

3   Which wines do you prefer?

4   How often do you drink wine?

5   How much do you usually spend on a bottle of wine?

6   Do you have a personal wine cellar at home?

7   How many bottles of wine have you bought during the last year?

8   Which wine-growing areas do you know?

9   When selecting wine, do you take into account the various growing areas?

10 Which taste do you prefer?

C

- If you or your students would prefer to do an exercise that doesn't involve wine, ask students instead to substitute fruit juice. Use the following replacement questions and answers for questions 3–8 and skip questions 9 and 10. You may need to teach that a *juicer* is a machine that makes fruit juice from raw fruit.

3   which / do / you / prefer / fruit juices /?

citrus (orange, grapefruit) ☐ tropical (mango, pineapple) ☐ grape ☐

4   how / do / you / drink / often / fruit juice /?

seldom ☐ occasionally ☐ once a week ☐ every day ☐

5   do / you / spend / usually / how / much / of / fruit juice / on / a / carton / ?

up to €1.50 ☐ €1.50 to €2.50 ☐ more than €2.50 ☐

6   do / have / you / a / juicer / at / home / ?

yes ☐ no ☐

7   many / cartons / of / juice / how / you / have / bought / during / the / last / year / ?

0–12 ☐ 13–24 ☐ 25–36 ☐ more than 36 ☐

LESSON NOTES

8   taste / which / you / prefer / do / ?

very sweet ☐ sweet ☐ medium ☐ a bit sour ☐
very sour ☐

- Get students in pairs to ask each other the questions and note the answers. Circulate, monitor and assist if necessary, especially with the question forms. If pairs are not discussing wine, check the questions they are asking.

- With the whole class, clarify points that are causing general difficulty. Get individual students to say the correct forms.

D

- With the whole class, give your students an example of a product and the questions they could ask about it, for example:

Flowers

- How often do you buy flowers?

- Do you buy flowers for particular occasions or with no particular reason in mind?

- How much do you spend, on average, when you buy flowers?

- Divide the class into groups and get them to work on the questions for their surveys. Circulate, monitor and assist if necessary.

- Bring the class to order and work on question forms that are still causing difficulty.

- Then get the students to form new groups. The members of each group administer their survey to each other. Circulate, monitor and assist if necessary. Note down language points for praise and correction afterwards.

- Bring the class to order. Praise strong points and work on half a dozen or so points that still need improvement.

- Then ask some individual students to talk about a person they spoke to, being careful with the third person. For example: *Agneta buys flowers once a week for her house. She spends up to $10 each time.*

Skills: Telephoning: exchanging information

Students listen to calls and note down specific information relating to numbers, names, etc.

A 🔊 CD2.20

- Get your students to listen and tick the correct option. Point out the use of *double* and *O* (mainly in BrE): *two three double nine.* Americans would say *two three nine nine.*

- Also point out groupings within numbers, with falling intonation at the end of the last group to show that that is the end of the number.

- Then get individual students to repeat the numbers.

1 b   **2** a   **3** b   **4** b

B

- Explain what your students have to do: they have to exchange numbers in pairs.

- Circulate, monitor and assist if necessary, especially with groupings within numbers and falling intonation at the end.

- Ask students to say what techniques they used for making sure they had heard their partner correctly.

- With the whole class, work on any remaining difficulties.

C – **D** 🔊 CD2.21

- The International Civil Aviation Organization (ICAO) spelling alphabet (also called the international radiotelephony spelling alphabet) is the most widely-used such alphabet and was introduced in 1951. It gives code words to the letters of the English language so that critical differences and combinations of letters can be pronounced and understood by those who transmit/receive voice messages over the radio/phone, regardless of their native language.

- With the whole class, get students to listen to the recording of the ICAO alphabet.

- Point out letters that speakers from your students' language background(s) tend to confuse. For example, French speakers confuse *a* and *r*, *e* and *i*, *g* and *j*.

- Then get your students to dictate addresses to each other in pairs. (If they come from different language backgrounds, and your students' level requires something more challenging, get them to use addresses from their own countries – this can be quite difficult.) Circulate, monitor and assist if necessary.

- With the whole class, go through common confusions and difficulties.

LESSON NOTES

E ◀)) CD2.22

- Explain the situation and ask your students to look at the four questions.

- Play the recording once or twice. Explain any difficulties, but don't give the answers to the questions.

- Go through the answers with the class.

> 1 Yes
>
> 2 It has increased by 2%.
>
> 3 Over £1.2 million
>
> 4 £250,000

F ◀)) CD2.23

- Explain the situation and ask your students to look at the information they will have to complete.

- Play the recording once or twice. Explain any difficulties, but don't give the answers to the questions.

- Then play the recording again, stopping after each piece of information required by the students and eliciting the answer.

> 1 Mrs Young Joo Chan
>
> 2 Korean
>
> 3 82 2 0735 8879
>
> 4 y.joochan1@bhds.com
>
> 5 Friday 18th

- Work on dates. Ask students about dates for the first three days of the month, as they may have a tendency to write *1th*, *2th*, *3th* rather than *1st*, *2nd*, *3rd*. (The same goes for *21st*, *22nd* and *23rd* and *31st*.) Point out that it is acceptable to write *1 December*, as well as *1st December*. Tell them that this way they won't make any mistakes!

G ◀)) CD2.22, 2.23

- Play the recordings once or twice more and ask students to tick the expressions that they hear in the Useful language box.

> Sorry, did you say ... ?
>
> Sorry, I didn't catch that.
>
> Let me read that back to you.
>
> Could you give me a few details?
>
> What about the new range?
>
> Did she say when she'd like to meet?
>
> OK, I think I've got all that.
>
> Right, I think that's everything.

- Check the answers with the whole class. Work on the intonation of the expressions by getting individual students to repeat them after you.

H

- Give students the background to the role play and allocate the roles. Explain that a focus group is a group of consumers who share their opinions about a product to help the manufacturers improve and/or market the product. Tell them that during the role play they should use the language from the Useful language box.

- Get students to prepare their roles. Circulate, monitor and assist if necessary.

- When they are ready, start the role play. Use telephone equipment if available. Otherwise get pairs to sit back-to-back.

- Circulate and monitor. Note language points for praise and correction afterwards, especially in relation to language used whilst telephoning.

- Bring the class to order. Praise strong language points you heard, and bring students' attention to points that need improving, getting individual students to say the correct forms.

➡ Resource bank: Speaking (page 184)

CASE STUDY

Wincote International

Students analyse the reasons for the underachievement of an outdoor-clothing company's key product range, and propose corrective action.

Stage 1: Background and listening 🔊 CD2.24–2.28

- Give your students some very general information about the case study: an outdoor company's range of jackets has not sold well. Tell them that they will have to make decisions about how to relaunch it.

- Before they read the background, ask your students to look at the information in the two charts and make statements about it, for example:
  - *The Wincote XWS costs $110.*
  - *It's less expensive than all of the other coats.*
  - *Its market share is 2%.*

- Ask your students to read the background and information about the launch. Meanwhile, write the headings on the left of the table below on the board. Then elicit information to complete the column on the right.

Made by	US company Wincote International
Company's base	Colorado
Targeted at	Mountaineers, hikers, snowboarders and anyone participating in extreme sports or outdoor activities
Sales	Below target/forecast
Consumer awareness (teach this term if necessary)	Low

- Tell the students to read the four Ps information (product, price, promotion and place) and to look again at Charts 1 and 2.

- Get students in pairs to discuss the question (Why do you think sales have been so poor?).

- Ask one or two pairs for their opinions and encourage discussion with the whole class.

Suggested answers

Consumers are not aware of the new product because the company probably has not promoted it effectively.

The company has probably not drawn sufficient attention to the innovative new material used to make the product.

- Tell students they are going to hear five consumers giving their opinions.

- Play the recordings, stopping after each consumer and asking your students to suggest notes that summarise the views of each consumer, like the ones below.

Consumer 1	Good for cold weather but not good for summer
Consumer 2	Doesn't fit well; warm in winter, but not fashionable (black is a dull colour)
Consumer 3	Perfect for canoeing and snowboarding; zip is awful; hood difficult to fold; jacket too bulky to pack neatly
Consumer 4	The look is good but it was hard to find; good for winter, not good for summer
Consumer 5	Delivery slow; likes the jacket a lot

Stage 2: Task

- Divide the class into small groups to carry out part 1. Explain that they should use the questions in the box as an agenda for their meeting.

- Circulate, monitor and assist if necessary. Note down language points for praise and correction afterwards, especially ones relating to marketing.

- Bring the class to order. Praise strong language points and work on half a dozen points that need improving, getting students to say the correct forms.

- For part 2, get a spokesperson for each group to present the group's ideas to the other groups. Encourage discussion with the whole class. (If the class is very big, this can be two parallel discussions.)

- Again, note down language points for praise and correction afterwards, especially ones relating to marketing.

- Praise strong language points and work on half a dozen points that need improving, getting students to say the correct forms.

- For part 3, ask one student (or one from each group) to say what their group's final conclusion was or to summarise the differing views. Then have the whole class make a list of things the company must do to improve the sales of Wincote XWS.

One-to-one

This case study can be done as a discussion between teacher and student and then as a basis for a presentation by the student. Don't forget to note language points for praise and correction afterwards. Also point out some of the key language you chose to use.

CASE STUDY

◎ You can also refer to the *Case study commentary* section of the DVD-ROM, where students can watch an interview with a consultant discussing the key issues raised by the case study.

Stage 3: Writing

● Make sure that your students understand what they have to do: as Marketing Director, write an e-mail to the CEO of Wincote summarising changes to the product and its marketing when it's relaunched. Tell them it can be written on the basis of the ideas for the relaunch that they had in their group or, if they prefer, on their own ideas for the relaunch. This can be done for homework.

➡ Writing file, page 126

➡ Resource bank: Writing (page 210)

Planning

AT A GLANCE

	Classwork – Course Book	Further work
Lesson 1 *Each lesson (excluding case studies) is about 45–60 minutes. This does not include administration and time spent going through homework.*	**Starting up** Students look at the different factors in planning various things, from a holiday to a career. **Vocabulary: Making plans** Students look at various nouns and the verbs that typically precede them.	**Practice File** Vocabulary (page 36) **Practice exercises:** **Vocabulary 1 & 2** (DVD-ROM) **i-Glossary** (DVD-ROM)
Lesson 2	**Listening: How important is planning?** A business consultant talks about how far ahead businesses should plan, and about successful and failed plans. **Reading: To plan or not to plan** How a software development company became one of Microsoft's key partners without ever writing a business plan.	**Resource bank: Listening** (page 197) **Practice exercises:** **Listening** (DVD-ROM) **Text bank** (pages 148–151)
Lesson 3	**Language review: Talking about future plans** Students look at the use of the present continuous and of *going to* for future plans, and of verbs such as *plan, hope, expect, would like* and *want*. **Skills: Meetings: interrupting and clarifying** Students listen to a meeting, identify expressions for interrupting and clarifying, and use them in a role play.	**Practice File** Language review (page 36) **Practice exercises:** **Language review 1 & 2** (DVD-ROM) **ML Essential Business Grammar and Usage** (Units 18, 19, 20 & 73) **Resource bank: Speaking** (page 185) **Practice exercises: Skills** (DVD-ROM)
Lesson 4 *Each case study is about 1 to 1½ hours.*	**Case study: European Press and Media Corporation** After analysing market research, students plan the first issue of a new health-and-fitness magazine.	**Case study commentary** (DVD-ROM) **Resource bank: Writing** (page 212) **Practice File** Writing (page 38) **Test file: Progress test 3**

For a fast route through the unit focusing mainly on speaking skills, just use the underlined sections.

For one-to-one situations, most parts of the unit lend themselves, with minimal adaptation, to use with individual students. Where this is not the case, alternative procedures are given.

BUSINESS BRIEF

Planning is about resource allocation, the way that individuals and organisations deploy their (by definition) limited resources such as time, money and expertise.

In the case of individuals, you could say that there is a worldwide planning industry, with its calendars, diaries, electronic personal organisers and **time management** training. These (often very expensive) courses tend to hand out some fairly obvious advice.

- Make lists of things you have to do. Classify them in terms of urgency and priority.

- Pursue tasks single-mindedly. Do not allow yourself to waste time through distractions and interruptions.

- Delegate. Do not try to do everything yourself.

- Do not try to be a perfectionist in everything. Do each task so that it is 'good enough' for the circumstances.

But all these things are easier said than done.

For complex projects involving many people and tasks, the **Gantt chart** is the tool of choice. This is a diagram that shows the different stages of a project, indicating the tasks that can be done at the same time as others, and those that must wait until other tasks are completed. Originally conceived about 100 years ago, Gantt charts are now produced using computer software. Other computer-based **project management tools** have been developed by particular companies or are available commercially.

Companies also have to plan for events that they do not want, such as disasters. **Contingency planning** is designed to prepare for the worst, with specific plans of action for **disaster recovery**, including handling of the media and protecting, as far as possible, the company's reputation.

Organisational planning in its grandest form is one element of **strategy**, where companies make long-term plans about the future development of their activities. Here, they have to anticipate competitors' activities as well as trends in the general economic and political **environment.** Very large organisations have teams of **scenario planners** trying to predict how this environment may change and how they might prepare for and perhaps influence this change.

Read on

Dr Mike Clayton: *Brilliant Time Management – What the Most Productive People Know, Do and Say*, Prentice Hall, 2010

James Lewis: *Project Planning, Scheduling and Control – The Ultimate Hands-On Guide to Bringing Projects in On Time and On Budget,* 5th edition, McGraw-Hill, 2010

Dr Piers Steel: *The Procrastination Equation – How to Stop Putting Things Off and Start Getting Things Done,* 2nd edition, Prentice Hall Life, 2011

LESSON NOTES

Warmer

- Write the word *planning* in big letters on the board.

- Ask students for words that they think of when they see the word. They will hopefully come up with things like *plan*, *proposal*, *forecast*, *intention*, *objective*, *goal*, *aim*. If they have trouble coming up with words, put hints on the board, for example for *plan*, you could write *pl _ _* , for *proposal*, write *propos _ _* . Give definitions of the words you are looking for, for example: *This is what you call something you think will happen*, *like a particular level of sales*. (Answer: *forecast*.)

- Write these words on the board and explain any unfamiliar ones.

Overview

- Ask students to look at the Overview section on page 82. Tell them a little about the things you will be doing, using the table on page 81 of this book as a guide. Tell them which sections you will be covering in this lesson and which in later lessons.

Quotation

- Write the quotation on the board and ask students to discuss it briefly in pairs.

- With the whole class, ask pairs what they understand by the quote.

- The photo shows a complex road system. Ask students why they think planning is important in this situation.

Starting up

Students think about the factors involved in planning various things, from a holiday to a career.

A

- To make the activity concrete, get students in pairs to make a complete list of stages for one of the four 'events', as in the example below. Allocate an event to each pair.

> **Holiday**
>
> Consult those going about the destination and dates. Phone or go to a travel agent to obtain brochures. Look at prices and special offers online. Check availability, etc.

- Circulate, monitor and assist if necessary.

- With the whole class, ask the pairs to present their lists and compare different approaches to the same 'event' by different pairs.

B

- Do this as a quick-fire activity with the whole class. Compare the approaches of different people.

C

- Get your students in pairs to discuss the statements. Circulate, monitor and assist if necessary.

- With the whole class, compare and discuss the students' opinions.

Vocabulary: Making plans

Students look at various nouns and the verbs that typically precede them (operating verbs).

A – B

- Get students to work in pairs to match the verbs and nouns, using a bilingual or monolingual dictionary. Circulate, monitor and assist if necessary.

- With the whole class, go through the answers.

> **Exercise A**
>
> **1** estimate   **2** forecast   **3** do   **4** collect
> **5** consider
>
> **Exercise B**
>
> The most likely combinations are:
>
> arrange a meeting / a schedule / a deadline
>
> implement a plan / a schedule /a budget / a report
>
> keep to a budget / a deadline / a plan / a schedule
>
> meet a deadline
>
> prepare a budget / a plan / a report / a schedule
>
> rearrange a meeting / a deadline / a schedule
>
> write a plan / a report / a schedule

C

- Go through the nouns from Exercises A and B and check that the students understand and can pronounce them all.

- Tell students the subject of the text in Exercise C and ask them to complete it in pairs with nouns from Exercises A and B. Circulate, monitor and assist if necessary.

> **1** meeting   **2** budget   **3** information
> **4** options   **5** research   **6** report
> **7** costs   **8** budget   **9** schedule
> **10** deadline   **11** sales

LESSON NOTES

D 🔊 CD2.29

- Play the recording and get students to check their answers as they listen.

- Check answers with the whole class and clarify any difficulties.

E

- Tell students they have to plan a particular type of event. Divide the class into pairs and allocate a particular task to each pair.

- Circulate, monitor and assist if necessary, for example with vocabulary relating to their event.

- With the whole class, ask some of the pairs to give details of their plans. Try to persuade them to use some of the word combinations from this section in describing their plans.

 i-Glossary

Listening: How important is planning?

Ian Sanders is a business consultant and the author of *Unplan your business*. Students listen to him talking about how far ahead businesses should plan, and about a successful plan and a failed plan.

A 🔊 CD2.30

- Ask students to read the five notes on what Ian says and to guess what the missing words might be. If they struggle with this, ask them to identify what parts of speech are missing (e.g. 1 noun phrase; 2 noun phrase; 3 adjective, etc.).

- Play the recording several times for students to complete the notes. Remind them that some of the gaps may have more than one word.

- Go through the answers, playing the recording again if necessary and clarifying any difficulties.

> **1** the size of the business   **2** three years
> **3** smaller   **4** technology   **5** three-month
> **6** manageable   **7** guessing

B 🔊 CD2.31

- Explain that in the second part of the interview, Ian gives an example of successful planning.

- Ask students to read the paragraph.

- Play the recording for students to fill in the gaps.

- Play the recording a second time for students to check their answers.

> **1** simple   **2** flexible   **3** fixed   **4** stone
> **5** technology

C

- Tell students to compare their answers in pairs, then check with the whole class.

> Able to change easily = flexible
>
> Not able to change easily = fixed, set in stone

D 🔊 CD2.32

- Explain that in the third part of the interview, Ian gives an example of a failure in planning.

- Ask students to read the questions.

- Play the recording and give students a few minutes to note their answers.

- Go through the answers, playing the recording again if necessary to focus on the correct information.

> **1** To learn lessons and adapt things that aren't right
>
> **2** A web-based company for producing business cards
>
> **3** Because he learned from a business plan that failed.

E

- Ask students to work in pairs to discuss the question. Circulate, monitor and assist if necessary.

- After a few minutes, ask students to call out their ideas as you write them on the board.

- Finish by taking a vote: Is it better to have a detailed business plan or no plan at all?

➡ Resource bank: Listening (page 197)

Reading: To plan or not to plan

How a software development company became one of Microsoft's key partners without ever writing a business plan.

A

- Ask students to discuss the question in pairs, then elicit answers and write them on the board.

> **Suggested answers**
>
> 1, 4, 6

B

- Ask students to look at the chart.

- Give them five minutes to scan the article and find the answers.

- Get them to check answers in pairs, then check answers with the group.

LESSON NOTES

name	job/position	company	type of company	location
Dan Scarfe	Chief Executive	Dot Net Solutions	software development	Windsor
David Hieatt	co-founder	Howies	ethical clothing manufacturer	Cardigan
Rajeeb Dey		Enternships	student internship matching service	
Paul Maron-Smith	Managing Director	Gresham Private Equity	private equity	

C

- Ask students to read the six questions.
- Give students time to read the article again in more detail and to answer the questions.
- Go over the answers, explaining any difficulties.

> 1 Two: Dan Scarfe and Rajeeb Dey
> 2 Dan Scarfe
> 3 David Hieatt
> 4 Rajeeb Dey
> 5 Rajeeb Dey and Dan Scarfe
> 6 Paul Maron-Smith

D

- Before discussing the questions, have students brainstorm business sectors (e.g. services, consumer goods, financial services, technology, healthcare, industrial goods, utilities, transport, etc.) for use in answering question 1.
- Go through the answers with the class.

> **Sample answers**
> 1 Transport (because of fuel costs), financial services (because of market fluctuations)
> 2 Students' own answers
> 3 Students' own answers
> 4 For: A business plan guides an entrepreneur to success.
>   Against: A business plan is only a guess. It can be limiting.
> 5 Students' own answers

- This exercise leads into the Language review, so you may want to ask students to note the expressions used to talk about planning for the future. You can also point out the different structures used with each verb (*intend to* + infinitive, *hope to* + infinitive, *plan to* + infinitive, *focus on* + *-ing* form) and the use of the present continuous.

➡ Text bank (pages 148–151)

Language review: Talking about future plans

The use of the present continuous and of *going to* for future plans, and of verbs such as *plan*, *hope*, *expect*, *would like* and *want*.

- Go through the examples and the explanations, dealing with any difficulties. Point out that *going to* and the present continuous are often interchangeable in talking about the future.

A

- Go through the text with the whole class, getting students to underline the plans mentioned by the speaker.

> 'Well, as you all know, we are hoping that the World Cup spirit will get more customers through our doors. <u>We are planning a wide range of activities to capitalise on our football links</u> and <u>are expecting to sell more televisions, food and drink.</u> <u>We are also going to sell official merchandise before and during the tournament.</u> <u>We would like to get some big-name endorsements and want to sell stickers and trading cards.</u> Then <u>we are going to launch a digital site to promote our association with football legends.</u> We are hoping to be the supermarket of choice for our country's football fans.'

LESSON NOTES

B – C

- Do these exercises as quick-fire activities with the whole class. In Exercise C, get students to read through the whole text so as to avoid jumping to conclusions.

Exercise B

1 c   **2** a   **3** b

Exercise C

1 hoping   **2** expecting   **3** planning

D

- Demonstrate the activity with one student, using the example.

- Then get your students to do the exercise in pairs. Circulate, monitor and assist if necessary. Note language points for praise and correction afterwards, especially in relation to the verbs in this section.

- Bring the class to order. Praise some of the good uses of the verbs that you heard and work on others that require it.

- Then get one or two pairs to give examples of their exchanges.

Skills: Meetings: interrupting and clarifying

Students listen to a meeting, identify expressions for interrupting and clarifying and then use them in a role play.

A 🔊 CD2.33

- Tell students the subject of what they are about to hear: a planning meeting at a company that is about to move. Get them to look at the different points they will hear discussed.

- Play the recording once or twice and elicit the answers to the questions.

---

a) 6   **b)** 1   **c)** 5   **d)** 4   **e)** 2   **f)** 3

B

- Get your students to work in pairs. Ask the pairs to read the utterances aloud and decide whether the expressions in italic are used for interrupting or clarifying. Circulate, monitor and assist if necessary.

---

1 b   **2** a   **3** b   **4** a   **5** b

C

- Get your students to look at the Useful language box. Ask them to repeat the expressions, concentrating on good intonation.

- Then explain the situation to your students and divide the class into groups of three or four. Get each group to quickly appoint a chair, who uses the seven points as an agenda.

- If you choose, you could give students additional information, e.g. the VIPs are arriving at the airport on Monday afternoon (16.00). They will leave on Thursday morning (9.00).

- During and after the discussion, encourage students to plan and produce an itinerary for the visit using the above as starting and ending times.

- Circulate, monitor and assist if necessary. Note language points for praise and correction afterwards, especially in relation to the language of interrupting, dealing with interruptions and clarifying from the Useful language box.

- Bring the class to order. Praise some of the good language that you heard and work on other points that require it.

- Ask one or two groups for an outline of the farewell event they have planned.

➡ Resource bank: Speaking (page 185)

CASE STUDY

European Press and Media Corporation

After analysing market research, students plan the first issue of a new health-and-fitness magazine.

Stage 1: Background, planning and listening

🔊 CD2.34

- Get students to read the background. Explain any difficulties and then check their understanding by getting one or two students to summarise it as a series of key points.

> **Key points**
>
> EPMC produces magazines, TV, radio
>
> New health and fitness magazine
>
> Launch in UK, then sell overseas if successful
>
> Website support
>
> Teams are competing for cash prize for best plan

- In groups, students first brainstorm topics for the magazine, then evaluate these topics using the chart in the book.
- Circulate, monitor and assist if necessary.
- The groups then read and note their answers to the six questions.
- Play the recording once or twice and get students to note the main points.
- Check the answers with the class.

> **Key points**
>
> The market is there, the timing is good, but it must be different from other magazines.
>
> Target consumer: men, women age 20–40
>
> Sections should be clear and well-organised.
>
> A celebrity feature should be included.
>
> Website: some free, some subscription content

- In the same groups, students discuss how to promote the first issue.
- Circulate, monitor and assist if necessary.

Stage 2: Task

- Students work in the same groups. Each group should quickly appoint a chair, who should use points 1 to 3 and the list of key questions as an agenda.
- To begin part 1, tell the groups to start their discussions. Then circulate and monitor. Note language points for praise and correction afterwards, especially in relation to the language of planning.
- When the groups have finished their plan, bring the class to order.
- Praise some of the good language that you heard and work on half a dozen other points that require it.
- Then do part 2. Ask different groups to present their plans for the first programme.
- After all the groups have presented, ask the class to vote on the best plan.

> **One-to-one**
>
> This case study can be done as a discussion between teacher and student and then as a basis for a presentation by the student. Don't forget to note language points for praise and correction afterwards. Also point out some of the key language you chose to use.

⊚ You can also refer to the *Case study commentary* section of the DVD-ROM, where students can watch an interview with a consultant discussing the key issues raised by the case study.

Stage 3: Writing

- Explain the writing task to your students, pointing out especially the form it should take: a letter to a famous business person asking for an interview. This can be done as homework.

➡ Writing file, page 128

➡ Resource bank: Writing (page 212)

WORKING ACROSS CULTURES 3

International conference calls

This unit features extracts from international conference calls and a talk by an expert on conference calls.

A

- Get students to discuss the points in groups of three or four. Circulate, monitor and assist if necessary.
- Share answers and discuss as a class.

B ◀)) CD2.35–2.40

- Explain that students are going to hear extracts from six conference calls, and that in each case there is a problem.
- Play the recordings while students listen and note the problems.

C ◀)) CD2.35–2.40

- Have students look at the six problems (a–f).
- Play the recording a second time for students to match each recording with a problem.
- Check the answers with the whole class.

> **1** f **2** c **3** d **4** e **5** a **6** b

D ◀)) CD2.41

- Have students read the two questions.
- Play the recording while students take notes.
- Play the recording a second time for students to check their answers.
- Check the answers with the whole class.

> **1**   a, b, c
>
> **2**   Technology going wrong / causing problems

E ◀)) CD2.42

- Ask students to guess the words to complete the exercise.
- Play the recording for students to complete their answers.
- Play the recording again for students to check their answers.
- Check the answers with the whole class.

> **1** quiet place   **2** eating; drinking   **3** advance
> **4** topic   **5** say   **6** interrupt   **7** comment

F

- Give students time to read through the notes and complete the exercise.
- Circulate, monitor and assist if necessary.
- Have students first check answers in pairs, then check with the whole class.

> **1** T   **2** F   **3** T   **4** F   **5** T

Task

- Students work in groups of four. While students study their role cards, circulate, monitor and assist if necessary.
- If possible in your classroom, have students either arrange their four chairs back-to-back or stand back-to-back to simulate the situation of a phone call (you can hear but not see the other participants).
- When the students have done the role play, praise strong points and mention one or two things that students should pay attention to.
- After completing the role play, get students to complete their list of dos and don'ts. Circulate and monitor.
- Get students to share their lists with the whole class.

UNIT C Revision

This unit revises and reinforces some of the key language points from Units 7–9 and from Working across cultures 3. (Course Book page numbers are given below.)

7 New business

Vocabulary (page 67)

> **1** domestic **2** unemployment **3** labour
> **4** tax **5** government **6** foreign **7** balance
> **8** interest **9** exchange **10** inflation

Time clauses (page 70)

> **1** As soon as **2** after **3** as soon as **4** before
> **5** until **6** while **7** Until **8** before **9** after
> **10** When **11** when **12** while

Writing

> **Sample answer**
>
> Dear Alan,
>
> I've recently become the European distributor for ChuTools, a new Chinese power-tool manufacturer based in Shenzen. The company produces a range of DIY power tools – drills, saws and garden tools. The prices are mid-range, but the quality is very high for the price. They have received excellent reviews in the trade press. The company wants to support retailers with marketing and promotion, including prizes and special offers.
>
> Can we get together to discuss a deal?
>
> All the best,

8 Marketing

Vocabulary (page 75)

> **1** share **2** launch **3** goods **4** segment **5** range

Questions (page 78)

A

> **1** Is the market research complete?
> **2** When do you want to do it?
> **3** Do you have time to look at the new website?
> **4** Did you read the survey?
> **5** Have you seen the sales figures?
> **6** How should we describe the new model?

B

> **1** b **2** d **3** f **4** a **5** c **6** e

Skills (page 79)

> **1** Sorry, did you say
> **2** Could you give me
> **3** What about
> **4** I didn't catch
> **5** Did they say when
> **6** I'll e-mail you to
> **7** Thanks very much
> **8** I should

9 Planning

Vocabulary (page 83)

> **1** arranged **2** prepare **3** meet **4** keep
> **5** consider **6** do **7** forecast **8** estimated
> **9** write **10** implement

Skills (page 87)

> **1** c **2** f **3** b **4** k **5** a **6** j **7** i **8** h **9** e
> **10** g **11** d

Cultures 3: International conference calls

> **1** Be on time for the call.
> **2** Make sure you are in a quiet place.
> **3** If possible, use a headset for the call.
> **4** Use the 'mute' button when you are not speaking.
> **5** Avoid eating, drinking or chewing gum while on a conference call.
> **6** If you really need to have a drink, remember to use the 'mute' button.
> **7** Prepare for the call in advance. Plan what you may need to say.
> **8** Have any documents you may need close to hand.
> **9** Listen carefully and wait to be invited to comment by the call leader.
> **10** When speaking, it can be helpful to say who you are each time you speak.
> **11** When you speak, stay on topic.
> **12** Make short contributions rather than long speeches.
> **13** Try not to interrupt people when they are speaking.
> **14** Avoid taking notes on a computer, as typing will be noisy for the other participants.

Managing people

AT A GLANCE

	Classwork – Course Book	Further work
Lesson 1 *Each lesson (excluding case studies) is about 45–60 minutes. This does not include administration and time spent going through homework.*	<u>**Starting up**</u> Students discuss the qualities and skills needed by good managers. **Vocabulary: Verbs and prepositions** Students work on the prepositions that follow certain verbs.	Practice File Vocabulary (page 40) Practice exercises: Vocabulary 1 & 2 (DVD-ROM) **i-Glossary** (DVD-ROM)
Lesson 2	**Listening: Managing people** A management expert talks about managers who have impressed him. **Reading: Management and motivation** Students read an article about employee engagement.	Resource bank: Listening (page 198) Practice exercises: Listening (DVD-ROM) Text bank (pages 152–155)
Lesson 3	**Language review: Reported speech** Students look at the structures used when reporting what other people have said. <u>**Skills: Socialising and entertaining**</u> Students look at punctuality, dress, gifts, small talk, invitations and other cross-cultural issues when people from different cultures meet.	Practice File Language review (page 41) Practice exercises: Language review 1 & 2 (DVD-ROM) **ML Essential Business Grammar and Usage** (Units 74, 75 & 76) Resource bank: Speaking (page 186) Practice exercises: Skills (DVD-ROM)
Lesson 4 *Each case study is about 1 to 1½ hours.*	<u>**Case study: Ashley Cooper Search Agency**</u> Students consider how to improve staff performance at a property-finding agency.	Case study commentary (DVD-ROM) Resource bank: Writing (page 213) Practice File Writing (page 42)

For a fast route through the unit focusing mainly on speaking skills, just use the underlined sections.

For one-to-one situations, most parts of the unit lend themselves, with minimal adaptation, to use with individual students. Where this is not the case, alternative procedures are given.

BUSINESS BRIEF

In the 1960s, Douglas McGregor, one of the key thinkers in this area, formulated the now famous **Theory X** and **Theory Y**. Theory X is the idea that people instinctively dislike work and will do anything to avoid it. Theory Y is the more enlightened view that everyone has the potential to find satisfaction in work. (Others have suggested Theory W (for 'whiplash'), the idea that most work since the beginning of human society has been done under conditions of total coercion, i.e. slavery.)

In any case, despite so much evidence to the contrary, many managers still subscribe to Theory X, believing, for example, that their **subordinates** need constant **supervision** if they are to work effectively, or that decisions must be **imposed** from above without **consultation**. This, of course, makes for **authoritarian** managers.

Different cultures have different ways of managing people. Some cultures are well known for the consultative nature of decision-making – all members of the department or work group are asked to contribute to this process. This is management by **consensus**. Many western companies have tried to imitate what they see as more **consensual** Asian ways of doing things. Some commentators say that women will become more effective managers than men because they have the power to build consensus and common goals in a way that traditional male managers cannot.

A recent trend has been to encourage employees to use their own **initiative**, to make decisions on their own without asking managers first. This **empowerment** has been part of the trend towards **downsizing**: reducing the number of management layers in companies. After **delayering** in this way, a company may be left with just a top level of senior managers, **front-line** managers and employees with direct contact with the public. Empowerment takes the idea of **delegation** much further than has traditionally been the case. Empowerment and delegation mean new forms of **management control** to ensure that the overall business plan is being followed, and to ensure that operations become more profitable under the new organisation, rather than less.

Another trend is **off-site** or **virtual management**, where teams of people linked by e-mail and the Internet work on projects from their own premises. Project managers judge the performance of the team members in terms of what they produce and contribute to projects, rather than the amount of time they spend on them.

Read on

Jo Owen: *How to Manage – The Art of Making Things Happen*, Prentice Hall Business, 2009

Professor Neil Thompson: *People Skills*, 3rd edition, Palgrave Macmillan, 2009

Stuart Wyatt: *The Secret Laws of Management – The 40 Essential Truths for Managers*, Business Plus, 2010

Laurie J Mullins: *Management and Organisational Behaviour,* Financial Times Press/Prentice Hall, 2010

LESSON NOTES

Warmer

- Write the word *managing* on the left of the board. On the right put the word *people*. Add lines underneath *people* and, if you think your students need more help, add initial letters as clues.

- Ask students for other things that managers have to manage, apart from people. The board might end up looking like this.

managing	people
	schedules
	resources
	budgets
	conflict

Overview

- Ask students to look at the Overview section on page 96. Tell them a little about the things you will be doing, using the table on page 90 of this book as a guide. Tell them which sections you will be doing in this lesson and which in later lessons.

Quotation

- Write the quotation on the board. Ask students to discuss it in pairs and think of problems that could arise if there are two captains on one boat.

- With the whole class, ask pairs for their opinions. They might mention the need for one person to lead, make final decisions, resolve conflicts, and so on.

Starting up

Students discuss the qualities and skills needed by good managers.

- With the whole class, look through the list of qualities required by managers. Ask students in pairs to choose the six most important. Circulate, monitor and assist if necessary.

- Ask pairs about their selections. You could get pairs to 'vote' for six qualities and write up the scores on the board. Above all, encourage discussion by getting students to say why they have chosen particular qualities.

B

- Do this exercise as a whole class discussion. Again, ask *why* these qualities are needed.

- You could suggest: *patience, language ability, flexibility, sense of humour, curiosity, optimism, tolerance, awareness of your own cultural assumptions* and *expectations*. Explain these words and expressions if necessary.

C

- You could start by giving students a few examples from your own experience. However, don't talk negatively about your current manager or anyone the students might be able to identify.

- Do this exercise as a quick class discussion.

Vocabulary: Verbs and prepositions

Students work on the prepositions that follow certain verbs.

A – B

- Get students to focus on the subject of this section, prepositions that follow certain verbs, by writing on the board: *respond to employees' concerns promptly*.

- Do the exercise with the whole class, explaining any vocabulary difficulties.

> **1** c **2** g **3** e **4** a **5** b **6** d **7** f

- Then ask individual students to say which are the three most important qualities for them and encourage discussion with the class.

C – D

- Write up the two example sentences on the board. Point out that in a business context, we usually talk about *reporting to* someone. It is possible to *report on* someone, but this usage is restricted to specific contexts, for example a journalist reporting on a news item or a detective reporting on a criminal.

- Explain to your students what they have to do and then ask them to work on the exercises in pairs. Circulate, monitor and assist if necessary.

Exercise C

1 a) someone b) something

2 a) both b) someone

3 a) someone b) both

4 a) both b) something

5 a) both b) someone

- Underline that you say *to agree with someone, to agree on something*. Try to eliminate any tendency for students to say *I am agree with you*.

Exercise D

1 with **2** to **3** about **4** for **5** about

6 with **7** to **8** on

- Go through the answers with the whole class. Clarify any problems.

LESSON NOTES

E

- Write an example question or two on the board to show your students the sort of thing that you want, for example: *When you make a mistake, do you apologise for it? Do you argue with your colleagues a lot?*

- Get students to write their own questions. Circulate, monitor and assist if necessary.

- Then get students to work in pairs and ask and answer their questions.

- Bring the class to order and get some of the pairs to ask and answer the questions they wrote.

- Deal with any persistent problems in this area, getting students to say the correct forms.

F

- The pairs from Exercise E join up with another pair to form groups of four. Ask them to make a list of the qualities of their ideal manager, including whether the ideal manager is male or female.

- Circulate, monitor and assist where necessary.

- Ask some students to share their group's ideas with the whole class.

 i-Glossary

Listening: Managing people

A management expert talks about managers who have impressed him.

A ◀))) CD2.43

- Ask students to look at the four questions before listening.

- Play the recording and allow students a minute to note their answers.

- Check their answers, playing the recording again if necessary for clarification.

1	Lord Sieff
2	S-I-E-F-F
3	Former Chairman of Marks and Spencer
4	quality control, profit, staff welfare

B ◀))) CD2.44

- Tell students to read the notes and remind them that these are summaries, i.e. that they will not hear these exact words in the recording.

- Play the recording twice, giving students a minute in between to complete the notes.

- Elicit the answers from the class.

1	1976	7	Virgin
2	caring attitude	8	1970
3	social	9	360
4	aid	10	entrepreneurial
5	environmental	11	concern
6	profit		

C ◀))) CD2.45

- Ask students to read the summary and clarify any problems with vocabulary (e.g. *genuine*) and pronunciation (e.g. *engender*).

- Play the recording. Students complete the summary.

- Go through the answers with the class, playing the recording again for clarification if necessary.

1	communication	5	contact
2	availability	6	commitment
3	visibility	7	respect
4	approach	8	trust

D

- Divide the class into pairs for the discussion. Encourage students to think about the points raised by Laurie Mullins, as well as contributing their own ideas.

- Circulate, monitor and assist where necessary. Note good uses of language, and also weak points that need further practice, and feed back on these at the end of the discussion.

➡ Resource bank: Listening (page 198)

Reading: Management and motivation

Students read an article about employee engagement.

A

- Students discuss the question quickly in pairs, then share their answers with the whole class.

B

- Ask students to read the extract and answer the question.

- Take a vote in the class on which theory is better, and give students a chance to say why they prefer their choice.

LESSON NOTES

C

- Tell students to skim the article to determine which theory Ruby's company would most likely support.

> Ruby's company probably supports Theory Y;
> Geraldine's company probably supports Theory X.

D

- Students read the article closely to decide whether the nine statements are true, false, or not mentioned in the article.
- Students check their answers in pairs.
- Check the answers with the whole class.

> **1** T **2** T **3** F **4** T **5** F **6** F **7** DS **8** T **9** DS

E

- Students work in pairs. Circulate, monitor and assist where necessary. Note good uses of language, and also weak points that need further practice, and feed back on these at the end of the discussion.

➡ Text bank (pages 152–155)

Language review: Reported speech

Students look at the structures used when reporting what other people have said.

- Parts of this are difficult, so take it easy. Go through the explanations and the examples slowly. Write the examples on the board to draw students' attention to their features.
- *Say*, *tell* and *ask* can in themselves be difficult, but concentrate here on the reported speech aspect.
- Point out how the verb in reported speech goes one tense back, except where things are very recent or generally true.

A

- Do this activity with the whole class. Work on the *process* of finding the right answer, rather than just asking for the answer and moving on to the next question.

> **1** said   **2** told   **3** told   **4** said   **5** told   **6** said

B

- Have a few students take turns reading a sentence aloud to the class. Ensure they know the gender of all the names (male: Hamza, Pierre, Justin; female: Adela, Eleanor).
- Get students to do the exercise in pairs. Circulate, monitor and assist if necessary.

- Check the answers with the whole class.

> **1** He said (that) he wasn't enjoying his job very much.
>
> **2** She said (that) she wanted to listen to her staff more.
>
> **3** They said (that) they needed to invest in the development of staff.
>
> **4** He said (that) he was feeling under pressure at work.
>
> **5** He said (that) the company had been performing badly.
>
> **6** She said (that) she was going to look for a new job.

C 🔊 CD2.46

- Explain the context to your students and play the recording once or twice, stopping after each message. Use the example to show students what you are after. Clarify any difficulties.
- Elicit the answer and have students come forward to write sentences on the board.

> Anna said the level of absenteeism had gone up over the month. She said we needed to monitor sickness levels more closely. Kurt said motivation was the biggest issue. He said that staff felt that no one listened to them. The union representative said that the unions wanted more days' holiday per year. He/She said this would lead to lower sickness levels. Barbara said our staff had more days' holiday than any of our competitors. She said there was no excuse for the present level of absenteeism.

- Explain any remaining difficulties.

Skills: Socialising and entertaining

Students look at punctuality, dress, gifts, small talk, invitations and other cross-cultural issues when people from different cultures meet, and the language needed in these situations.

A

- Talk about the importance of socialising and ask your students to do the exercise in pairs. If possible, form pairs with members from different countries, who then explain the situation in their countries to each other.
- Circulate, monitor and assist if necessary.
- With the whole class, go through the various points, inviting comments and encouraging discussion.

LESSON NOTES

1 What counts as 'being on time'? How late do you have to be before you're considered 'late'? Discuss this in relation to different business and social situations, such as meetings and dinner parties. Is the answer the same in all cases?

2 Again, refer to different situations. Teach the expression *smart–casual*: dressing smartly but in casual clothes, perhaps with 'designer' names. Does the concept of smart–casual exist in your students' countries? Do 'dress-down' Fridays exist, where companies allow their employees to dress less formally than on other days? (A phenomenon of the dot-com boom era, this trend may be disappearing – ask your students about this if you think they will be aware of it.)

3 Most people have outside interests, and most of these are fairly natural to talk about: playing a sport, playing a musical instrument, travel, and so on.

4 You could also talk about how to introduce yourself. Do you say (e.g. for John Smith): *Smith*, *John Smith* or just *Smith* or just *John*? Does this vary depending on the degree of conservatism of the organisation?

5 When do you give gifts? What should you give? Does the recipient unwrap them immediately or wait till later? Teach the expression *That's very kind of you.*

6 How often do people shake hands? Every day on meeting, as in France, or less often? When is kissing or hugging appropriate, if at all? Should Westerners in Asia bow (practise the pronunciation of this word) or just use the universal gesture of shaking hands?

B – C 🔊 CD2.47

- Ask students to look at the two questions in Exercise B and play the recording. Explain any difficulties, but don't give the answers to the questions.

- Elicit the answers to Exercise B.

Exercise B

1 To have dinner with him and his friend Abdullah

2 No, he doesn't

- Ask your students to look at the exchanges in Exercise C. Play the recording again once or twice and get students to complete the exchanges.

Exercise C

1 it's very kind of you   2 if you don't mind
3 quite understand

- Ask your students to read this part of the conversation in pairs. Point out the usefulness of the expressions used.

D 🔊 CD2.48

- Explain the situation and play the recording once or twice. Help with any difficulties, but don't give the answers to the exercise.

- Elicit the questions from the whole class.

1 What do people like doing here in their spare time?

2 What about you, Paul, what do you usually do after work? How do you spend your evenings?

3 How about you, Mohammed? What's your favourite pastime?

E 🔊 CD2.49

- Play the recording once or twice. It doesn't matter if students don't understand every word. The idea is for them to get the gist in order to answer the question.

Paul has come to Damascus to find a company to supply carpets for his store. Abdullah knows someone who runs a family business specialising in traditional carpet designs. He will put Paul in touch with him.

F 🔊 CD2.49

- Play the recording again once or twice and get students to number the sentences in the order they hear them. Clarify any difficulties.

a) 3   **b)** 6   **c)** 2   **d)** 5   **e)** 1   **f)** 4

G

- Explain that students should imagine that they're travelling abroad on business.

- Go through the different things students have to find out. Remind them that one of the aims of the role play is to use as many of the expressions from the Useful language box as possible.

- Then get students to do the role play in pairs. Circulate and monitor. Note down language points for praise and correction afterwards, especially in relation to language used whilst socialising and entertaining.

- Bring the class to order. Praise strong language points and work on half a dozen points that need improving, getting students to say the correct forms.

- Get one of the pairs to do their role play again for the whole class.

➡ Resource bank: Speaking (page 186)

CASE STUDY

Ashley Cooper Search Agency

Students consider how to improve staff performance at a property-finding agency.

Stage 1: Background 🔊 CD2.50

- Get students to read the information, then go through it with the whole class, eliciting the key points.

> ACSA in London finds top-class UK, France and Germany properties for wealthy clients from all over the world.
>
> Database needs building up.
>
> London has six multilingual consultants. They only search for properties at €1 million and above.

- Ask the question to the whole class.

> **Possible answers**
>
> ACSA has a good network for finding top-class properties.
>
> Consultants are paid a salary rather than a commission, so they may not try to offer clients the most expensive properties, but may instead look for the most suitable one.

- Get students to read the section about the staff payment system. Elicit the following information.

> Current system: Salary based on service, bonus decided by manager
>
> Proposed system: Salary only (to be adjusted), no bonus

- Play the recording while students make notes about the two consultants.

- Elicit the descriptions of the two new consultants. Make notes on the board.

> **Adriana**
>
> Youngest team member
>
> Economics graduate – good with figures
>
> Meeting sales targets
>
> Good ideas and adding clients to database
>
> Lacks social skills
>
> Doesn't get on well with the team
>
> Presentations not up to standard
>
> Doesn't like payment system
>
> **Ahmed**
>
> Good sales record
>
> Not in office enough
>
> Not a team player – doesn't attend meetings or build up database
>
> Is happy with payment system

- Working individually, students read the summaries of the other four consultants and the sales chart, and list problems Diana might have as she becomes manager of the team.

- Students share answers with the group as you make notes on the board.

> **Possible answers**
>
> Daria, Jackie and Ahmed have consistently improved, while Peter and Klaus's sales have diminished. (There's no trend for Adriana because she has only one year's performance data.) This means that the newer employees are performing better than the ones who've been with the company longer.
>
> The men are all happy with the current system, but the women don't like it. This will be especially tricky with Daria, who already thinks the women are treated unfairly.
>
> Jackie performs very well, but isn't popular with colleagues.

Stage 2: Task

- Explain to students that as a director of ACSA, you need to give Diana some advice about how to improve the team's performance and motivation.

- Students work in small groups to discuss the questions, including the question in part 2 regarding who should be made redundant.

- When the discussions are under way, circulate and monitor. Note down language points for praise and correction afterwards.

- When the groups have come to some sort of conclusion, bring the class to order.

- Praise strong language points and work on half a dozen points that need improving, getting students to say the correct forms.

- Ask what conclusions the different groups came to.

> **One-to-one**
>
> This case study can be done as a discussion between teacher and student and then as a basis for a presentation by the student.

◎ You can also refer to the *Case study commentary* section of the DVD-ROM.

Stage 3: Writing

- Make sure that your students understand what they have to do: write the recommendation section of a report to the CEO of ACSA. This can be done as homework.

➡ Writing file, page 129

➡ Resource bank: Writing (page 213)

AT A GLANCE

	Classwork – Course Book	Further work
Lesson 1 *Each lesson (excluding case studies) is about 45–60 minutes. This does not include administration and time spent going through homework.*	**Starting up** Students do a quiz to find out how good they are at dealing with conflict. **Vocabulary: Word-building** Students look at related nouns and adjectives and their opposites.	Practice File Vocabulary (page 44) Practice exercises: Vocabulary 1 & 2 (DVD-ROM) i-Glossary (DVD-ROM)
Lesson 2	**Listening: Resolving disputes** An expert in handling business conflict talks about common causes of conflict in organisations. Students then talk about their own experiences in this area. **Reading: Conflict management** Students read an article on conflict management.	Resource bank: Listening (page 199) Practice exercises: Listening (DVD-ROM) Text bank (pages 156–159)
Lesson 3	Language review: Conditionals Students look at the first and second conditional, and their use in negotiating. **Skills: Negotiating: dealing with conflict** Students look at ways of defusing conflict and the language to use in this situation.	Practice File Language review (page 45) Practice exercises: Language review 1 & 2 (DVD-ROM) ML Essential Business Grammar and Usage (Units 79, 80 & 82) Resource bank: Speaking (page 187) Practice exercises: Skills (DVD-ROM)
Lesson 4 *Each case study is about 1 to 1½ hours.*	**Case study: Herman & Corrie Teas** Students analyse an offer from a large multinational drinks company to buy a relatively small, privately-owned tea importer and packager.	Case study commentary (DVD-ROM) Resource bank: Writing (page 214) Practice File Writing (page 46)

For a fast route through the unit focusing mainly on speaking skills, just use the underlined sections.

For one-to-one situations, most parts of the unit lend themselves, with minimal adaptation, to use with individual students. Where this is not the case, alternative procedures are given.

BUSINESS BRIEF

Conflict may well be productive in some cases. In any business situation, there are often a number of different ideas about the way to proceed. Usually only one way can be chosen, so conflict is inevitable. Ideally, airing the different ideas in discussion will lead to the best one being chosen. But the process may become political, with an idea being defended by the person or group putting it forward after it has become apparent that it is not the best way to go. Those defending a long-cherished idea are unwilling to lose face by abandoning it. There may be conflict between different levels in an organisation's **hierarchy** or between different departments, with hostility to ideas from elsewhere – the **not-invented-here syndrome**.

Examples of unproductive conflict include disputes between colleagues or between managers and subordinates that go beyond ideas and become personal. Companies can spend a lot of time and energy resolving these disputes. In countries with high levels of **employee protection**, dismissing troublesome employees can lead to a long process of consultation with the authorities and even litigation, for example where an employee sues their company for **unfair dismissal**. Defending an action like this is of course costly and a distraction from a company's normal business.

Labour–management conflict in the form of tactics such as **strikes** and **go-slows** can also be very expensive and time-consuming. The goodwill of a company's customers, built up over years, can be lost very quickly when they are hurt by such a dispute. But there are sometimes cases where the public sympathise with the employees and don't mind the disruption. Both sides may put a lot of effort into presenting their case and gaining public sympathy with the use of advertising, public-relations firms, and so on. Many countries have legislation with compulsory **cooling-off periods** before strikes can begin, official procedures for **arbitration** between the two sides, and so on.

In dealings between companies, **supplier–customer relationships** can degenerate into conflict. Conflict seems to be endemic in some industries, for example construction, where contractors are often in dispute about whether the work has been performed properly or whose responsibility a particular problem is. This can lead to protracted legal proceedings.

More and more companies in the US are specifying in contracts that any disputes should be settled using **alternative dispute resolution (ADR)**, avoiding expensive legal wrangling. Specialised organisations have been set up to facilitate this.

Read on

Shay McConnon and Margaret McConnon: *Managing Conflict in the Workplace – How to Develop Trust and Understanding and Manage Disagreements*, 4th revised edition, How To Books Ltd, 2010

Kenneth Cloke, Joan Goldsmith: *Resolving Conflicts at Work – Ten Strategies for Everyone on the Job*, 3rd edition, Jossey Bass, 2011

Steve Gates: *The Negotiation Book – Your Definitive Guide to Successful Negotiating*, John Wiley & Sons, 2010

Professor David A Buchanan and Dr Andrzej A Huczynski: *Organizational Behaviour*, Financial Times Press/Prentice Hall, 2010

Laurie J Mullins: *Management and Organisational Behaviour*, Financial Times Press/Prentice Hall, 2010

Ed Rose: *Employment Relations*, Financial Times Press, 2009

LESSON NOTES

Warmer

- Write the word *conflict* in big letters on the board.
- Ask students for the things that they think of when they see the word. They will probably come up with things like *disagree*, *disagreement*, *dispute*, *argue*, *argument*, *war*, etc.

Overview

- Ask students to look at the Overview section on page 104. Tell them a little about the things you will be doing, using the table on page 97 of this book as a guide. Tell them which sections you will be doing in this lesson and which in later lessons.

Quotation

- Write the quotation on the board and ask students to discuss it briefly in pairs.
- With the whole class, ask pairs what they think it means (that simply winning an argument may not achieve anything, but that arguing to achieve progress has a better chance of giving the desired result).
- Ask students if they agree with this view, and whether it applies to all areas of life.

Starting up

Students do a quiz to find out how good they are at dealing with conflict.

- Tell your students to do the quiz in pairs. Each member of the pair asks the other member the questions. Both then work out their individual scores. Circulate and monitor to check they have understood the procedure and to help with any vocabulary or pronunciation problems, such as the pronunciation of *criticise*.
- Bring the class to order and go round the pairs asking them to talk about each person's answer for a particular question, for example: *I'm in a meeting and people cannot agree. I suggest a ten-minute break. Paula proposes something new.* Then ask another pair about the next question, and so on.
- Then ask the whole class to say with a show of hands which score they got and which profile they have. Discuss the results tactfully.

Vocabulary: Word-building

Students look at related nouns and adjectives and their opposites.

- If possible, ensure that your students have a good monolingual dictionary, such as the *Longman Active Study Dictionary*, or a good bilingual dictionary for this exercise.

- As professional language trainers, we take word classes such as nouns and adjectives for granted, but be sure that your students understand the difference. One obvious advantage of using bilingual dictionaries is that students can see very clearly the equivalent words in their own language. If your students are all from one language background, you could get them to say what the translations are.

- Do the first item as an example for the whole class. Then get your students to fill in the first two columns of the chart in pairs. Circulate, monitor and assist if necessary.

- Bring the class to order and ask for the answers, clarifying any difficulties. Practise the pronunciation of nouns and adjectives. You may want to point out that other forms exists (e.g. 5 *emotive* and 10 *creation*) but that these words aren't applicable to people's character.

> **2** calm **3** weak **4** flexible **5** emotional
> **6** consistent **7** sympathetic **8** formality
> **9** enthusiastic **10** creativity

B 🔊 CD2.51

- Students do the exercise. Play the recording for them to check their answers. Then have them practise in pairs.

1	'patience	'patient
2	'calmness	'calm
3	'weakness	'weak
4	flexi'bility	'flexible
5	e'motion	e'motional
6	con'sistency	con'sistent
7	'sympathy	sympa'thetic
8	for'mality	'formal
9	en'thusiasm	enthusi'astic
10	crea'tivity	cre'ative

C

- Now point out how the opposites are formed. (It's probably easier to tell your students to learn the opposites one by one rather than try to apply 'rules'.) Get your students to complete the third column in pairs.

> **1** impatient **4** inflexible **5** unemotional
> **6** inconsistent **7** unsympathetic
> **9** unenthusiastic **10** not (very) creative

LESSON NOTES

- Point out the difference between *sympathetic* (= trying to understand someone's problems and give them help) and *nice* (= generally friendly).

- Go through the answers, explaining any difficulties. Practise the pronunciation of the opposites with the whole class.

D

Do this as a quick-fire activity with the whole class.

1 impatient	**2** creative	**3** unemotional
4 flexible	**5** unsympathetic	**6** calm
7 weak	**8** inconsistent	

E – F

- Get students to work in pairs on this. Tell them to note down the things they agree and disagree about. Circulate, monitor and assist if necessary. Be sure to get your students to distinguish correctly between nouns and adjectives, for example: *Patience is a very important quality* but *It's important to be patient.*

- When they have reached an agreement about the answers to Exercise E, they should move on to discuss the question in Exercise F. Give them a few minutes to discuss it.

- Get students to join up with another pair to discuss their answers to E and F.

- Bring the class to order. Help with any general difficulties. Then get some of the pairs to summarise their views, for example: *Paula thinks that calmness is important, but I totally disagree with her. I think it's important to show emotions such as anger and impatience. But we agree that it's important to be strong and not to show weakness in negotiations.*

- ◎ i-Glossary

Listening: Resolving disputes

An expert in handling business conflict talks about common causes of conflict in organisations.

A ◀)) CD2.52

- Tell students they are going to listen to someone who specialises in helping companies resolve conflicts.

- Go through the questions with the class. Then play the recordings while students note their answers.

- Check the answers with the class.

1	20 years ago
2	London
3	It makes businesses aware of more effective ways of dealing with conflict
4	Up to 40,000

B ◀)) CD2.53

- Ask students to read the paragraph and see if they can guess what the missing words are.

- Play the recording for them to confirm their guesses and to complete the gaps.

- Check their answers and address any difficulties.

1 communication	**2** communication	**3** dealing
4 unfair	**5** workplace	**6** culture	**7** employees

- The missing words are all multisyllabic – do a quick test by asking students which syllable is stressed in each one (*communi'cation, 'dealing, 'unfair, 'workplace, 'culture, em'ployees* or *emplo'yees*).

C ◀)) CD2.54

- Ask students to read the notes and see if they can guess what the missing words are.

- Play the recording and ask students to complete the notes.

- Check the answers with the class.

1 dialogue	**2** problem	**3** process	**4** time
5 agenda	**6** talked about	**7** communication	
8 solution			

D

- To give your students the idea, tell them (without naming names, of course) about conflicts you have been involved in and how you tried to deal with them.

- Then ask your students tactfully about conflicts they have been involved in and how they dealt with them. Get them to use correctly some of the vocabulary from this section.

➡ Resource bank: Listening (page 199)

Reading: Conflict management

Students read an article on conflict management.

A

- This may be best done as a class discussion. First, define *bullying* (= using your strength or power to frighten or hurt a weaker person). Encourage students to imagine situations where joking or teasing becomes bullying.

B

- In pairs, students brainstorm sources of conflict at work.

- Ask pairs to share their ideas with the whole class. Write the ideas on the board.

LESSON NOTES

C

- Students read the text quickly to see if their ideas are mentioned.

- Give them a few minutes to read, then have students share their findings with the class. Note any ideas that are in the article that weren't mentioned in class.

D

- Go over the questions with the class.

- Students read the article more closely to answer the questions.

- Have them check their answers in pairs or small groups. Then check answers with the whole class.

> 1 Managers should be sensitive. They should be prepared to step in and have a quiet word with the team members involved. They should inform those involved that, while plenty of communication is encouraged, it's important that there is respect for other people and that certain standards of behaviour are expected at work.
>
> 2 So that those involved will understand what is unacceptable.
>
> 3 To prevent habits from being formed and to ensure that the manager is taken seriously.
>
> 4 If managers ignore unacceptable behaviour, problems will get worse until the disciplinary process has to be used or a formal complaint is made, by which time it will be much harder to achieve a successful resolution.
>
> 5 They are a good opportunity for managers to ask questions about any conflict issues that might be worrying employees.

E

- Have students find the words. Check the answers with the whole class.

> 1 inappropriate (lines 13–14)
>
> 2 unacceptable (lines 15, 31, 45)
>
> 3 impolite (line 65)
>
> 4 informal (line 70)

F

- Students work in pairs or small groups. If students are not in work, get them to think about other situations where they may have faced similar problems.

- Circulate, monitor and assist if necessary.

➡ Text bank (pages 156–159)

Language review: Conditionals

Students look at the first and second conditional, and their use in negotiating.

- Go through the explanations, writing the examples on the board and underlining the verbs.

A

- Go through the sentences with the class, getting students to comment on them and correct them.

> 1 If you **paid** in dollars, we would deliver next week.
>
>   OR If you pay in dollars, we **will** deliver next week.
>
> 2 If I **had** his number, I would phone him.
>
> 3 If the goods ~~will~~ arrive tomorrow, I'll collect them.
>
> 4 If the cars **were** more reliable, more people would buy them.

B

- With the whole class, explain any unfamiliar vocabulary (e.g. *signing-on bonus*). Explain the idea of the exercise, using the example as an illustration. Write it on the board in order to focus students' attention on it. Also point out that *If you pay in dollars* could be followed by b, c, e, f, as well as g.

- Get your students to do the rest of the exercise in pairs, thinking about the context of each exchange. Circulate, monitor and assist if necessary.

- Bring the class to order and clarify any general difficulties. Ask students for their answers.

- Tell students that all the combinations are grammatically possible if the verb tenses are correct, but that the following are the most probable from the point of view of meaning.

> **Suggested answers**
>
> 1 f, h – Buyer talking to seller
>
> 2 a, b, c, d, f, g – Someone in a company working on a distribution agreement talking to a possible distributor
>
> 3 a, b, c, d, e, f, g – Seller talking to buyer
>
> 4 a, b, c, d, e, f – Seller in a commercial negotiation talking to the buyer
>
> 5 a, b, c, d, e, f – Seller talking to buyer
>
> 6 f, h – Buyer talking to seller
>
> 7 f, h – Buyer to seller
>
> 8 d – Employer talking in a recruitment interview *or* a, b, c, e, f, g – Seller talking to buyer

C ◀)) CD2.55

- Explain that you're going to play a recording of two people negotiating and that they have to listen out for every time an offer is made.

- Read the rubric with the students. Explain to them that they need to underline two sentences and circle two sentences in the audio script.

- Check answers with the whole class.

Underline:	If I reduced the price by 7%, would you give me a firm order?
	If we increased our order, would you give us a bigger discount?
Circle:	If you increase your order to 1,000 units, we'll give you a 10% discount.
	If you give us 90 days' credit, we'll sign the order today.

D

- Go through the example with the whole class, explaining any difficulties. Work on the pronunciation of *wouldn't*.

- Ask your students to work on the activity in pairs. Circulate, monitor and assist if necessary.

- Bring the class to order and ask students for their answers. Write one answer for each question on the board as a model.

- If there is time, make a link back to the quiz in the Starting up activity at the beginning of the unit. This time, students could answer the questions with conditionals, for example: *In a meeting, if two people cannot agree, Paula would intervene and propose something new, but I would say nothing.* Go through some of the questions and answers with the whole class.

Skills: Negotiating: dealing with conflict

Students look at ways of defusing conflict and the language to use in this situation.

A

- Go through the first two or three points with the whole class, without being prescriptive. Good ways of defusing conflict in some places may be considered bad in others, and vice versa – see what your students think about this. Deal with any vocabulary difficulties in the remaining points.

- Then ask your students to discuss the remaining points in pairs. Circulate, monitor and assist if necessary.

- Bring the class to order and discuss the points with the whole class.

1 There is more eye contact in some cultures than others. Where there is little eye contact to begin with, there may be even less when there is conflict, but it's hard to imagine a situation where no eye contact at all would help. At the other end of the scale, staring at one's counterpart across the table wouldn't be helpful either.

2 Some places may consider this conciliatory, others provocative. If in doubt, don't smile too much.

3 Again, this may be considered provocative. Discuss with your students if it is possible to have a facial expression and body language that are 'neutral' in all cultures.

4 It depends – if the conflict is about a major issue, there might be no point in discussing anything else until it is resolved.

5 In some cultures, silence is a sign of respect, a sign that you are thinking carefully about what has been said. But there must always be a point at which it becomes uncomfortable.

6 Some cultures might find this strange – the implied idea being that, if you saw what the other person meant, you wouldn't be in conflict with them. Tell students not to use this expression too often.

7 Information gathering is always useful, but persistent questioning about points that have already been covered and that are perfectly clear will cause irritation and may cause further conflict.

8 Easier said than done. A good idea in principle, but ideas are often inextricably bound up with the person expressing them.

9 Humour is appropriate in some cultures and not in others. It could help to defuse a situation of conflict in some places, but in others it might aggravate it.

10 Good idea, but don't overdo it. It could sound patronising.

B ◀)) CD2.56

- Give the background to the situation. Play the recording once or twice and clarify any difficulties.

- Elicit the answers from the class.

LESSON NOTES

1 a) Rachel's current salary
   b) The salary that Rachel is asking for

2 a) Thinks she's undervalued; has done well in last two years (exceeded her targets by almost 40%); none of sales staff has done better than that; Sophie Legrand got a raise to over $100,000 and hasn't been getting as good results; could move to another company
   b) Company in difficult economic situation; got to cut costs; won't discuss other people's salaries

3 To raise her salary to $80,000 now and review it again in six months' time

C 🔊 CD2.56

- Play the recording again and get students to complete the extracts.

> **1** worth **2** targets **3** economic
> **4** saying; view **5** compromise **6** covered

D

- Go through the expressions in the Useful language box, working on intonation.

- Discuss the extracts in Exercise C with your students and get them to classify them.

> **Expressing your point of view**
>
> I think I'm worth a lot more than that to the company.
>
> My work's greatly undervalued at the moment.
>
> I've exceeded my targets by (almost 40 per cent).
>
> Put yourself in our shoes.
>
> We're facing a difficult economic situation.
>
> **Calming down**
>
> I understand what you're saying.
>
> I can see your point of view.
>
> **Creating solutions**
>
> Let me suggest a compromise.
>
> How about if we ...
>
> **Closing a negotiation**
>
> I think we've covered everything.

E

- Tell students that they should try to use the expressions from the Useful language box in the role play.

- Give the background information and explain any difficulties, for example *middle-of-the-range car*.

- Divide the class into pairs, allocate roles and get your students to prepare them. Circulate, monitor and assist if necessary.

- When students are ready, get them to start the role play. Circulate and monitor. Note language points for praise and correction afterwards, especially in relation to the language in the Useful language box.

- When the pairs have finished, bring the class to order. Praise strong language points that you heard and go through half a dozen that need improvement, getting individual students to say the correct forms.

- With the whole class, ask some of the pairs what happened in their negotiations and encourage general discussion about the outcomes.

➡ Resource bank: Speaking (page 187)

CASE STUDY

Herman & Corrie Teas

Students analyse an offer from a large multinational drinks company to buy a relatively small, privately-owned tea importer and packager.

Stage 1: Background 🔊 CD2.57

- Tell your students to silently read the background. Meanwhile, write the headings on the left of the table below on the board.

- Ask students for key points to complete the first five items in the column on the right of the table with information from the reading.

- Explain that students are going to listen to a recording of a radio report about the company. Have them listen and complete the remainder of the table with information from the recording. Encourage them to suggest notes similar to the ones here, rather than longer sentences.

Company	Herman & Corrie Teas
Activities	Importing and packaging tea
Based in	Rotterdam, the Netherlands
Main markets	Europe, the US, Australia
Potential buyer of the company	UCC
Analysts' opinion of the company	Could be doing a lot better
Company values	'Green'; one of the first to get fair trade certificate
Staff profile	Very loyal

- Have students read the question (How might Herman & Corrie Teas benefit from the sale?).

- Brainstorm answers as a class.

Possible answer

They might have access to a larger market and better marketing and distribution.

Stage 2: Conflict

- Get your students to silently read the e-mail and note the key points.

- Check the key points with the whole class.

Key points

A decision hasn't been made

Profits are down

Range of suppliers and products is limited

Financial press has been critical

Difficult to fill management posts

Stage 3: Task

- Explain what will happen in the role play. Allocate roles. In a large class, the Chief Executive could be supported by other directors who would give their opinions and participate in the final vote.

- When the groups are ready, tell them to start the role play. Circulate and monitor. Note down language points for praise and correction afterwards, especially in relation to the language of conflict.

- When the groups have come to a conclusion, bring the class to order. Praise strong language points and work on half a dozen points that need improving, getting students to say the correct forms.

- Ask some of the students what happened in their role plays. Compare and contrast the different outcomes and encourage discussion.

One-to-one

This case study can be done as a discussion between teacher and student and then as a basis for a presentation by the student. Don't forget to note language points for praise and correction afterwards. Also point out some of the key language you chose to use.

🔘 You can also refer to the *Case study commentary* section of the DVD-ROM, where students can watch an interview with a consultant discussing the key issues raised by the case study.

Stage 4: Writing

- Make sure that your students understand what they have to do: write a letter to the shareholders as if from the CEO of Herman & Corrie Teas, telling them the outcome of the meeting. This can be done for homework.

➡ Writing file page 128

➡ Resource bank: Writing (page 214)

12 Products

	Classwork – Course Book	Further work
Lesson 1 *Each lesson (excluding case studies) is about 45–60 minutes. This does not include administration and time spent going through homework.*	**Starting up** Students talk about products that they like and their attitudes to companies that make products. **Vocabulary: Describing products** Students look at some adjectives that can be used to describe products.	Practice File Vocabulary (page 48) **Practice exercises:** **Vocabulary 1 & 2** (DVD-ROM) **i-Glossary** (DVD-ROM)
Lesson 2	**Listening: Favourite products** Students listen to four people talk about their best purchases, and to an interview with a lifestyle trends expert. **Reading: Launching new products** Students read about Casio, the Japanese consumer-electronics company	Resource bank: Listening (page 200) **Practice exercises:** **Listening** (DVD-ROM) **Text bank** (pages 160–163)
Lesson 3	**Language review: Passives** Students look at passives in the context of where goods are made and produced. **Skills: Presenting a product** Students listen to a sales manager presenting a product to buyers and then present a product themselves.	Practice File Language review (page 49) **Practice exercises:** **Language review 1 & 2** (DVD-ROM) **ML Essential Business** **Grammar and Usage** (Units 21 & 22) **Resource bank: Speaking** (page 188) **Practice exercises: Skills** (DVD-ROM)
Lesson 4 *Each case study is about 1 to 1½ hours.*	**Case study: The George Marshall Awards** Students present ideas for new products to the selection committee for an award that recognises innovative goods. The selection committee decides which is the best.	Case study commentary (DVD-ROM) **Resource bank: Writing** (page 215) Practice File Writing (page 50) **Test file: Progress test 4**

For a fast route through the unit focusing mainly on speaking skills, just use the underlined sections.

For one-to-one situations, most parts of the unit lend themselves, with minimal adaptation, to use with individual students. Where this is not the case, alternative procedures are given.

BUSINESS BRIEF

When we think of business, we usually think of **tangible products** that we can see and touch: computers on the desk or cars in the showroom. We may also think of **primary products** like coal or agricultural goods. But manufacturing forms a diminishing part of most advanced economies: only 17 per cent of the US economy, for example. What manufacturing there is is increasingly **lean**, with 'Japanese' techniques such as **just-in-time (JIT)** ordering of components and **total quality management (TQM)** becoming widespread.

There is an unresolved argument about whether economies need manufacturing at all to survive and flourish. In many people's minds, nevertheless, there is great regret when a factory closes in a 'traditional' industry: there is something more 'real' about work in a car plant than in a call centre. Call centres typically sell intangible products such as mortgages (more and more services are described in product terms). However, car plants are likely provide more work indirectly than call centres, for example at the component manufacturers that supply them.

We define ourselves partly by the products we own and use, wherever they are made. Economies in different parts of the world are at different stages of development in the way products are bought and perceived. In newly industrialised countries, such as some of those in Asia, more and more people are now able to afford **consumer durables** like washing machines for the first time, and companies that sell these types of goods can make large amounts of money. In the West, the market for televisions or washing machines is basically one of **replacement**. In a situation like this, **design**, **brand** and **image** become more important. Previously prestigious products, like certain makes of luxury car, become increasingly affordable, and manufacturers have to be careful to stay ahead of the game to avoid their brands being perceived as 'ordinary'.

The cars, televisions and washing machines of the 1950s may have had more style, but modern products are technically far better now than they were then. Consumers can complain about **designed-in obsolescence** and unnecessary **sophistication** of products with too many features that are never used, and manufacturers may have started to take this into account, simplifying their features. Consumers are also able to obtain and compare information about different products more and more easily. **Consumerism** is a force that manufacturers increasingly have to reckon with.

Read on

Lonnie Wilson: *How to Implement Lean Manufacturing*, McGraw-Hill Professional, 2009

James H. Gilmore: *Authenticity – What Consumers Really Want*, Harvard Business School Press, 2007

Philip Kotler, Hermawan Kartajaya and Iwan Setiawan: *Marketing 3.0 – From Products to Customers to the Human Spirit*, John Wiley & Sons, 2010

LESSON NOTES

Warmer

- Write the words *a product* in big letters on the right of the board.

- Ask students for verbs that can come in front of the word. The board could end up looking like this:

invent develop make distribute market sell buy improve	a product

- Tell students they will see more verbs like this in the Vocabulary section of the unit.

Overview

- Ask students to look at the Overview section on page 112. Tell them a little about the things you will be doing, using the table on page 105 of this book as a guide. Tell them which sections you will be doing in this lesson and which in later lessons.

Quotation

- Write the quotation on the board and ask students to discuss it briefly in pairs.

- With the whole class, ask pairs for their opinions.

Starting up

Students talk about products that they like and their attitudes to companies that make products.

A – **B**

- To give students the idea, talk about a product that you like and what it says about you.

- Then with the whole class, ask your students what products they like, why, and what they say about them; also ask what types of cars, clothes, music or food they prefer, and what items they could not live without. Elicit some opinions about personal tastes in design and function: iPhone versus Blackberry, Mac versus PC, and so on.

C

- Get your students to look at the statements and then discuss them in pairs. Circulate, monitor and assist if necessary.

- Bring the class to order and ask the pairs for their opinions. Encourage discussion.

1 On the one hand, it's good to support your local/national economy, but on the other, if you believe in the free market, then buying cheaper imported goods is a valid choice, and businesses that can't compete have to change.

2 While this statement is no doubt true in some cases, students should also consider cost beyond the financial price paid for items. The world is full of products that have a relatively cheap price tag, but the cost to the environment is high in terms of consuming limited resources and creating pollution. There is an increasing awareness that everyone pays the price of damage to the environment.

3 Some students may complain about high marketing and advertising costs that add to the 'real' cost of goods. Others may say that competition depends on good communication and marketing, and that this competition drives down the cost of products in the long run. See what they think.

4 This is one of the key issues in the globalisation debate. Pro-globalisers say that this is a good way of getting countries onto the development ladder: after assembling multinationals' products, countries with the right business and political leadership will move on to developing and manufacturing their own. Anti-globalisers say that multinationals take advantage of low wage costs and then move on somewhere else if they rise too high.

5 There are many sides to this debate. Communications technology has allowed us to be connected to other people all of the time (receiving e-mail by phone, and so on). Some would say this is a great improvement, while others would say the opposite – that we have become slaves to our technology.

Vocabulary: Describing products

Students look at some adjectives that can be used to describe products.

- Go through the words and check their meanings and pronunciation (especially stress) with your students.

- Ensure especially that your students understand the difference between *economical* and *economic*. *Economic* is the adjective related to *economy*: for example *economic issues*. Give students an example with *economical*, which means getting good value for money, for example *Buying in bulk is economical*.

LESSON NOTES

- Get your students to work in pairs and to think of specific products that match the adjectives. Get them to develop a context for the example, as in the box that follows. Give them one or two of these sample answers to give them the idea. Circulate, monitor and assist if necessary.

> **Sample answers**
>
> I think French clothes are so *attractive* – I really like this year's summer collection in the La Redoute catalogue.
>
> The main thing about Nike trainers is that they are *comfortable* – I can't wear ordinary shoes any more.
>
> The new Mini is very *economical* – it does 100 kilometres on six litres of petrol.
>
> Hybrid cars are very *efficient*. They use far less petrol than normal cars.
>
> Rolex watches are *expensive* – but they're worth the money.
>
> Flared jeans are very *fashionable* at the moment – Levi's new range is very good.
>
> Milk is often advertised as a *healthy* drink option.
>
> If you want an example of a *popular* newspaper, look at *The Sun* in the UK – it sells over three million copies a day and is read by more than five million people.
>
> The furniture at Ikea is *practical* – you take it home and put it together yourself, so you don't have to wait for it to be delivered.
>
> Bottled water companies usually claim that their product is very *pure*.
>
> Japanese cars are famous for being *reliable* – I've had a Toyota for 10 years and it has never broken down.
>
> Organic cleaning products for the home are *safe* to use.

- With the whole class, gather ideas from the different pairs.

B

- Do this as a quick-fire activity with the whole class. Write the words in the table on the board.

- Get students to practise saying them with the correct stress.

un-	in-	im-
unattractive	inefficient	impractical
uncomfortable	inexpensive	impure
uneconomical		
unfashionable		
unhealthy		
unpopular		
unreliable		
unsafe		

- Ask students if they notice the 'rule' about when *im-* is used (before *p*).

C – **D**

- Again, go through the words and check their meanings and pronunciations (especially stress) with your students.

- Get students to work on the exercise in pairs and then go round the class asking for the answers.

> **Exercise C**
>
> **1** high   **2** hard   **3** high   **4** best   **5** long
> **6** well   **7** high

- Get your students in pairs to think of specific companies and products that match the adjectives. Circulate, monitor and assist if necessary. (After the activity in Exercise A, they should have the idea.)

> **Exercise D: Possible answers**
>
> 1 Siemens makes *high-tech* healthcare equipment among many other products.
>
> 2 Gore-Tex produces *hard-wearing* materials for outdoor clothes.
>
> 3 John Lewis sells *high-quality* furniture.
>
> 4 Dell assembles the world's *best-selling* PCs.
>
> 5 Cummins makes *long-lasting* diesel engines.
>
> 6 Gucci shoes are *well-made* and fashionable.
>
> 7 Nike makes *high-performance* athletic clothing.

- With the whole class, ask pairs for their ideas.

E

- Have students do this in pairs. Some descriptions are obvious, for example *fashionable jeans*. However, students may want to make a case for less obvious collocations such as *fashionable bottled water* (perhaps a film star has been seen drinking it), or *a hard-wearing perfume* (maybe the scent doesn't fade quickly), and so on.

> **Possible answers**
>
> Bottled water: popular, pure, best-selling
>
> MP3 player: high-tech, best-selling, fashionable
>
> Soap: expensive, pure, high-quality
>
> Pair of jeans: fashionable, popular, expensive
>
> 4WD car: comfortable, economical, efficient
>
> Perfume: attractive, expensive, best-selling
>
> Fast-food product: popular, unhealthy
>
> Laptop: high-performance, efficient, inexpensive

LESSON NOTES

F

- Do the matching as a quick-fire activity with the whole class.

- Then get students to call out the correct order. Some students may point out that it is possible to have other orders, for example when a product is promoted before it is launched or is modified after it is launched.

> **1** c **2** e **3** g **4** b **5** d **6** a **7** f **8** h
>
> Suggested order: design, test, modify, manufacture, launch, distribute, promote, discontinue

 i-Glossary

Listening: Favourite products

Students listen to four people talk about their best purchases and to an interview with a lifestyle trends expert.

A 🔊 CD2.58–2.61

- Tell students that they will hear four people talking about the best things they have bought.

- Play the recordings once or twice and ask students to note what the speakers say about the things they bought.

- Check answers with the whole class.

> **1** Ford Mustang: it's eye-catching; fast and furious; virtually maintenance-free; comfortable; reliable; gives great performance; has great interior and exterior; is fun to drive
>
> **2** Trampoline: had hours of fun; been good for parties; weather-proof and durable; lasted over 12 years; good form of exercise; strong rigid frame, high-quality springs
>
> **3** Laptop chair: copies shape of your body when stretched out; aluminium and plastic frame; lots of pillows to support body; monitor suspended in front to prevent neck strain; keyboard and mouse designed for user's lap; curved frame provides back support; eye-catching; popular with design-conscious friends
>
> **4** Arab scarf: can be a sarong, scarf, turban, beach towel, bath towel, bag; dries in 15 minutes

B 🔊 CD2.62

- Explain that students are going to listen to an interview with James Wallman, an editor who follows trends and innovations in the retail and technology sectors.

- Ask your students to look at the notes and try to guess the words that might go in the gaps.

- Play the recording while students complete the notes.

- Go through the answers.

> **1** use
>
> **2** problem; need; electric car
>
> **3** functional; helpful; easier; better

C 🔊 CD2.63

- Explain that the text contains three mistakes. Ask students to read the text to themselves, then play the recording while students listen for the mistakes.

- Have students check their answers in pairs, then check the answers with the whole class.

> It's the Tesla Roadster. This is the new **electric** vehicle which goes from 0 to 60 mph in **3.4** seconds. I drove one from **Nice** to Cannes, and it was very exciting. The response from the accelerator is instant.

D 🔊 CD2.64

- Have students read the questions to themselves.

- Play the recording while students note their answers.

- Play the recording again for students to check their answers, then check answers with the whole class.

> **1** The driverless car
>
> **2** Can be boring
>
> **3** In cities
>
> **4** General Motors, Google, Audi
>
> **5** You will be able to either drive the car yourself or let the car drive itself, just like a 747 plane.

E 🔊 CD2.65

- Get students to look at the chart.

- Play the recording while students note their answers.

- Play the recording again for students to check their answers, then check answers with the whole class.

his favourite product	Mac computer
the colour of this product	black
his job	journalist
what he is writing	a novel
uses Skype to talk to friends where?	New York and Australia

LESSON NOTES

F 🔊 CD2.65

- Ask your students to read the extracts and try to guess the words that might go in the gaps.
- Play the recording while students complete the extracts.
- Go through the answers.

> **1** e-mail   **2** Wi-Fi   **3** café   **4** holiday   **5** computer
> **6** Internet   **7** people   **8** connected   **9** fun

➡ Resource bank: Listening (page 200)

Reading: Launching new products

Students read about Casio, the Japanese consumer-electronics company.

A

- Students discuss the questions in small groups.
- Circulate, monitor and assist if necessary.
- Ask a few students to share their group's ideas with the whole class.

B

- Students scan the article to find the information. You could do this as a competition to see who can find each piece of information first.
- Go through the answers quickly with the class.

> **1** The yen's strength, the economy's weakness, the collapse in Japanese mobile phone sales
>
> **2** radio-controlled watch, G-Shock watch, high-speed "burst" digital camera, electronic calculator
>
> **3** Canon and Nikon
>
> **4** 'resist preconceived ideas', 'from zero to one'
>
> **5** Taiwan, China, South Korea

C

- Tell students to read the article again more closely and decide whether the statements are true, false or not mentioned.
- Give students a reasonable amount of time to do this, then go through the answers.

> **1** NM   **2** T   **3** F   **4** NM   **5** T   **6** T   **7** F   **8** F

D

- Students discuss the question in groups of three or four. Circulate, monitor and assist if necessary.
- Writing this up could be set for homework or a mini-project.

➡ Text bank (pages 160–163)

Language review: Passives

Students look at passives in the context of where goods are made and produced.

- Go through the examples and explanations. Remind students that the past participle is the third form that they see in verb tables, for example *make*, *made*, *made*. (The other three verbs in the examples are regular: *use*, *used*, <u>*used*</u>; *dominate*, *dominated*, <u>*dominated*</u>; *test*, *tested*, <u>*tested*</u>.)

A

- Go through the products on the left of the table, explaining meanings and practising pronunciation where necessary.
- Ask your students to work on the exercise in pairs. Circulate, monitor and assist if necessary.
- When the pairs are ready, ask them for their answers. The following answers are not complete. Ask your students about other places where things are produced. Ensure they use the correct verbs.

> **Possible answers**
>
> Diamonds are mined in South Africa.
>
> Microchips are produced/manufactured/made in the United States.
>
> Semiconductors are produced/manufactured/made in Malaysia.
>
> Electronic goods are produced/manufactured/made in Japan.
>
> Coffee is produced/grown in Brazil.
>
> Leather goods are produced/manufactured/made in Spain and Zambia.
>
> Oil is produced/refined in Kuwait.
>
> Rice is produced/grown in China.
>
> Watches are produced/manufactured/made in Switzerland.
>
> Coal is mined in Poland.
>
> Mobile phones are produced/manufactured/made in Finland.

LESSON NOTES

B

- Do this as a quick-fire activity with the whole class.

1   The Channel Tunnel was opened in 1994.

2   The new design has been chosen.

3   This website is seen by thousands of people every day.

4   The staff were asked for their opinions (by the employers).

5   My car is being repaired at the moment.

6   The missing file has been found.

7   This watch was made in Switzerland.

C

- Students work on the exercise in pairs.
- With the whole class, ask pairs for the answers.

1 were launched	11 are melted
2 has been controlled	12 is cooled
3 are performed	13 is tested
4 are reduced	14 are fed
5 have been manufactured	15 are modified
6 is/has been designed	16 is cut
7 are weighed	17 are loaded
8 are blended	18 are distributed
9 (are) fed	19 has been/was promoted
10 is also fed	

Skills: Presenting a product

Students listen to a sales manager presenting a product to buyers and then present a product themselves.

A 🔊 CD2.66

- Play the recording once or twice and get students to say which words they hear.

stylish, well-designed, elegant, popular, sturdy, reliable, versatile

- Practise the stress and intonation of these words with your students.

B 🔊 CD2.66

- Play the recording again, this time getting students to concentrate on the missing words and phrases.

1 features   2 well-designed   3 stainless steel
4 reliable   5 selling points   6 economical
7 benefits   8 versatile
9 expensive; retail price   10 guarantee

- With the whole class, ask for the answers. Work on any remaining difficulties.

C

- Tell your students that they will be presenting a product themselves. Go through the language in the Useful language box, explaining any difficulties and working on stress and intonation.

- Get your students to work in groups of three or four. Get each group to select one of the products and prepare a presentation about it. (Tell your students to invent any missing information.)

- Circulate, monitor and assist if necessary. Note down language points for praise and correction afterwards, especially language used for product presentations.

- When the groups are ready, bring the class to order. Praise strong language points and work on half a dozen points that need improving.

- Then get your students to form new groups, ideally with members who worked on different products. Each student should give a product presentation to the new group they are in. If possible they should stand up and pretend to show the actual product or even draw it on a sheet of cardboard which they stick to the wall. Again, note down language points for praise and correction afterwards.

- Bring the class to order and again praise strong language points and work on half a dozen points that need improving, getting students to say the correct forms.

➡ Resource bank: Speaking (page 188)

CASE STUDY

The George Marshall Awards

Students present ideas for new products to the selection committee for an award that recognises innovative goods. The selection committee decides which is the best.

Stage 1: Background 🔊 CD2.67

- Get your students to read the background. Meanwhile, write the headings on the left of the table on the board. When the students have finished reading, elicit information to complete the table.

Organisation	George Marshall Foundation
Based in	Melbourne, Australia
Event	George Marshall Awards: Recognise innovation and creativity in developing, marketing and launching new products
Benefit for winners	An award badge for their products, which appeals to consumers and boosts sales

- Explain to students that they're going to hear a conversation between two members of the selection committee. Have students note down the key points of the conversation. Check answers with the class.

Key points

Looking for products that show originality and creativity

Winning product must improve customers' lifestyle

Winning product must not harm the environment

Winning companies have to explain their marketing plans

Winning product must be profitable

Winning product must make interesting or exciting use of technology

Stage 2: New products

- Get students to work in pairs and look at the products being entered for the award. Allocate each pair to a particular product.

- Bring the class to order and ask one of the pairs to talk about each product: *Company B is offering a Password Memory File. It generates passwords and keeps them safe. You can view your passwords on the LCD screen. It costs 70 US dollars.*

Stage 3: Task

- Get your students to work in groups of three or four. Ask each group to select one of the products and prepare a presentation about it. One group member will present to the committee. The presenter can draw and label the product on a sheet of cardboard.

- Circulate, monitor and assist if necessary. Note down language points for praise and correction afterwards.

- When the groups are ready, bring the class to order. Praise strong language points and work on half a dozen points that need improving, getting students to say the correct forms.

- Then ask the product presenters from the old groups to stand to one side for the moment. Get the remaining students in the class to form new groups of three or four. Explain that these groups are Selection Committee members.

- Each Selection Committee group will get a presentation about each of the five innovative products in turn. Tell the presenters that they should present the product in such a convincing way that the committee will choose the product for its top award. The committee should ask questions about the products after each presentation.

- Presenting students go round the class to different groups of committee members. Each presentation should last 10 minutes, including questions. When each presentation is over, bring the class to order and send the presenters round to a new group of committee members.

- During the presentations note down language points for praise and correction afterwards.

- Bring the class to order, praise strong language points and work on half a dozen points that need improving, getting students to say the correct forms.

- Then ask each Selection Committee group to discuss the products they have seen and then say which product most impressed them, and why.

One-to-one

This case study can be done as a discussion between teacher and student and then as a basis for a presentation by the student.

⊙ You can also refer to the *Case study commentary* section of the DVD-ROM.

Stage 4: Writing

- Make sure your students understand what they have to do: as a member of the Selection Committee, write a short report on one of the products you saw presented. This can be done as homework.

⇨ Writing file, page 129

⇨ Resource bank: Writing (page 215)

Preparing to do business internationally

This unit features a questionnaire that highlights cultural differences.

A

- Get students to discuss the questions in groups of three or four. Circulate, monitor and assist if necessary.

- Share answers and discuss as a class.

B

- Explain that students are going to complete a questionnaire about their own culture.

- Have students work alone. Circulate, monitor and assist if necessary.

- Students then work in pairs to compare their answers.

- If you have a mix of cultures represented in your class, invite students to share their answers with the class and note any interesting differences.

C

- Students work in pairs to discuss the questions.

- Share answers and discuss as a class.

D

- Give students time to read the seven statements and do the matching exercise.

- Have them check answers first in pairs. Then check the answers with the whole class.

> **1** g **2** d **3** a **4** e **5** b **6** f **7** c

E

- Ask students to discuss the two questions in pairs or small groups.

- Share answers and discuss as a class.

F

- Do this as a quick brainstorming activity with the whole class. Note answers on the board.

> **Possible answers**
>
> Hairstyles, written language, the way people drive, the style of buildings, the way people greet each other, personal space, body language, different roles of men and women

G 🔊 CD 2.68

- Play the recording. Compare the list of ideas your students generated with the ideas mentioned in the recording.

> The recording mentions: weather, food, written language, the way people drive, the style of buildings, the way people greet each other, personal space, body language, different roles of men and women

H 🔊 CD 2.69

- Ask students to look at the five topics and try to guess what the speaker might say about them.

- Play the recording. Students listen and note what the speaker says about each topic.

> **1** a) How important the individual, the family, the team or groups is
>
>   b) May be more important than getting instant results
>
>   c) May take longer to make decisions, depending on attitude to risk-taking
>
>   d) Affects attitudes to deadlines and also whether thinking is long- or short-term
>
>   e) Status can be linked to age and connections, not just talent/ability.
>
> **2** Be aware of your own culture, be sensitive, try and notice things, be flexible

Task

- Students work in pairs or small groups. In monolingual classes, encourage students to imagine visitors from different countries to ensure variety.

- While students prepare their short presentations, circulate, monitor and assist if necessary.

- When the students are ready, have them give their presentations in their pairs or small groups while the other students ask questions. Circulate, monitor and assist if necessary. Note language points for praise and correction afterwards.

- After all students have presented, get students to write their list of dos and don'ts for their partner's country. Circulate and monitor.

- Get students to share their lists with the whole class.

This unit revises and reinforces some of the key language points from Units 10–12 and from Working across cultures 4. (Course Book page numbers are given below).

10 Managing people

Vocabulary (page 97)

1 to **2** with **3** about **4** to **5** in **6** in **7** with **8** about **9** with **10** for

Reported speech (page 100)

1 she wants **2** were **3** was **4** had been **5** had been **6** we needed

Skills (pages 100–101)

1 d **2** b **3** g **4** f **5** a **6** h **7** e **8** c

11 Conflict

Vocabulary (page 105)

1 nervous **2** calm **3** not credible **4** patience **5** sympathetic **6** formal **7** weakness **8** consistent

Conditionals (page 108)

1 offer **2** 'd start **3** deliver **4** 'd give **5** spoke **6** 'll start **7** ordered **8** 'll place

Skills (page 109)

1 I believe **2** Why don't **3** I've got **4** I know **5** I've always met **6** let's look **7** I'd like **8** Let's have

12 Products

Vocabulary (page 113)

1 fashionable **2** unreliable **3** hard-wearing **4** uncomfortable **5** high-performance **6** economical **7** high-tech **8** best-selling **9** unsafe **10** long-lasting

Passives (page 116)

1 was made **2** was opened **3** were marketed **4** were bought **5** was launched **6** were worn **7** was moved **8** are loved

Writing

- In this final writing task, students can choose any product they use and like.

Sample answer

Dear Mr Singh,

I think the iPhone case that I use could be successful in our shop. It's made of leather. It weighs only a few grams, and its dimensions are just a bit bigger than the phone – about 60 mm x 10 mm x 115 mm. It comes in red, blue, black and yellow.

It's designed to look smart and also to protect the phone, even if it's dropped. The case clips around the phone firmly, but it's also easy to release if necessary. I paid less than £10 for mine, so it's great value for money.

If you have any questions, let me know.

All the best,

Cultures 4: Preparing to do business internationally

Exercise A

1 f **2** g **3** a **4** h **5** b **6** d **7** e **8** c

Exercise B

1 Meals out

2 emotion

3 Socialising

4 personal space

5 Body language

6 relationships

7 Risk-taking

Text bank

TEACHER'S NOTES

Introduction

The Text bank contains articles relating to the units in the Course Book. These articles extend and develop the themes in those units. You can choose the articles that are of most interest to your students. They can be done in class or as homework. You have permission to make photocopies of these articles for your students.

Before you read

Before each article, there is an exercise to use as a warmer that helps students to focus on the vocabulary of the article and prepares them for it. This can be done in pairs or small groups, with each group then reporting its answers to the whole class.

Reading

If using the articles in class, it is a good idea to treat different sections in different ways, for example reading the first paragraph with the whole class, and then getting students to work in pairs on the following paragraphs. If you're short of time, get different pairs to read different sections of the article simultaneously. You can circulate, monitor and give help where necessary. Students then report back to the whole group with a succinct summary and/or their answers to the questions for that section. A full answer key follows the articles.

Discussion

In the *Over to you* sections following each article, there are discussion points. These can be dealt with by the whole class, or the class can be divided, with different groups discussing different points. During discussion, circulate, monitor and give help where necessary. Students then report back to the whole class. Praise good language production and work on areas for improvement in the usual way.

Writing

The discussion points can also form the basis for short pieces of written work. Students will find this easier if they have already discussed the points in class, but you can ask students to read the article and write about the discussion points as homework.

OVERSEAS EXPERIENCE

Before you read

Is it part of your career plan to work abroad one day? If you have worked abroad, was it good for your career? Why? / Why not?

Reading

Read this article from the *Financial Times* by Rhymer Rigby and answer the questions.

FT

LEVEL OF DIFFICULTY ● ● ○

Working abroad

By Rhymer Rigby

A period overseas is seen by many as an important addition to your CV. But how do you make sure that it really works to your advantage?

1 _____

"Think carefully about the job," says executive coach, Nicola Bunting. "Does it fit in with your career goals or are you being attracted by the lifestyle? Also before you go, you need to have a re-entry plan." Kevan Hall, chief executive of the international people management group, Global Integration, says you shouldn't underestimate the culture shock. "Go out there beforehand. See what you're getting into."

2 _____

Nigel Parslow, UK managing director of Harvey Nash executive search, says staying where you are may not be possible if you work for an organisation that has overseas operations. He adds that the experience you gain is also very attractive.

3 _____

The biggest is family. This can be particularly hard for people in the middle of their careers who may have children at school. Ms Bunting says: "There's your partner's career too. Some people's spouses try and commute back and I'd really advise against this as it makes an already stressful situation even more difficult."

4 _____

Mr Hall says: "There's been a power shift to Asia, and that, coupled with low growth in America and Europe, means that particularly if you're ambitious you might want to spend some time there."

5 _____

Many people say two to three years. But this will vary according to the country and organisation. Mr Parslow thinks that if you spend too long abroad, you can end up with a not entirely positive expat* label attached to you.

* An expat is someone who lives and works abroad, often for a long period.

1 **Find the correct place in the article for each of these questions.**

a) Is there an ideal length of time?

b) What about the destination?

c) What are the advantages and disadvantages?

d) What are the personal considerations?

e) What should I consider before I go?

2 **Look through the whole article and match each person 1–3 with their organisation a)–c), and their opinions/advice i)–viii). (Each person has more than one opinion/ piece of advice.)**

1	Nicola Bunting	a) Global Integration	i) Don't stay abroad too long.
2	Kevan Hall	b) Harvey Nash	ii) Make sure the overseas job suits your career goals.
3	Nigel Parslow	c) not mentioned	iii) Think about your partner's career.
			iv) Don't underestimate the culture shock.
			v) You may have no choice about going abroad or not.
			vi) Think about what you will do when you get back.
			vii) Go to work in Asia.
			viii) Go to the place beforehand to check it out.

3 **Read paragraph 2 and decide if these statements about expressions are true or false.**

If you …

a) consider if a job *fits in with your career goals* (lines 8–9), you think about the long-term consequences of taking the job.

b) go to work abroad and have *a re-entry plan* (line 12), you have an idea about what you are going to do when you get back.

c) *underestimate* something (line 16), you give it more importance that it really has.

d) suffer from *culture shock* (line 17), you find it easy to get used to another culture.

e) *get into* a situation (line 19), you get involved in it.

4 **When you work overseas, …** *the experience you gain is … very attractive.* **(lines 26–27) Attractive to whom?**

5 **Find the answers to these questions in paragraphs 4, 5 and 6. Start your answers with *Because* …**

When considering a job abroad …

a) why is it especially hard for people in the middle of their careers?

b) why should married people consider the issues carefully?

c) why is it a bad idea for the husband or wife to commute back to the home country?

d) why is Asia a good place to go and work for a while?

e) why is it a good idea not to stay there too long?

Over to you 1

Imagine that a colleague of yours is going to work or study abroad for two years. What advice would you give them?

Over to you 2

Some say that the business world is becoming more or less the same everywhere, and that people should have less and less trouble adjusting to work in a new country. Do you agree or disagree? Give your reasons.

PERFORMANCE REVIEWS

Before you read

In a performance review or performance appraisal, your boss tells you
how well you are doing your job, and things that you must improve.
Are these reviews useful? Why? / Why not?

If you're a student, what forms of appraisal are there for your work?

Reading

Read this article from the *Financial Times* by Lucy Kellaway and
answer the questions.

LEVEL OF DIFFICULTY ● ● ○

TEXT BANK

It's time to sack job appraisals

By Lucy Kellaway

Last week an e-mail went round the office asking for suggestions on ways to improve our performance appraisal system. 5 My suggestion is dead easy and dirt cheap: get rid of the whole thing and replace it with nothing at all.

Over the past 30 years, I 10 have been appraised 30 times – as banker, journalist and non-executive director. I've lived through the fashion for long, complicated forms. I've also 15 survived the fashion in which appraisals are called "career chats". I've done appraisals across a table, on a sofa, even over a meal.

20 But I have never learnt anything about myself as a result. I have never set any target that I later hit. Instead I always feel as if I am playing a particularly bad 25 party game that isn't fun and that doesn't answer the most basic question: am I doing a good job? The resulting form is then put on file even though you know from 30 experience how much attention will be paid to it later: none at all.

At least I've only had to suffer one side of the process. I have never – thank goodness – 35 had to appraise anyone else. This must be even worse, as you have to perform the same operation with each employee in turn. You have to let people believe they are 40 doing more or less okay, because it's too tiring to tell them that they aren't doing okay at all.

1 **Read through the whole article. Is the writer for or against job appraisals?**

2 **Complete the table with words from paragraphs 1, 2 and 3.**

verb	noun
suggest	....
....	improvement
appraise	....
....	replacement
....	survival
target	....
....	answer
file	....
experience	....

3 **Now match the nouns in Exercise 2 to their definitions.**

a) what you give when someone asks a question

b) when something gets better

c) something that takes the place of another

d) the act of giving an opinion about someone or something

e) something that you aim at or for

f) advice about what to do

g) sheets of paper with information, kept together

h) knowledge of what has happened in the past

i) continuing to exist, despite difficult conditions

4 **Choose the correct alternative to complete these statements about the expressions in italic from paragraphs 2 and 3.**

a) If something is *dead easy* (line 5), it is ...
   i) not so easy.
   ii) very easy.
   iii) quite easy.

b) If something is *dirt cheap* (line 6), it is ...
   i) very cheap.
   ii) quite cheap.
   iii) not at all cheap.

c) If you *get rid of* something (line 6), you ...
   i) keep it.
   ii) throw it away.
   iii) prevent it.

d) If you *live through* something (lines 12–13), you ...
   i) experience it.
   ii) ignore it.
   iii) realise it.

e) If something is *complicated* (line 14), it is ...
   i) easy.
   ii) nice.
   iii) difficult.

f) A *chat* (line 17) is a type of ...
   i) speech.
   ii) interview.
   iii) conversation.

5 **Match the verbs from paragraph 3 with the things that they go with.**

1	learn	a)	a party game
2	set	b)	something on file
3	play	c)	a basic question
4	answer	d)	a target
5	put	e)	attention to something
6	pay	f)	something about yourself

6 **Read paragraphs 3 and 4 and decide if these statements are true or false.**

The writer of the article ...

a) found out things about herself thanks to job appraisals.

b) set targets for herself, but didn't hit them.

c) compares job appraisals with party games.

d) has found out if she has done a good job during job appraisals.

e) has done job appraisals of people working for her.

f) thinks that it's easy to tell people that they are not performing well.

Over to you 1

After reading the article, do you think that performance appraisals are a) less useful, or b) more useful than you did before you read it? Give your reasons.

Over to you 2

Give suggestions on how to tell an employee in a performance appraisal that their work is not good enough.

TEXT BANK

LOOKING AFTER EMPLOYEES

Before you read

What's the best way to keep a company's employees happy and motivated?

Reading

Read this article from the *Financial Times* by Stefan Stern and answer the questions.

FT

LEVEL OF DIFFICULTY ● ● ○

The real value of managing information and people

By Stefan Stern

SAS has been a pioneer in the business of "analytics". This involves not just gathering information, but also processing it and getting the value from it. Its chief executive, Jim Goodnight, says: "When the economic downturn started I told everyone there would be no job losses, that we might have lower profits but that was fine with me," he says. "I didn't care because I prefer keeping everybody's jobs. I think everybody actually worked harder to save money, to cut expenses, to try to bring in more revenue, and we actually ended up growing last year by 2.2 per cent. I always say if you treat people like they make a difference they will make a difference."

SAS has just been named by Fortune magazine as the best company to work for in the US. The on-site perks and benefits at SAS headquarters are remarkable. Medical care, childcare, sports centres, massage, food, hairdressers and a 35-hour week: these all form part of the employee package.

There is a downside. SAS does not pay the highest wages in its sector. But it is a successful business with low staff turnover. Most employees seem happy with the deal, which is designed to make working life easier. It is these software programmers who in turn keep SAS's clients happy.

TEXT BANK

1 **Look through the whole article. Which organisation is it about?**

2 **Complete these statements with words from paragraph 1, as they are used in the article.**

   a) A .... is a person or organisation that does something that has not been done before. (7 letters)

   b) If you collect information, you .... it. (6 letters)

   c) If you .... information, you try to make it easier to use, understand, etc. (7 letters)

   d) An economic .... is a time when business activity goes down. (8 letters)

   e) You say that something .... happened when you want to talk about what really happened, not what might have happened. (8 letters)

   f) .... is another word for 'costs'. (8 letters)

   g) .... is money from sales. (7 letters)

   h) If you .... people in a particular way, you manage them in that way. (5 letters)

3 **Read paragraph 1 and choose the best summary.**

   SAS got through the economic downturn ...

   a) but profits increased and some employees lost their jobs.

   b) but it made a loss; however, everyone kept their jobs.

   c) and the company even grew during that time.

4 **Now answer these questions about paragraph 1.**

   a) What does SAS do?

   b) During the downturn, why didn't Jim Goodnight worry about having lower profits?

   c) How did his employees manage to get the company to grow?

   d) What is his 'philosophy' in relation to employees?

5 **Read paragraph 2. Imagine that SAS employees make the comments below. Which perk or benefit is each employee referring to?**

   a) 'I like being able to leave work at 5.30!'

   b) 'If I get ill, I can always go and see the company doctor.'

   c) 'I can leave my kids in the crèche and pick them up when I leave work.'

   d) 'It's great to be able to play tennis at lunchtimes.'

   e) 'I can always get my hair cut without going into town.'

   f) 'The hamburgers are delicious.'

6 **Choose the alternative with the closest meaning to the expression in italic.**

   a) There is a *downside*. (line 32)
       i) disadvantage
       ii) disagreement
       iii) disappointment

   b) SAS does not pay the highest *wages* ... (line 33)
       i) earning
       ii) salaries
       iii) payments

   c) ... in its *sector*. (line 34)
       i) segment
       ii) industry
       iii) area

   d) But it is a successful business with *low staff turnover*. (line 35)
       i) few employees who leave
       ii) low sales per employee
       iii) few employees who sell

   e) Most employees seem happy with the *deal*, ... (line 37)
       i) location and salary
       ii) healthcare and sports centres
       iii) pay and benefits

Over to you 1

Think about your own organisation or one you would like to work for. What perks and benefits would you most like to have?

Over to you 2

SAS is based on a 'campus' outside Raleigh, Virginia. (A campus is a kind of park, often on the edge of a city, where a company has its offices.) Would you prefer to work on a campus like this, or in a city centre office? Give your reasons.

ITALIAN COMPANIES

Before you read

What products do you think of when you think of Italian companies?

Reading

Read this article from the *Financial Times* by Rachel Sanderson and answer the questions.

FT

LEVEL OF DIFFICULTY ● ● ●

Value of being 'Made in Italy'

By Rachel Sanderson

In Palazzo Strozzi, a Renaissance palace overlooking Florence's Arno River, Ferruccio Ferragamo, owner of luxury shoe brand
5 Salvatore Ferragamo, is explaining why his shoes are "Made in Italy". Mr Ferragamo's father, Salvatore, put handmade shoes on the feet of Marilyn
10 Monroe and Sophia Loren, Lauren Bacall and Judy Garland. But many people might think that his son is living in different times, with rising Chinese and Indian
15 manufacturing companies putting Italian companies out of business.

A decade ago, many economists, in Italy and outside, were convinced that the small
20 and medium-sized businesses that make up a large part of the country's economy were in decline. The Italians could not compete with rival manufacturing
25 countries in Asia. Their productivity was too low and too costly. But the country's exports are estimated to have grown 12.5 per cent this year, with forecasts
30 of 8 per cent for next year's growth.

The surge has been caused by the attraction of "Made in Italy" goods to the middle classes of
35 rapidly growing economies, including Brazil and China. And whether it is sending furniture to Russia, textiles to Egypt, rubber and plastic products to Turkey
40 or winemaking equipment to Chile, emerging markets are proving increasingly important for Italy's entrepreneurs.

The place where a product is
45 made is very important for Chinese consumers. By some estimates, China is now the world's biggest luxury market. This has allowed the industry to
50 raise prices by 10 per cent in the past 12 months. As Mr Ferragamo says, "We cannot make enough to keep up with the demand from the Chinese. They want their shoes
55 not just made in Italy, but often made in Florence."

1 **Look through the first paragraph to find the names of:**

a) a luxury Italian shoe company.

b) its current owner.

c) the name of his father.

d) the names of four actresses who have worn its shoes.

2 **Choose the alternative with the closest meaning to the expression in italic.**

a) *A decade* (line 17) ago, ...
   i) five years
   ii) ten years
   iii) twenty years

b) ... many economists, in Italy and outside, were *convinced* (line 19) that the small and medium-sized businesses ...
   i) unsure
   ii) secure
   iii) sure

c) ... that make up a large part of the country's economy were *in decline*. (lines 22–23)
   i) getting smaller and less important
   ii) getting bigger
   iii) staying the same

d) The Italians could not compete with *rival* (line 24) manufacturing countries in Asia.
   i) similar
   ii) competing
   iii) helpful

e) Their *productivity* (line 26) was too low and too costly.
   i) sales
   ii) profits
   iii) output per person

f) But the country's exports are *estimated* (line 28) to have grown 12.5 per cent this year, ...
   i) known
   ii) calculated
   iii) guessed

g) ... with *forecasts* (line 29) of 8 per cent for next year's growth.
   i) predictions
   ii) promises
   iii) plans

3 **Read paragraphs 3 and 4 and decide if these statements about expressions are true or false.**

a) A *surge* (line 32) is an increase.

b) If something has an *attraction* (line 33), people like it.

c) *Emerging markets* (line 41) have existed as markets for a long time.

d) *Entrepreneurs* (line 43) are people who start new businesses and have new ideas for existing businesses.

e) *Demand* (line 53) for something is the amount of it that is available to buy.

4 **List all the products mentioned in paragraph 3.**

5 **Choose the best summary of the whole article.**

Italian manufacturing companies ...

a) have been successful because they have higher productivity than Chinese or Indian companies.

b) were expected to do badly, but have been successful because of demand from emerging markets.

c) do well because customers in emerging markets want their shoes made in Florence.

Over to you 1

Why is the place where luxury goods are made so important?

Over to you 2

Describe areas in your country that specialise in making particular goods. How are they doing now in relation to the past?

BUSINESS-TO-BUSINESS SELLING

Before you read

When businesses sell services to other organisations, what skills do the salespeople need?

Reading

Read this article from the *Financial Times* by Stefan Stern and answer the questions.

FT

LEVEL OF DIFFICULTY ● ● ●

The days of amateur selling are over

By Stefan Stern

Don't you just love it when you come through the arrivals gate at the airport and you see a driver there waiting for you, holding up a board with your name on it? How much is that service worth to you? If it is a business trip and your company is paying, do you know what price you will be charged?

I didn't think so. The individual customer doesn't have this sort of information. The travel department in your company can handle it. But what if the travel agency that they are buying from doesn't know the price either? Good news for your company's purchasing department: they can get a better all-in deal. But the travel agency, through its amateur approach to buying and selling, is throwing away a large amount of money.

That is the story of a real travel business as told to me by Michael Moorman, head of ZS Associates, a Chicago-based sales and marketing consultancy. Mr Moorman is critical of some of the old-fashioned, amateur selling techniques that go on in many businesses, that are unsuited to today's commercial environment.

A new report from the UK's Cranfield School of Management has also described some of the problems. "The average sales person is a pleasant individual who knows a lot about their products," the report says, "but is not able to show how their products are different from the competition, or to solve the customer's problems."

This game has changed. "Today sales people have to go in and negotiate with professional negotiators," Mr Moorman says. "You have to be able to speak the language of finance." It is not good enough to be a "born salesman" any more. It is the smart salesmen and women who will keep their businesses afloat in the months ahead.

1 **Look through the whole article. It's about the way that companies buy products and services. Which type of product or service is mentioned in particular?**

a) cars   b) travel   c) computers

2 **Give your own personal answers to the three questions in paragraph 1. For the third question, think of a particular place that you have visited and give details of prices, if you can.**

3 **Read paragraph 2 and answer the questions.**

a) What two expressions are used to refer to the department that buys travel services in a company?

b) What expression is used to refer to the organisation selling these services?

c) What is the organisation in question b) above doing wrong? Why?

4 **Complete the table with words from paragraphs 4 and 5, in the form they are used in the article.**

verb	noun
report	....
manage	....
compete	....
....	solution
negotiate	negotiation, ... (people)

5 **In what order do these items of information appear in paragraphs 4 and 5?**

Sales people ...

a) have to know about finance.

b) are usually nice people.

c) have to be intelligent.

d) should be able to say why their products are different from the competition.

e) are often highly informed about their products.

f) should be able to provide answers to the customer's problems.

g) have to be able to negotiate skilfully.

6 *It is the smart salesmen and women who will keep their businesses afloat in the months ahead* (lines 53–56). The writer is comparing these businesses to:

a) planes   b) trucks   c) ships

Over to you 1

The average sales person is a pleasant individual who knows a lot about their products. Is this your experience when buying things as a consumer?

Over to you 2

Who is responsible for buying products and services in your department or school? Who are the main suppliers? What could be done to negotiate lower prices with them?

CLOSING THE SALE

Before you read

What is the most difficult thing about selling?

Reading

Read this article from the *Financial Times* by Mike Southon and answer the questions.

FT

LEVEL OF DIFFICULTY ● ● ●

TEXT BANK

What to do at closing time

By Mike Southon

The most difficult sales task is asking for money, or, to use the technical term, "closing". Even experienced sales people will do [5] anything to avoid this unpleasant part of the job. So, for a business owner, an important part of sales management is to encourage, or even threaten, sales people to get [10] them to ask for orders.

Part one of the sales cycle is the qualification process: the sales person should listen carefully to the customer's needs and find [15] a solution that can be delivered quickly. The larger the order, the more likely it is that the buyer may have to get authorisation from someone higher in the [20] organisation, perhaps even the purchasing director. This is probably someone who is only interested in big discounts. It is a good idea to ask a possible buyer [25] how much they are allowed to spend. Then you can offer them products or services that they can afford.

It's useful to practise a good [30] closing technique in advance of the key moment. This will include a positive summary of the sales process, explaining the benefits for the customer that the proposed [35] solutions will bring.

Then there is the most difficult part of the script, a final question in the style of, "So, do we have a deal?" This should be [40] followed by silence, which may feel uncomfortable, but if the sales person breaks that silence, the deal could easily disappear. Ideally, the customer will break [45] the silence and say yes, a positive outcome for all concerned. But even if the customer says no, it is reasonable to ask why and perhaps work out how to change [50] their mind.

1 Put the paragraph headings in the correct order.

a) Checking you have got the sale

b) Finding out about customers

c) Getting orders is hard

d) Practise what to say at the end, to get the sale

2 Match the expressions (1–6) from paragraphs 1 and 2 with their definitions (a–f).

1	business owner	a)	deciding how likely it is that someone will buy something
2	sales management	b)	the different points in the process of selling something
3	sales people	c)	members of the sales force
4	sales cycle	d)	someone whose job is to buy goods and services for an organisation
5	qualification process	e)	someone who owns a company
6	purchasing director	f)	the way that sales are organised and controlled

3 Complete the answers to the questions, using appropriate forms of expressions from paragraphs 1 and 2.

a) Is the point where you ask someone to buy something called 'ending'?

– No, it's called '........................'.

b) Is it always a nice experience?

– No, it can be ....

c) Is it enough just to encourage sales people to get orders?

– No, sometimes it's necessary to .... them.

d) Does the writer talk about delivering products and services?

– No, he talks about a '........................'.

e) Is the buyer always able to place the order?

– No, sometimes they have to get ....

f) Are purchasing directors usually interested in the personal qualities of sales people?

– No, they are only interested in ....

4 Complete these statements with appropriate forms of words from paragraphs 3 and 4.

a) A way of doing something is a t........................ (9 letters)

b) A short speech, description, etc. giving the key points of something is a s........................ . (7 letters)

c) The advantages of a product or service for the customer are its b........................ (8 letters)

d) Something that is suggested is p........................ (8 letters)

e) A d........................ is an agreement to buy something. (4 letters)

f) If something no longer exists, it has d........................ (11 letters)

g) The result of a process is its o........................ (7 letters)

h) If something is acceptable, it is r........................ (10 letters)

5 Which one of these statements about the whole article is true?

a) Sales people always have to be threatened before they go out and close a sale.

b) Qualification and using the final closing script are two key stages in the sales process.

c) Sales to companies always have to be authorised by the purchasing manager.

Over to you 1

Describe the sales process in your organisation, or one that you would like to work for.

Over to you 2

Some say that good sales people are born and that it's impossible to train others to become good sales people. What do you think? Give your reasons.

PARTNERSHIPS IN INNOVATION

Before you read

Where do companies usually get their ideas from?

Reading

Read this article from the *Financial Times* by Jonathan Birchall and answer the questions.

FT

LEVEL OF DIFFICULTY ● ● ○

Innovation brings growth

By Jonathan Birchall

Procter & Gamble, the world's largest consumer goods company, is a global industry leader in new consumer product innovation.
5 According to data from IRI, the market research firm, it produced five of the top 10 US non-food product launches last year. Its goal is to add another
10 1bn customers to the estimated 4bn it already reaches. Bob McDonald, its chief executive, says that the road to more innovation should increasingly
15 include other people's good ideas. "We need bigger innovations that create more value," Mr McDonald told this year's annual awards event for companies and
20 research centres that work with P&G. "We want you to come to us with your big ideas first."

External co-operation has delivered a stream of successful
25 "big idea" products. Last year, IRI's list included Tide Total Care, a premium version of its Tide detergent. This product was number two by sales on
30 IRI's top 10 list of non-food products. It was developed with external research from Sweden's University of Lund and from two small chemical companies.

35 P&G's list of partners includes other large corporations, such as food groups ConAgra and General Mills, and rivals, including Clorox. P&G is developing a joint
40 venture with Clorox to produce Glad brand plastic bags. Its most unexpected government research partner may be the Los Alamos National Lab, the US defence
45 technology research centre. Los Alamos initially helped P&G to produce one of the chemicals used in babies' nappies, using data analysis systems developed
50 for weapons technology.

One of the programme's early success stories was its Olay Regenerist anti-ageing creams, which was built around a chemical
55 process developed by Sederma, a French company. "As a small company, we had little chance of getting in there until P&G changed its policy," says Karl Lintner,
60 who headed Sederma at the time.

1 Look through the whole article to find the names of:

a) a consumer goods company.

b) its CEO.

c) a market research organisation.

d) a Scandinavian university.

e) two big food companies.

f) a competitor of the company in item a) above.

g) a military research laboratory.

h) a French company.

2 Now look through the whole article again to find the products developed in partnership with the organisations in items d), f), g) and h) in Exercise 1 above.

3 Find expressions in paragraph 1 with the number of words shown in brackets that mean the following.

a) the biggest organisation anywhere in the world that makes products for the general public (6)

b) the biggest and best company of its kind anywhere in the world (3)

c) developing new products for the general public (3)

d) an occasion every year where prizes are given (3)

4 Read paragraphs 3 and 4 and decide if these statements about expressions are true or false.

a) *External co-operation* (line 23) is when a company develops a new product by itself.

b) The word *stream* (line 24) is used here to refer to water.

c) A *premium version* (line 27) of a product is less good and costs less than the ordinary version.

d) The word *chemical* is used in line 34 as an adjective and in line 47 as a noun.

e) A *corporation* (line 36) is usually a small business.

f) A *joint venture* (lines 39–40) is when two companies work together on a particular project.

g) The word *data* (line 49) refers to information, especially information analysed on computers.

5 Choose the best summary for the whole article.

Procter and Gamble ...

a) has always welcomed co-operation with other companies to develop new products.

b) only works with American companies to develop new products.

c) has realised the importance of working with other organisations, not only companies, on new products.

Over to you 1
What are the risks of working on new products with competitors in joint ventures?

Over to you 2
Is there co-operation in your country between businesses and universities to develop new products and services? If there is, give some examples. If not, try to explain why.

ACCEPTING NEW IDEAS

Before you read

The expression 'Not invented here' is used by someone to say that an idea or new product did not start in their department or company. Why is it difficult for organisations to accept ideas that are 'Not invented here'?

Reading

Read this article from the *Financial Times* by Stefan Stern and answer the questions.

FT

LEVEL OF DIFFICULTY ● ● ●

TEXT BANK

Open your mind to the idea of innovation

By Stefan Stern

The three most dangerous words in management? "Not invented here". As Henry Chesbrough, executive director of the Center for Open Innovation at the University of California, Berkeley, has pointed out, senior management teams can fail to spot important innovations because the new ways of doing business do not easily fit in with the way they are doing things now.

Researching the performance of Xerox, the copier and printer company, Prof Chesbrough found that, out of 35 projects that had been rejected as part of a review process, 10 had gone on to become highly successful businesses. Indeed, the combined value of these 10 new projects was twice that of Xerox itself. He calls these rejections "false negatives": the innovations had looked bad, but that was because senior managers did not recognise their benefits.

Prof Chesbrough was one of the speakers at last week's Financial Times innovation conference in London. The conference also heard from Brian Dunn, chief executive of Best Buy, the electrical goods retailer. He told a story of how his company had in the past 20 years brought in new ways of doing things again and again.

Whether it was ending commissions for sales staff, starting to sell on the Internet, or renewing the company's approach to customers, or expanding abroad: each time, Best Buy's leadership did not make the decisions easily. Each time, there were smart people at the top who resisted change, he said. Necessary innovations are hard to introduce when, as in Best Buy's case, the business seems to be doing fine.

1 Put the paragraph headings in the correct order.

a) Best Buy's difficult innovation decisions

b) Company managers can fail to see new ideas

c) The innovation process at Xerox

d) Regular innovations at Best Buy

2 Read paragraphs 1 and 2 and decide if these statements about expressions and related expressions are true or false.

a) An *innovation* (line 9) is a new idea, product, etc. *Innovation* (line 5) is new ideas, products, etc. in general.

b) If you *point* something *out* (line 7), you don't talk about it.

c) If you *spot* something (line 9), you don't see it.

d) If something *fits in* (line 11) with something else, it's acceptable.

e) If something is *rejected* (line 18), it is accepted.

f) In a *review process* (lines 18–19) things, ideas, etc. are judged.

3 Find expressions in paragraphs 3 and 4 with the number of letters shown in brackets that mean the following.

a) boss (5, 9)

b) introduced (7, 2)

c) repeatedly (5, 3, 5)

d) payments in addition to salary (11)

e) senior managers considered as a group (10)

f) fought (8)

g) needed (9)

4 Read paragraphs 2, 3 and 4 and choose the correct answer.

a) How many of the new business projects rejected in Xerox's review process went on to become successful businesses?
   i) most of them
   ii) more than half of them
   iii) nearly a third of them

b) How much were the businesses worth in relation to the value of Xerox?
   i) twice as much
   ii) the same
   iii) half as much

c) Why had Xerox managers rejected the new business ideas?
   i) Because the ideas were not explained properly.
   ii) Because the managers couldn't see their value.
   iii) Because the managers didn't understand the ideas.

d) What does Best Buy do?
   i) It's a wholesaler of electrical goods.
   ii) It's a retailer of electrical goods.
   iii) It makes electrical goods.

e) Why is Best Buy mentioned?
   i) Because it is similar to Xerox in its approach to innovation.
   ii) Because it did not innovate at all.
   iii) Because it does accept new ideas, but only after a lot of disagreement and discussion.

f) Why was it particularly difficult to introduce new ways of doing things at Best Buy?
   i) Because it was already a successful company.
   ii) Because most of its senior managers resisted them.
   iii) Because it did not need them.

5 Choose the best summary for the whole article.

Companies ...

a) do not find it easy to accept new ideas.

b) do not accept new ideas because many managers are stupid.

c) accept and develop new ideas easily.

Over to you 1

What does your own school or organisation do to keep itself open to new ideas?

Over to you 2

What do you do to keep yourself open to new ideas?

TECHNIQUES FOR DEALING WITH STRESS

Before you read

What do you do when you feel stressed?

Reading

Read this article from the *Financial Times* by Rhymer Rigby and answer the questions.

LEVEL OF DIFFICULTY ● ● ○

Beating stress

By Rhymer Rigby

Cary Cooper, professor of organisational psychology and health at Lancaster University, says you need to learn to
5 differentiate between stress and pressure, which can be thought of as "good stress". "Pressure is motivating and it makes you more productive," he says. "But when
10 the pressure becomes greater than your ability to cope, then you're in the bad stress area."

Jessica Colling, product director at corporate well-being
15 consultancy Vielife, says, "Learn to recognise your early warning signs – for instance, being irritable, suffering from headaches or a sudden lack of
20 confidence." As many people are poor judges of themselves, she suggests asking a friend or family member to help you spot signs of stress.

25 "There have been so many job cuts that workloads have increased massively," says Prof Cooper. "People feel guilty about leaving work on time."

30 Create time to organise your thoughts, plan your tasks and understand what is going on around you. If you are constantly working long hours, then create
35 good reasons to leave work on time. "Think of this as a kind of emotional exercise," says Prof Cooper. "Even if you enjoy working from eight until eight,
40 in the long term it's not good for you."

1 **Read through the whole article and match each question (a–d) to the paragraph (1–4) that answers it.**

a) What should I look out for?

b) What are some of the causes?

c) Is all stress bad?

d) How do I manage it?

2 **Complete the table with words from paragraph 1.**

noun	adjective or *-ing* form
organisation	....
....	psychological
....	healthy
....	stressed, stressful
motivation	....
production	....
....	able

3 **Now match the adjectives in Exercise 2 to their meanings.**

This adjective is used to describe someone who ...

a) is doing a lot and getting results.

b) feels worried and tired because they have too much work.

c) is in a good physical and mental condition.

d) can do something.

This adjective is used to describe ...

e) a situation where someone feels out of control.

f) companies, departments, etc.

g) work that is interesting and that makes you want to do it.

h) the mind.

4 **Find expressions in paragraphs 2 and 3 with the number of letters shown in brackets that mean the following.**

a) the state of feeling good (4-5)

b) things that show you that something is going wrong (7, 5)

c) describes someone who easily gets angry or annoyed (9)

d) the state of not having something (4)

e) the feeling of being able to do something (10)

f) If you see that something is happening, you .... it. (4)

g) amounts of work that people have to do (9)

h) If something increases a lot, it increases .... (9)

i) If you feel responsible for something bad, you feel .... (6)

5 **Choose the alternative with the closest meaning to the expression in italic.**

a) *Create* (line 30) time ...
   i) make
   ii) do
   iii) get

b) ... to organise your thoughts, plan *your tasks* (line 31) and understand what is going on around you.
   i) what you did
   ii) what you have to do
   iii) what you want

c) If you are *constantly* (line 33) working long hours, then create good reasons to leave work on time.
   i) always
   ii) often
   iii) sometimes

d) "Think of this as a kind of emotional *exercise* (line 37)," says Prof Cooper.
   i) activity
   ii) plan
   iii) project

e) "Even if you enjoy working from eight until eight, in the *long term* (line 40) it's not good for you."
   i) long time
   ii) long period
   iii) long run

Over to you 1

Is work more stressful, on average, than it was 15 years ago? Give reasons for your opinions.

Over to you 2

One of Prof Cooper's tips for avoiding stress is to *create good reasons to leave work on time*. Is this always possible in your job or one that you would like to have? Why? / Why not?

STRESS IN THE PUBLIC SECTOR

Before you read

Are jobs in the public sector (schools, hospitals, social work etc.) more or less stressful than those elsewhere? Why? / Why not?

Reading

Read this article from the *Financial Times* by Brian Groom and answer the questions.

LEVEL OF DIFFICULTY ● ● ●

TEXT BANK

Stress-related absence rises

By Brian Groom

Staff absence levels remain higher in the public sector than in the private sector, with stress levels likely to grow as the
5 government's spending cuts take effect, according to a report by the Chartered Institute of Personnel and Development (CIPD). Its survey of 573 organisations with
10 1.5m employees found that the recession has had an effect on the whole economy, with a third of all employers reporting an increase in stress-related absence.
15 More than a third of employers noted an increase in mental health problems such as anxiety and depression – a big rise on last year's survey, when one-fifth reported
20 an increase. But only one-fifth of organisations had increased their focus on employee well-being and health promotion, suggesting that more could be done.
25 The survey found that average absence was three days higher in the public sector than in private sector services, at 9.6 days per employee per year compared
30 with 6.6 days. Stress was the main cause of high levels of long-term public sector absence, with three-quarters of public sector organisations putting stress among
35 the top five causes of absence. More than half of public sector employers rated organisational change and restructuring as one of the leading causes of work-related
40 stress, compared with fewer than 40 per cent in other sectors.

Jill Miller of the CIPD said: "The survey shows why closing the gap between public and
45 private sector absence has proved so difficult for all governments over the years. Compared to the private sector, more public sector employees are in challenging jobs
50 such as social work, policing, teaching and nursing, where they often have to deal with people in emotionally difficult situations."

1 Look through the whole article and match the figures to the things that they refer to.

1 573   a) the average number of days of absence of public sector workers per year

2 1.5m   b) the number of public sector organisations who think stress is an important cause of absence

3 9.6   c) the average number of days of absence of private sector workers per year

4 6.6   d) the number of companies in the CIPD survey

5 three-quarters   e) the number of public sector employers who think change in their organisation is an important cause of stress

6 more than half   f) the number of workers in the private sector who think change in their organisation is an important cause of stress

7 fewer than 40 per cent   g) the number of employees covered in the CIPD survey

2 Match the two parts to make expressions from paragraph 1.

1 Staff absence   a) spending cuts

2 public   b) levels

3 private   c) levels

4 stress   d) sector

5 government's   e) sector

6 stress-related   f) absence

3 Read paragraphs 2 and 3 and decide if these statements are true or false.

a) Anxiety and depression are mental health problems.

b) About 20 per cent of employers say that mental health problems have increased in the past year.

c) About 20 per cent of employers said last year that mental health problems had increased in relation to the previous year.

d) About 80 per cent of employers have started thinking more about the well-being of their staff in the past year.

e) Private sector workers take more days of absence than public sector ones.

f) More than 60 per cent of public sector employers think that changes in their organisation cause stress.

g) Fewer than four in ten employees in the private sector think that changes in their organisation cause stress.

4 Complete these statements with expressions from paragraph 4.

a) If you want to make the difference between two things smaller, you try to .... between them. (3 words)

b) A .... job is a difficult one, but it might be difficult in an interesting way. (1 word)

c) If you work to solve problems, you try to .... them. (2 words)

d) Situations where people's feelings are very strong are .... ones. (2 words)

5 Stress is increasing in all UK organisations and it is...

a) higher in the private sector than the public sector.

b) higher in the public sector than the private sector.

c) the same in both sectors.

Over to you 1

Go back to the answer you gave in 'Before you read'. Would it be the same now that you have read the article? Why? / Why not?

Over to you 2

What can companies do to focus on employees' well-being and health?

TEXT BANK

UNUSUAL ENTERTAINMENT

Before you read

If you were invited to an evening of cutting up raw meat, would you go? Why? / Why not?

Reading

Read this article from the *Financial Times* by Samantha Pearson and answer the questions.

LEVEL OF DIFFICULTY ● ● ○

TEXT BANK

Bankers turn to corporate butchery

By Samantha Pearson

Nine men dressed in expensive suits and white coats covered with blood gather round a table. Among the group are bankers, a
5 property developer and some of England's richest men. This is corporate entertainment in the post-banking crisis era and they are learning the art of butchery
10 at an evening class in central London.

The class at the Ginger Pig butcher's shop in Marylebone has become a popular way for
15 City institutions to entertain their clients in the recession, as many cut back on expensive parties. Tim Wilson, the Yorkshire farmer who owns the shop and four
20 others in the capital, says that one of his butchers started offering one-off classes three years ago after requests from customers. Now there are three sessions a
25 week and half of the places are taken up by corporate bookings.

Borut, a Slovenian butcher who jointly runs the class, starts off by teaching the group how to
30 tell rump from ribeye steak. After completing a three-year degree in butchery in Ljubljana, Borut came to London to follow the profession that has been in his
35 family for generations. During the past six months, he says, the class has become particularly popular with companies wanting to entertain clients. "You could take
40 them to an expensive restaurant, but they want to do something different. We've even had some vegetarians come."

Later on in the evening, the
45 men are challenged to hold up a 45kg side of beef in the air for 20 seconds as their colleagues and friends count down, cheer and take pictures with their
50 BlackBerrys. The prize is a ribeye steak to take home. Equipped with saws and knives, they then go about trying to prepare the final cut of beef.

1 Choose the alternative with the closest meaning to the expresion in italic.

a) Nine men *dressed in* (line 1) expensive suits and white coats covered with blood gather round a table.
   i) carrying
   ii) wearing
   iii) clothing

b) This is corporate entertainment in the *post-banking crisis era* ... (line 8)
   i) period following the banking crisis
   ii) term after the banking crisis
   iii) stage next to the banking crisis

c) ... and they are learning the art of *butchery* (line 9) at an evening class in central London.
   i) selling meat
   ii) eating meat
   iii) cutting up meat

d) The class at the Ginger Pig butcher's shop in Marylebone has become a popular way for *City institutions* ... (line 15)
   i) banks and other organisations in London as a whole
   ii) banks and other organisations in cities around the world
   iii) banks and other organisations in the City of London

e) ... to entertain their clients in the recession as many *cut back on* (line 17) expensive parties.
   i) increase the number of
   ii) reduce the number of
   iii) reduce the size of

f) Tim Wilson, the Yorkshire farmer who owns the shop and four others in the capital, says that one of his butchers started offering *one-off classes* (line 22) three years ago after requests from customers.
   i) courses
   ii) single classes, not part of a course
   iii) one-to-one teaching

g) Now there are three sessions a week and half of the places are taken up by *corporate bookings*. (line 26)
   i) company reservations
   ii) reserves for companies
   iii) company books

2 Answer these questions about paragraph 3.

a) Where does Borut come from?

b) Is he the only teacher in the class?

c) What are rump and ribeye?

d) What is Borut's qualification?

e) What is his background?

f) Why have butchery classes become popular?

g) Do vegetarians ever come to the classes?

3 Correct these expressions used in paragraph 3 by crossing out the unnecessary word in each expression.

If you ...

a) *run in a class*, you teach it.

b) can *tell one thing from of another*, you know what the difference is between them.

c) *complete off a course*, you finish it successfully.

d) *come to on a place*, you arrive there.

e) *follow up a profession*, you have a job in that profession.

f) *entertain out clients*, you take them to restaurants, special events, etc.

4 Complete these statements with words or expressions from paragraph 4.

a) If you are asked to do something difficult, you are c........................ to do it.

b) If you keep something in the air with your hands, you h........................ it u........................ .

c) The people that you work with are your c........................ .

d) If you say, 'five, four, three, two, one', you c........................ d........................ from five to one.

e) If you have tools to do a job, you are e........................ with these tools.

f) If you start to do something, you g........................ a........................ doing it.

5 Choose the best summary of the whole article.

Butchery classes are ...

a) a new form of corporate entertainment, following the banking crisis.

b) an ideal form of corporate entertainment for rich meat-eaters.

c) only popular as corporate entertainment because this is not a good time for expensive parties.

Over to you 1

Go back to the answer that you gave in 'Before you read'. Have you changed your mind now that you have read the article? Give your reasons.

Over to you 2

Think of some other unusual forms of corporate entertainment that would be suitable for clients in an industry that you are interested in.

IS HOSPITALITY A CRIME?

Before you read

Bribery is when someone offers money or a gift to someone, for example in order to obtain a contract. Could some corporate hospitality for clients be a form of bribery?

Reading

Read this article from the *Financial Times* by Bob Sherwood and answer the questions.

FT

LEVEL OF DIFFICULTY ● ● ●

Bribery law threat to business hospitality

By Bob Sherwood

Businesses are reviewing their corporate hospitality plans as they are worried that some forms of hospitality could be illegal
5 under new UK bribery laws. Lawyers say they have been asked by companies who fear that they may have to cancel bigger hospitality events after
10 the Bribery Act comes into force. Many City institutions consider luxury entertaining, which can include international flights and free tickets to sporting events, as
15 a normal part of business.

Stephen Morrall, corporate partner at Dawsons Solicitors, said: "We have talked to a lot of people about this. They are
20 very worried and they should be worried. People are asking whether they should be holding corporate entertainment events."

Two UK banks said they were
25 looking at how entertaining would be affected by the legislation. Some lawyers are advising that breaking the law could depend on the type of hospitality. So,
30 for example, offering lunch at a Twickenham rugby match may be fine, but flying clients to Australia to watch cricket could be risky. "Until clear guidelines are
35 published, people should be very careful about any lavish form of entertainment, because there's clearly a risk that an offence could be committed," added
40 Mr Morrall.

Gary Miller, fraud specialist at lawyers Mishcon de Reya, believed many companies were unnecessarily worried and
45 executives needed only to take a "commonsense" approach to hospitality. If they had always offered hospitality as routine then it was unlikely to attract
50 attention, he suggested, but entertaining clients at a sensitive time, such as when a contract was due for renewal, would be riskier.

1 Look through the whole article and decide what the word *hospitality* refers to.

   a) hospital management
   b) hotel management
   c) entertaining clients

2 Complete the table with words from paragraph 1, in the form they are used in the article.

verb	noun
....	review
bribe	bribe, ...
....	fear
....	cancellation
entertain	....
fly	....

3 Now match the nouns in Exercise 2 to their meanings.

   a) an illegal gift
   b) the crime of giving illegal gifts
   c) the state of feeling afraid
   d) trips by plane
   e) when something that was going to happen does not take place
   f) when you look again at a situation and examine it
   g) inviting clients to a special event

4 Read paragraphs 1 and 2 and decide if these statements are true or false.

The new UK laws on bribery ...

   a) are causing businesses to check their policies on hospitality.
   b) mean that some hospitality events may be cancelled.
   c) may affect giving free international flights to clients.
   d) are not causing a lot of worry among businesses.

5 Complete these statements with appropriate forms of expressions from paragraph 3.

   a) A law or set of laws are referred to as l......................... (11 letters)
   b) If someone doesn't obey a law, they b......................... it. (5 letters)
   c) If there's a chance of something bad happening, the situation is r......................... (5 letters)
   d) Advice may be given in the form of g......................... (10 letters)
   e) Entertainment that is expensive and luxurious is l......................... (6 letters)
   f) A formal expression meaning 'to break a law' is 'to c......................... a......................... o.........................'. (6, 2, 7 letters)

6 Answer these questions about the expressions in paragraph 4 with *yes* or *no*.

   a) If you are *unnecessarily worried* (line 44) about something, do you really need to be worried?
   b) If you take a *commonsense approach* (line 46) to something, do you need a lot of technical knowledge to understand it and make a decision about it?
   c) If something is *unlikely to attract attention* (lines 49–50), will people probably not notice it?
   d) If something happens at a *sensitive time* (lines 51–52), do people involved need to be careful how they behave?
   e) Does a contract that is *due for renewal* (line 53) still have a long time to run?

Over to you 1

Describe the forms of corporate hospitality that are acceptable for clients in your country.

Over to you 2

...entertaining clients at a sensitive time, such as when a contract was due for renewal, would be riskier. How long before or after a contract's renewal would it be acceptable for the clients to be offered lavish hospitality? Give your reasons.

ADVERTISING NEW WEBSITES

Before you read

When you use the Internet, do you sometimes look for new websites, or do you always look at the ones you already know? Describe your Internet 'behaviour'.

Reading

Read this article from the *Financial Times* by Tim Bradshaw and answer the questions.

FT

LEVEL OF DIFFICULTY ● ● ○

Web start-ups buy more TV advertising

By Tim Bradshaw

More and more, small Internet start-ups are advertising on television, often within months of their launch. In the late 1990s,
5 many of the Internet's biggest brands – such as Google, Skype and Amazon – were built through word-of-mouth, without paying for offline ads. Today Google is
10 advertising on TV and billboards, and investors are encouraging more of their start-up companies to take advantage of television.

Index Ventures invests in
15 Internet start-ups. Saul Klein, a partner at Index, says: "Once you have a clear sense of how much it costs you to get a customer and the total lifetime value of

20 that customer, you should start experimenting with as many different marketing channels as possible." Recent e-commerce companies appearing on UK TV
25 include Spotify, the digital music service; Lovefilm, the DVD-rental and online-video service; Glasses Direct, which sells spectacles; Wonga, a loan provider; and
30 Just-Eat, which lets people order from local fast food takeaways online.

Such companies started off by advertising on Google's
35 search ads, which allow an exact analysis of how much each ad cost and how much the visitor who saw the ad went on to spend.

But search ads are most useful
40 when people know what they are looking for – so for companies trying to build awareness for a new kind of online service, TV ads can be more useful.

45 "Our goal on TV is to educate people that there is an alternative to the high street," says Kevin Cornils, chief executive of Glasses Direct. "Anyone can do an ad
50 online, but people trust TV." Mat Braddy, marketing chief at Just-Eat, buys TV advertising to target younger people in early evenings and at weekends. "If you're
55 clever about it, you can advertise at the times of day when people make the decision to eat," he says.

1 Look through the whole article and find the names of:

a) three 'old' Internet companies.

b) a company that invests in Internet start-up companies.

c) someone who works for the investment company in b).

d) five new Internet companies.

e) people who work for two of these companies.

2 Find three forms of advertising in paragraph 1.

3 Complete these expressions from lines 14–34 with the correct prepositions.

a) invest _ _ a start-up

b) experiment _ _ _ _ different things

c) appear _ _ TV

d) order something _ _ _ _ somewhere

e) start off _ _ doing something

4 Find expressions in paragraphs 2 and 3 that mean the following.

a) the total amount that a customer buys from a company
†_ _ _ _ l_ _ _ _ _ _ _ v_ _ _ _

b) different ways of advertising
m_ _ _ _ _ _ _ _ c_ _ _ _ _ _ _

c) glasses (to see with)
s_ _ _ _ _ _ _ _ _

d) a type of bank
l_ _ _ p_ _ _ _ _ _ _

e) ready meals you buy somewhere and eat elsewhere
†_ _ _ _ _ _ _ _

f) examination
a_ _ _ _ _ _ _

g) knowing about something
a_ _ _ _ _ _ _ _

5 Correct these statements about the expressions in italic as they are used in the article.

a) A *goal* (line 45) is only something that happens in football.

b) If you *educate* (line 45) people, this always happens in schools.

c) If you have an *alternative* (line 46), you have no choice.

d) *The high street* (line 47) is in the same place as a shopping mall.

e) If you *do* (line 49) an ad online, you read an ad on the Internet.

f) If advertisers *target* (line 52) particular people, they do not want to reach them and communicate with them.

6 Choose the best summary of the whole article.

a) Internet advertising will replace TV advertising in the long run.

b) TV advertising can be used to get people to look at particular websites.

c) TV advertising is only useful to get people to order takeaway food online.

Over to you 1

'People trust TV advertising.' Is this true in your country? Why? / Why not?

Over to you 2

Would you use the Internet to buy any of the products/ services sold by the companies in Exercise 1, question d) above? Why? / Why not?

TEXT BANK

Before you read

An entrepreneur is someone who starts a new business, or a series of new businesses. Are you / Could you be an entrepreneur? Why? / Why not?

Reading

Read this article from the *Financial Times* by Luke Johnson and answer the questions.

LEVEL OF DIFFICULTY ● ● ●

TEXT BANK

Rules of the game have been rewritten

By Luke Johnson

Entrepreneurs of the 21st century are different. The world of business has changed a lot since I entered it in the 1980s, and
5 the rules of the game have been totally rewritten. An important factor has been the influence of the Internet. Many start-ups are now online companies or use the
10 Internet in some way. A 26-year-old such as Mark Zuckerberg can create a community of 500 million users with Facebook – employing just 1,000 staff. Facebook is
15 also an example of how investors are willing – sometimes – to back projects that have almost no sales revenues, believing that a profitable business model will
20 come later, as it did with Google.

Every young company now uses social networking as one of its marketing tools. An understanding of how to use
25 Facebook, Twitter, Foursquare and the rest is important for the success of almost any brand targeted at the young. Each new wave of technology is accepted
30 very quickly. Things used to evolve much more gradually in the past.

Start-ups are far more likely to be founded by graduates than
35 they used to be. In the past six years in the UK, there has been a 46 per cent jump in the number of graduates describing themselves as self-employed. I am sure that
40 will continue, partly because comfortable jobs are much harder to get. Of course, many more people attend university now; yet when I left Oxford, it was seen
45 by many as "wasting" a degree to want to create a business.

Women entrepreneurs are much more common than in the past, with almost one in three UK
50 start-ups in 2009 founded by a woman. Now women are much more confident and ambitious in their careers, and there are plenty of role models of successful
55 women in the workplace.

1 Put the paragraph headings in the correct order.

a) Women entrepreneurs

b) The importance of social networking

c) Graduate entrepreneurs

d) Entrepreneurs and the Internet

2 Answer these questions about paragraph 1.

a) When did the writer arrive in the world of business?

b) What expression does the writer use to describe what has happened since then?

c) What does the expression in question b) above mean?

d) Why has this happened?

e) Are all start-ups now Internet companies?

f) How many people work at Facebook?

g) Why are investors willing to put money into companies with no sales revenues?

3 Choose the alternative with the closest meaning to the expression in italic.

a) An understanding of how to use Facebook, Twitter, Foursquare and the rest is important to the success of almost any brand *targeted at* (line 28) the young.
    i) made for
    ii) made by
    iii) presented to

b) Each new wave of technology is accepted very quickly. Things used to *evolve* (line 31) much more gradually.
    i) stay
    ii) event
    iii) change

c) Start-ups are far more likely to be founded by *graduates* (line 34) than they used to be.
    i) people with degrees
    ii) people with a gradual approach to business
    iii) people with doctorates

d) In the past six years in the UK, there has been a 46 per cent *jump* … (line 37)
    i) fall
    ii) decrease
    iii) increase

e) … in the number of graduates describing themselves as *self-employed*. (line 39)
    i) working for a company
    ii) working for themselves
    iii) working hard

f) I am sure that will continue, partly because comfortable jobs are much *harder* (line 41) to get.
    i) more difficult
    ii) easier
    iii) better paid

g) Of course, many more people *attend* (line 43) university now; …
    i) wait for
    ii) go to
    iii) drop out of

h) … yet when I left Oxford, it was seen by many as "wasting" a degree to want to *create* (line 46) a business.
    i) start
    ii) manufacture
    iii) invent

i) Women entrepreneurs are much more *common* (line 48) than in the past, with almost one in three UK start-ups in 2009 founded by a woman.
    i) ordinary   ii) often   iii) usual

4 Complete the table with words from paragraphs 2 and 3, in the form they are used in the article.

verb	noun
understand	....
succeed	....
....	target
jump	....
....	waste
....	creation

5 Now match the nouns in Exercise 4 to their meanings.

a) the act of starting something

b) the customers that something is made for

c) when you achieve what you wanted or hoped for

d) when you do not use something in an effective way

e) when you know what something means, know how it works, etc.

f) when something is more than before

6 Imagine a different headline for the article. Choose the best alternative from the following.

a) When I was a young man, business start-ups were easier

b) Thirty years of change in the world of entrepreneurs

c) Graduate start-ups are the way to go

Over to you 1

Is it possible nowadays to start a business that does *not* depend on the Internet in some way? Explain your ideas.

Over to you 2

Do you think that university graduates are 'wasting' their degree if they start a business? Give your reasons.

MARKETING SPORTS

Before you read

What are the traditional sports in your country a) to watch and
b) to participate in? Are you a fan of these sports?

Reading

Read this article from the *Financial Times* by Roger Blitz and Rose
Jacobs and answer the questions.

FT

The search for new sports fans

By Roger Blitz and Rose Jacobs

The National Basketball Association (NBA) has brought
its product to London, once
more pitching the game to an
5 overseas market in an attempt
to expand its product beyond its
North American homeland. The
NBA had insisted that the LA
Lakers–Minnesota Timberwolves
10 friendly last month would feel
just like a US-based NBA game.

American football is also in the
fourth year of its own export drive.
On Sunday, the San Francisco
15 49ers take on the Denver Broncos
at Wembley stadium in London
in the latest annual attempt to sell

the National Football League to
a new audience. Sports operators
20 face competition from other sports
for revenues as well as other
leisure interests and must find
new markets if they wish to grow.
Consumption can be measured
25 both by the numbers participating
in the sport and those watching it.

The NFL and NBA are not
the only sports trying to find
new markets. Bernie Ecclestone,
30 the Formula One motor racing
chief, has dropped some
venues and created new ones in
Singapore, Bahrain, Malaysia
and, most recently, South Korea.

35 Football, the most popular of
sports, still has the Indian and
Chinese markets to penetrate.
Expansion in these markets is left
to individual clubs to see what
40 new fan bases they can reach.

Sports that enter new markets
must bite into the leisure time
and income of people already
participating in or watching the
45 traditional main sports of their
countries. As David Stern of the
NBA puts it: "We just want one
in 10 people to bounce the ball
rather than kick it." However,
50 he concedes "the growth is
different market by market."

TEXT BANK

1 **Look through the whole article and find the names of:**

a) four types of sport.

b) two teams that play one of these sports.

c) two teams that play another of these sports.

d) three sports organisations.

e) two people who work for these organisations.

f) four countries mentioned in relation to a particular sport.

g) two countries mentioned in relation to another sport.

2 **Answer these questions about the expressions in italic in paragraph 1.**

a) What is the *product* referred to in line 3?

b) If a marketer *pitches* something to someone (line 4), what do they do?

c) If a marketer *expands* a market (line 6), what do they do?

d) Which countries are referred to in the expression *North American homeland*? (line 7)

e) If you *insist* something will happen (line 8), are you unsure that it will happen?

f) If x *feels like* y (lines 10–11), is x similar to y?

3 **Choose the alternative with the closest meaning to the expression in italic.**

a) American football is also in the fourth year of its own export *drive*. (line 13)
   i) road
   ii) lane
   iii) campaign

b) On Sunday, the San Francisco 49ers *take on* (line 15) the Denver Broncos at Wembley stadium in London ...
   i) play
   ii) carry
   iii) employ

c) ... in the latest annual attempt to sell the National Football League to a new *audience*. (line 19)
   i) listener
   ii) spectator
   iii) public

d) Sports operators face competition from other sports for *revenues* ... (line 21)
   i) income
   ii) costs
   iii) expenses

e) ... *as well as* (line 21) other leisure interests and must find new markets if they wish to grow.
   i) also
   ii) in addition to
   iii) too

f) *Consumption* (line 24) can be measured both by ...
   i) the popularity of a sport
   ii) the amount eaten at stadium restaurants
   iii) the number of spectators

g) ... the numbers *participating* (line 25) in the sport and those watching it.
   i) activating
   ii) taking part
   iii) gaming

4 **Complete the table with words from paragraphs 3 and 4, in the form they are used in the article.**

verb	noun
market	....
....	creation
....	penetration
....	reach
....	bite
....	bounce
....	kick
grow	....

5 **Now match the nouns in Exercise 4 to their meanings in the context of the article.**

a) when something gets bigger

b) when a product enters a new market

c) when a ball hits the ground and goes up again

d) how much a product is known about, bought, etc.

e) starting or making something for the first time

f) when someone hits a ball with their foot

g) the act of sinking your teeth into something

h) places where something is sold

Over to you 1

Why do you think baseball and American football are not (with some exceptions) generally as popular around the world as they are in the US?

Over to you 2

Think of a sport that is not popular in your country. How would you market it there?

MARKETING MACHINES

Before you read

Are coffee-making and tea-making machines for the home becoming popular?

Reading

Read this article from the *Financial Times* by Haig Simonian and answer the questions.

FT

LEVEL OF DIFFICULTY ● ● ●

Stirring up the tea market

By Haig Simonian

Competition in the hot drinks market reached boiling point on Wednesday, as a former Nestlé executive launched a new tea-making system to compete with the Swiss food group's own recently launched product. The move followed legal action, as Nestlé this week won a court battle to ban a rival product in its highly profitable Nespresso business.

Eric Favre, previously Nespresso's chief executive, and who is now an independent businessman, launched Tpresso, a new tea-making system which he said he wanted to make "the Nespresso of tea". The first machines, to be assembled in China from European components, will go on sale in China in April, with other Asian markets next year, and Europe possibly following.

The new system, to be sold in China for Rmb5,000 ($756), followed Nestlé's launch last year of Special T, a tea-making system designed to do for tea what Nespresso has done for coffee. Machines for Nestlé's Special T system, launched initially in France, cost €129 ($168), with a 10 capsule pack costing €3.50.

Over on the coffee front, a commercial court in the Swiss city of St Gallen gave Nestlé an important legal victory on Monday when it won its case against discount retailer Denner. Denner had been selling Nespresso-compatible coffee capsules for about half the Nestlé price. Last June Nestlé showed its willingness to defend Nespresso, which it says is protected by 1,700 patents. It took legal action against the US company Sara Lee, when it launched its L'Or Espresso machine.

1 Look through the whole article and find the names of:

a) a big Swiss food company.

b) a coffee machine that the company makes.

c) someone who used to work for the company.

d) a tea-making machine that he has launched.

e) a tea-making machine that the company in a) above has launched.

f) a retailer that sells at low prices.

g) a coffee-making machine that another company has launched, and the name of the company.

2 Match the two parts to make expressions from paragraph 1.

1	hot drinks	action
2	boiling	battle
3	tea-making	business
4	legal	market
5	court	product
6	rival	system
7	profitable	point

3 Now match the expressions in Exercise 2 to their meanings, as they are used in the article.

a) when someone tries to solve a disagreement by using the legal system

b) an example of item a) where the disagreement is very big

c) an extreme stage

d) a product that competes with another product

e) an activity that makes money

f) selling tea and coffee machines

g) a machine to make one of the drinks in item f)

4 Read paragraphs 2, 3 and 4 and decide if these statements are true or false.

a) Tpresso machines will be assembled in France.

b) The parts will be made in China.

c) Special T is designed to be a success for tea in the same way that Nespresso has been a success for coffee.

d) Special T was launched all over Europe at the same time.

e) Special T costs less than €130 and the capsules cost €0.35 each.

f) Denner has also launched a tea-making machine.

g) Other companies are free to copy the technology used in Nespresso.

5 Answer these questions about paragraph 4.

a) Who won the court case between Nestlé and Denner?

b) Why did Nestlé take legal action against Denner?

c) Which two other things show that Nestlé wants to protect its Nespresso machine?

6 Choose the best summary of the whole article.

a) The market for tea- and coffee-making machines is very competitive.

b) Company executives can always leave in order to start their own business.

c) Chinese companies are entering the market for tea- and coffee-making machines.

Over to you 1

Is it acceptable for an executive to leave a company and immediately start competing with it by marketing similar products? Why? / Why not?

Over to you 2

Coffee machines like Nespresso mean that Nestlé can continue to make money from sales of coffee capsules for each machine it sells. Make a list of other products where the manufacturer can continue to sell things after it sells the main product.

BUSINESS TRAVEL

Before you read

What is the most important thing to remember when planning a business trip?

Reading

Read this article from the *Financial Times* by Rhymer Rigby and answer the questions.

FT

LEVEL OF DIFFICULTY ● ● ○

TEXT BANK

Planning efficient business trips

By Rhymer Rigby

With business travellers expected to do more work in less time, how do you ensure that you use the time you have in the best way?

5   Although it is fashionable at the moment to take public transport to the airport and to fly economy, it might not be the best solution. "It might be better to be
10 driven to the airport if it means you can use the time to make calls," says Clare Evans, a time management coach. "It's the same with business class. If you're a
15 senior manager and it means you can be productive, it's potentially cheaper. Calculate what your time is worth."

It is better to get to the airport
20 an hour early and spend the time working. Ms Evans says: "Make sure you always have some work with you. With laptops and smart phones, a decent lounge isn't that
25 different to your office." Ensure that you are organised at the other end and don't take any more than carry-on luggage if you can help it. Sites such as Dopplr and TripIt
30 can help you organise your travel online and alert you to delays.

"Arrange meetings with jet lag in mind," says Ms Evans. "If you're on a long-haul flight from London
35 to Los Angeles, then mornings are going to be better for you." Spend the "lower quality" time on administrative tasks such as e-mail. Unless the flight is very
40 short, you do need to spend some time resting. "If you're away for four days, you may be better off spending the flight relaxing rather than working."

1 Put the paragraph headings in the correct order.

a) You will be tired after a long flight

b) Make best use of your travel time

c) Plan your journey

d) Time is money

2 Read paragraphs 1 and 2 and decide if these statements about expressions are true or false.

If ...

a) you are *expected* (line 1) to do something, this is what people want you to do.

b) you *ensure* (line 3) that something will happen, you make certain that it will happen.

c) something is *fashionable* (line 5), not many people are doing it.

d) you find a *solution* (line 9) to a problem, you find an answer to it.

e) you *are driven* (lines 9–10) somewhere, you drive yourself there.

f) you are *productive* (line 16), you don't do much useful work.

g) x is *potentially* (line 16) cheaper than y, it will certainly be cheaper.

h) your time is *worth* (line 18) a particular amount, that is its value.

3 Relate these traveller's thoughts to the advice given in paragraph 3. Put the thoughts into the same order as the pieces of advice given in the article.

a) 'I must check online to see if any of my flights are cancelled.'

b) 'I'm glad I brought the company's latest financial results to read.'

c) 'It's good that I only have hand luggage with me. I won't have to wait in the baggage hall.'

d) 'It's only four o'clock and the flight doesn't leave till six.'

e) 'This place is nice and I can sit here quietly and get through a lot of work.'

4 Match the two parts to make expressions from paragraphs 3 and 4.

1	carry-on	lag
2	jet	time
3	long-haul	tasks
4	lower quality	luggage
5	administrative	flight

5 Which one of these pieces of advice does not appear anywhere in the article?

a) Don't take too much luggage.

b) Organise meetings to take account of how you will be feeling when you arrive.

c) Don't eat or drink too much on the plane.

Over to you 1

What advice would you give for planning a) a successful business trip, or b) a successful holiday trip?

Over to you 2

This article is about time planning on business trips. What tips would you give for time management in relation to planning your work or studies?

TEXT BANK

BUSINESS IDEAS THAT TAKE OFF

Before you read

Why do some business ideas 'take off' and become successful, but most do not? Make a list of all the factors for success/failure that you can think of.

Reading

Read this article from the *Financial Times* by Alina Dizik and answer the questions.

LEVEL OF DIFFICULTY ● ● ○

TEXT BANK

When friendship and fashion equal success

By Alina Dizik

When launching Gilt Groupe, an online shopping site that currently has 3m members, the co-founders did not write a traditional
5 business plan. Instead, Alexis Maybank, 35, and Alexandra Wilkis Wilson, 33, took what they had learnt from Harvard Business School. "You could have taken a
10 good month to write a beautiful 40-page business plan, but you could have lost a critical month in getting your product to market," says Ms Maybank, who adds that
15 competition was coming quickly. "You don't really know if an idea is going to take off before putting it in front of customers."

And they did just that. The two
20 founders used a short presentation to convey their idea to the venture capitalists they had found through the business school network. They also talked about what it was like
25 to be two female entrepreneurs, pitching an idea to male-dominated venture capital firms. "Talking about women's fashion to a bunch of guys in Boston
30 was difficult and something that hadn't been pitched to them very many times," says Ms Maybank.

However, after initial investment, it took only two
35 months to build a site that was ready to test. Three years later,

in spite of intense competition from newer sale sites such as HauteLook or Rue La La in the
40 US, Gilt is still expanding quickly.

Launched just before the US recession in November 2007, the Gilt site offers limited-time fashion bargains to a restricted
45 list of customer members, and the site's members can invite new members to use the site. Gilt's business, dominated by its fashion sales, draws "hundreds
50 of thousands of people" checking its site each day, the group says, mostly at or soon after it opens its selected daily sales at noon New York time.

1 **Choose the alternative with the closest meaning to the expression in italic.**

a) When *launching* (line 1) Gilt Groupe, an online shopping site …
   i) continuing
   ii) starting
   iii) closing

b) … that *currently* (line 2) has 3m members, …
   i) at the time
   ii) during the period
   iii) now

c) to write a *traditional* (line 4) business plan.
   i) usual
   ii) normal
   iii) old-fashioned

d) "You could have taken a good month to write a beautiful 40-page business plan, but you could have lost a *critical* (line 12) month …
   i) a difficult
   ii) a serious
   iii) an important

e) … in *getting* (line 13) your product to market," says Ms Maybank, who adds that competition was coming quickly.
   i) bringing
   ii) obtaining
   iii) sending

f) "You don't really know if an idea is going to take off before *putting it in front of* (lines 17–18) customers."
   i) placing it to
   ii) making it available to
   iii) serving it to

2 **Find words and expressions in paragraph 2 with the number of letters shown in brackets that mean the following.**

a) A noun for people who start a business. (8)

b) A two-word combination for investors who put money into new businesses (7, 11)

c) A noun for a group of people who communicate with each other, help each other, etc. (7)

d) A two-word adjective used to describe a situation where there are more men than women. (4-9)

e) A three-word combination for the organisations that the people in b) above work for. (7, 7, 5)

f) A three-word expression used informally to refer to a group of men. (5, 2, 4)

g) A verb used twice in different forms to talk about explaining a new business idea to possible investors. (Give the infinitive.) (5)

3 **Read paragraphs 1 and 2. What does each word in italic below refer to?**

a) *They* didn't write a traditional business plan.

b) *They* gave *one* to venture capitalists. (2 expressions)

c) They found *them* through Harvard Business School.

d) *It* was difficult because *they* were not used to presentations like this. (2 expressions)

4 **Read paragraphs 3 and 4 and decide if these statements about expressions as they are used in the article are true or false.**

a) *Initial* (line 33) is used to describe something that relates to the beginning of something.

b) *Build* (line 35) is only used in relation to houses and other buildings.

c) *Intense* (line 37) competition is weak.

d) If something *expands* (line 40), it grows.

e) A *recession* (line 42) is a period when the economy gets smaller.

f) If goods are offered on a *limited-time* (line 43) basis, they are available for a very long period.

g) A *bargain* (line 44) is when you pay a lot for something, more than you think it is worth.

5 **What is the key message of the article? Choose the best summary.**

a) Successful businesses always start on the basis of a detailed business plan, detailed analysis and the opening of a number of stores.

b) Gilt Groupe was started by two women entrepreneurs who made short presentations to possible investors, obtained initial investment, and built a website to sell clothes at bargain prices.

c) Gilt Groupe could not have succeeded without the support of students from Harvard Business School.

Over to you 1

Think of a business you know that has started in the last ten years. (It could be anything from a local restaurant to an e-commerce site.) Imagine a short presentation that its founders might have made about their plans to get finance for the business.

Over to you 2

If you are doing business studies, economics, etc., think of a business case study that has particularly interested you. What questions about planning would you ask the business people involved?

If you are working in an organisation, identify one of its activities, products, markets, etc. that would be interesting for students in a business school. What key facts about the way it was planned would be useful for the students to know?

EMPLOYEES' OPINIONS OF MANAGERS

Before you read

What is the most important characteristic of a good manager?
Give reasons.

Reading

Read this article from the *Financial Times* by Brian Groom and answer
the questions.

FT

TEXT BANK

Do you like the way you are managed?

By Brian Groom

Research among 3,000 employees by the Chartered Institute of Personnel and Development (CIPD) found the proportion of people happy with their job had increased to +46 per cent (percentage satisfied minus percentage dissatisfied), compared with +26 per cent in a similar survey last year.

However, the CIPD's new quarterly Employee Outlook survey suggested problems were developing that would damage employee well-being, morale and commitment if not dealt with. Three-quarters of employees said their organisation had been affected by the recession, with 52 per cent saying that there had been increases in work-related stress as a consequence, and 38 per cent saying there had been an upsurge in office politics. The proportion of people who said their jobs made them worried or tense had also increased and nearly six in ten said they were worried by the future.

The survey also highlighted problems with how people are managed. Although most felt treated fairly by their line manager, they were less happy with how far their manager discussed their training and development, gave feedback or coached them. Employees were particularly critical of senior managers, with less than a fifth agreeing that they trusted them and only a quarter agreeing that they consulted employees about important decisions.

Ben Willmott, senior public policy adviser at the CIPD, said: "Employers must ensure arrangements for informing and consulting employees over major changes, such as redundancy, are effective, if they want to improve trust in senior management. They also need to invest in developing line managers' people management skills, particularly in coaching and performance management, if they want to boost employee commitment and productivity. They must ensure managers can spot the early warning signs of stress and provide support to help people struggling to cope."

1 Look through the whole article. What is it mainly about?

a) employees' opinions of their companies

b) managers' opinions of their employees

c) neither of the above

2 Look through the whole article and match the figures to the things that they refer to.

1	3,000	a)	those saying that stress levels had increased
2	+46 per cent	b)	those saying that they were consulted by senior managers when there were big changes
3	+26 per cent	c)	the number of people interviewed for the survey
4	three-quarters	d)	those saying there had been an increase in office politics
5	52 per cent	e)	those who said they trusted senior managers
6	38 per cent	f)	the difference between satisfied and dissatisfied employees this year
7	nearly six in ten	g)	those affected by the recession
8	less than a fifth	h)	those worried about the future
9	a quarter	i)	the difference between satisfied and dissatisfied employees last year

3 Complete the table with words from paragraph 2, in the form they are used in the article.

verb	noun
employ	....
survey	....
....	suggestion
....	development
commit	....
increase	....
stress	....

4 Now match the nouns in Exercise 3 to their meanings in the context of this article.

a) a set of questions that you ask a lot of people in order to find out about their opinions

b) continuous feelings of worry

c) when there is more of something than before

d) caring about your organisation and its success

e) improving employees' skills

f) something that may be true, but needs to be confirmed

g) someone who works for an organisation

5 Complete these statements with words from lines 24–43, using the correct form of the words.

If ...

a) you are involved in trying to get personal advantage in relation to others who work with you, you are involved in .... (6 letters, 8 letters)

b) you are unhappy because of a problem, you are .... about it. (7 letters)

c) a problem is ...., it is discussed and people pay attention to it. (11 letters)

d) people are treated in a proper way, they are treated .... (6 letters)

e) people talk about a problem, they .... it. (7 letters)

f) you give .... to someone, you tell them how they are doing, how good their work is, etc. (8 letters)

g) a manager .... an employee, he or she gives them help and advice about their career. (7 letters)

h) you are .... of something, you do not like it. (8 letters)

i) managers .... employees about changes, etc., they discuss the changes with them. (7 letters)

6 Relate the issues (1–4) from paragraph 4 to what different employees might have said to the researchers (a–d).

1	redundancy	a)	'I always believe what our Chief Executive tells us.'
2	trust in senior management	b)	'She goes round talking to herself the whole time.'
3	boosting productivity	c)	'A quarter of us are going to lose our jobs.'
4	early warning signs of stress	d)	'If they gave us better computers, we could do more work.'

Over to you 1

What are the biggest causes of stress in your organisation?

Over to you 2

What can senior managers do to increase employees' trust in them? Give five examples.

PEOPLE MANAGEMENT IN A CRISIS

Before you read

What products is Switzerland famous for?

Reading

Read this article from the *Financial Times* by Yih-teen Lee and Pablo Cardona and answer the questions.

FT

LEVEL OF DIFFICULTY ● ● ●

TEXT BANK

Victorinox

By Yih-teen Lee and Pablo Cardona

Victorinox is famous for its core product – the Swiss army knife. The company was founded in 1884 in Ibach, a small town in the German-speaking part of Switzerland, by Karl Elsener. He wanted to create jobs that would be long term. This has remained a cornerstone of the company culture.

After the terrorist attacks on the US in September 2001, new airline safety regulations around the world stopped passengers from taking knives on board. The rules had a serious effect on Victorinox, because sales of pocket tools at airports were important sales channels. Victorinox needed to find a way to survive and to deal with the fact that there were too many employees.

Victorinox decided not to get rid of workers. However, it stopped hiring new workers, cancelled overtime and reduced the workday by 15 minutes. Employees were encouraged to take vacation, sometimes in advance of when it was due. Victorinox kept all the employees on its own payroll, while lending 80 or so to other companies for up to six months.

Having committed workers who understand and share the company mission is the goal of many businesses. But few achieve this. The secret lies in the way that Victorinox has always treated its employees. It created some employee-oriented management systems, such as long-term employment, training and development opportunities, and a policy which aims to better integrate young and older workers, immigrants, and people with disabilities into its workforce. It also maintains a 5:1 salary ratio between the highest-paid and average-paid workers.

1 Put the paragraph headings in the correct order.

a) The strategic response

b) The key lessons

c) The challenge

d) Company history

2 Choose the alternative with the closest meaning to the expression in italic.

a) Victorinox is *famous* ...(line 1)

   i) infamous

   ii) well-known

   iii) interesting

b) ... for its *core* (line 1) product – the Swiss army knife.

   i) most important

   ii) most profitable

   iii) sharpest

c) The company was *founded* (line 3) in 1884 in Ibach, a small town in the German-speaking part of Switzerland, by Karl Elsener.

   i) begin

   ii) placed

   iii) started

d) He wanted to create jobs that *would be long term*. (lines 7–8)

   i) were necessary

   ii) were well-paid

   iii) would last

e) This has remained a *cornerstone* (line 9) of the company culture.

   i) one of the most important parts

   ii) one of the most interesting parts

   iii) one of the weakest parts

f) ... because sales of pocket tools at airports were important *sales* (line 18) channels.

   i) spreading

   ii) distribution

   iii) delivery

3 Read paragraph 3 and decide if these statements are true or false.

After 9/11, Victorinox ...

a) asked some of its employees to leave the company.

b) took no action at all.

c) stopped recruiting.

d) stopped asking employees to work more than the normal number of hours.

e) asked employees to work the normal number of hours.

f) told employees to go on holiday.

4 Find words in paragraph 4 with the number of letters shown in brackets that mean the following.

a) A word ending in -*ed* that describes employees who believe in their organisation, want to do their best for it, etc. (9)

b) A noun used to talk about the company's purpose. (7)

c) A noun meaning *objective*, also used in football. (4)

d) A verb used to talk about reaching objectives. (Give the infinitive.) (7)

e) A verb used here to talk about how the company considers its employees, what it does for them, etc. (Give the infinitive.) (5)

f) A word combination used to describe things that are good for workers. (8-8)

g) A noun used to talk about the way that employees can learn new skills, get more important jobs in the company, etc. (11)

h) A noun referring to people who come from other countries. (10)

i) A verb used to say that a situation is kept, not changed. (Give the infinitive.) (8)

5 Choose the best summary of the whole article.

Victorinox ...

a) has always had employee-oriented policies, and its actions after 9/11 were part of this long-term 'philosophy'.

b) treated its employees particularly well when sales fell after the 9/11 attacks.

c) is always willing for its employees to work for other companies, rather than lay them off.

Over to you 1

Why do you think many companies *don't* share Victorinox's values? What reasons might they give?

Over to you 2

Think about your organisation or one you would like to work for. If there was a sudden fall in its sales, which of the crisis management actions taken by Victorinox, if any, could be taken by it? Give reasons.

Before you read

Give some examples of family-owned companies in your country.

Reading

Read this article from the *Financial Times* by Rahul Jacob and answer the questions.

FT

LEVEL OF DIFFICULTY ● ● ○

TEXT BANK

Family conflicts in Asian companies

By Rahul Jacob

In Hong Kong, the man and woman on the street show more interest in the lives of the city's tycoons than perhaps anywhere
5 else in the world. On Tuesday, Walter Kwok, who, following a dispute with his brothers and sisters, lost his stake in one of the world's most valuable property
10 companies, Sun Hung Kai Properties, said that he had been offered HK$20bn ($2.6bn) to settle the dispute, but that it was not enough.

15 The family-controlled public companies of Hong Kong are characteristic of the Asian model of management, say observers. The Asian public company
20 is often an extension of the founding family. Asian business people typically trust an inner circle, which starts with the family. Moreover, in developing
25 countries, the personal contacts between founder and family are more important than they are in the west.

The disputes between the
30 two Indian billionaire brothers, Mukesh and Anil Ambani of Reliance Industries, over the past few years have been on an epic scale. In 2009, the younger
35 brother, Anil, even flew from Mumbai to the Himalayas seeking the god Shiva's help in the hope of resolving his dispute with his brother. The problem, says Joseph
40 Ngai, who heads the Hong Kong office of McKinsey, the consulting firm, is that in the typical family-run business, family, ownership and business issues are mixed
45 together. "The more you can separate these three, the longer your family business will last," says Mr Ngai.

Still, change is happening,
50 even in countries like India, long dominated by family companies. The founders of Infosys Technologies, the Bangalore-based software firm,
55 were so determined to create a professionally-run company that they ordered that none of the founders' children would be allowed to work in the business.

1 **Look through the whole article. Which headline (a–c) could be used instead of the existing headline?**

a) Family-run Asian companies and their problems

b) Family-run companies around the world

c) Family-run companies in India

2 **Look through the whole article and find the names of:**

a) a very rich property developer in Hong Kong.

b) the name of the company in which he had a stake.

c) two Indian billionaire brothers.

d) their company.

e) a god whom one of the brothers went to 'see' in order to help solve a dispute.

f) a consulting firm with an office in Hong Kong.

g) someone who works for it.

h) an Indian IT company.

3 **Find words and expressions in paragraph 1 that mean the following.**

a) ordinary people t..
   .... (7 words)

b) very rich business owners t............................

c) a conflict d........................

d) the percentage of a company that someone owns
   s........................

e) a verb used to talk about ending a conflict
   s........................

4 **Read paragraph 2 and decide if these statements about expressions are true or false.**

a) Something *characteristic* (line 17) of something is typical of it.

b) A *model* (line 17) is a way of doing something that is not copied by anyone else.

c) An *extension* (line 20) of something is another part of it.

d) In a company, the boss's *inner circle* (lines 22–23) consists of people that he or she doesn't know.

e) Your *personal contacts* (line 25) are people that you don't know.

f) Someone who takes over a company is its *founder*. (line 26)

5 **Answer these questions about paragraph 3, starting your answers with the words given.**

a) Have the disputes between the Ambani brothers been on a small scale? – No, they ...

b) Did one of the brothers seek outside help to resolve the dispute? – Yes, he even ...

c) Why are disputes so difficult to resolve in family-run businesses? – Because many different issues ...

d) What is the best way to resolve them? – By ...

e) What happens if you can resolve family business disputes? – The longer the business ...

6 **Complete the table with words from lines 40–58 in the form they are used in the article.**

verb	noun
....	head
....	separation
change	....
....	domination
found	....
....	order

7 **Now match the nouns in Exercise 6 with related points from the article (a–f).**

a) dividing family issues from business issues

b) the boss of McKinsey in Hong Kong

c) the position of family businesses compared to other businesses in India

d) the instruction that the founders' children should not take over Infosys

e) the way that even in India things are not the same as before

f) the brothers who started Infosys Technologies

Over to you 1

Why are family disputes, even non-business ones, so hard to resolve?

Over to you 2

What advantages do professional managers have over family members when running a business?

TEXT BANK

IS CONFLICT A GOOD THING?

Before you read

Do you like arguments, or do you try to avoid them? Give your reasons.

Reading

Read this article from the *Financial Times* by Stefan Stern and answer the questions.

FT

LEVEL OF DIFFICULTY ● ● ●

The challenge of conflict

By Stefan Stern

Robert McHenry, chief executive of OPP, the Oxford-based business psychology consultancy, says that some organisations may be hiding conflicts that should be out in the open. "Clients sometimes tell us that their biggest problem is the lack of conflict in their organisations," he says. "They say that senior leaders create a culture where people prefer to 'keep their head down' and not offer feedback or ideas: conflict damages performance."

OPP recently surveyed 5,000 employees in Europe and America to find out about their experience of conflict at work. They found that, on average, each employee spends 2.1 hours a week – roughly one day a month – dealing with conflict in some way. Most managers find this difficult to manage. Some, but not enough, receive training in the kind of communication skills that can help to resolve conflict.

It's not all bad news. According to another piece of new research, conflict might offer the chance to improve your company's performance. Early results from the research point to the role of successfully managed conflict in the development of effective corporate strategy. In their work with international businesses, the London-based consultancy Cognosis has found that managers who deal with conflict successfully will get better performance from their staff.

How can you benefit from disagreement? Conflict should be managed, Cognosis has found. In open corporate cultures, employees feel able to challenge senior managers. Indeed, managers will actively ask them for their views. "One of the characteristics of effective leaders is their ability to both challenge others and be challenged themselves in a positive way," says Richard Brown, managing partner at Cognosis.

1 **Look through the whole article. What is it mainly about?**

a) Marketing

b) Finance

c) Human resources

2 **Look through the whole article and find the names of:**

a) two people who work for consultancies.

b) their job titles.

c) the names of the two consultancies.

d) the places where they are based.

3 **Read paragraph 1 and decide if these statements about expressions are true or false.**

If ...

a) you *hide* (line 5) something, you do not discuss it.

b) something is *out in the open* (lines 5–6), it is not discussed.

c) there is a *lack* (line 8) of something, there is lots of it.

d) you *keep your head down* (line 12), you do not comment on things, make trouble, etc.

e) you *offer feedback* (line 13) on something, you give your opinion about it.

f) x *damages* y (line 14), it is good for y.

4 **Find words and expressions in paragraph 2 that mean the following.**

a) asked questions *s _ _ _ _ _ _ _*

b) workers *e _ _ _ _ _ _ _ _*

c) get information *f _ _ _ o _ _ a _ _ _ _*

d) typically *o _ a _ _ _ _ _ _*

e) managing *d _ _ _ _ _ _ w _ _ _*

f) type *k _ _ _*

g) solve *r _ _ _ _ _ _*

5 **Match the two parts to make expressions from paragraph 3.**

1	bad	conflict
2	new	businesses
3	successfully managed	research
4	effective	news
5	international	performance
6	better	corporate strategy

6 **Now match the expressions in Exercise 5 to their meanings.**

a) when employees produce improved results

b) when arguments are dealt with in a good way

c) information that was not available before

d) companies that operate in more than one country

e) a company's plans for its future that are successful

f) new information that is not good

7 **In what order do these points occur in paragraph 4?**

a) In these companies, bosses will ask employees for their opinions.

b) In some companies, workers are free to criticise their bosses.

c) How can you get an advantage from conflict?

d) Good bosses are able to criticise others, and able to accept criticism from others.

e) Disagreement is something that should happen in an organised way.

Over to you 1

Do you think that conflict in organisations can be a good thing, as the article says? Why? / Why not?

Over to you 2

... on average, each employee spends 2.1 hours a week – roughly one day a month – dealing with conflict in some way. Is this your experience? Why? / Why not?

TEXT BANK

WORKING WITH UNIVERSITIES

Before you read

Do universities work with companies in your country to develop new products? If so, give some examples (perhaps by doing some research on the Internet). If not, give some reasons why.

Reading

Read this article from the *Financial Times* by Andrew Jack and answer the questions.

LEVEL OF DIFFICULTY ● ● ●

TEXT BANK

GSK looks to universities for new drugs

By Andrew Jack

GlaxoSmithKline aims to start working this year with 10 university "superstar researchers" in long-term partnerships to help develop medicines more effectively and cheaply. The aim is to work closely with leading medical researchers over a decade, all the way to the launch of a new drug. This will allow GSK to use its knowledge while providing the university researchers with investment that will be more than paid back if a new drug is successful.

While big drug companies have often licensed ideas from universities and then take full control, GSK wants instead to continue working with leading medical researchers who prefer to remain in their current jobs rather than become employees of a biotechnology company.

Patrick Vallance, senior vice-president for drug discovery and development at GSK, said: "We want partnerships that allow university researchers to work all the way through to the end of the project, getting a big reward if a medicine is launched." The move comes as the UK pharmaceutical group cuts back on expensive but unproductive in-house research and attempts to change from investment in their own research centres towards partnerships with outside developers.

GSK has recently signed a contract with Professor Mark Pepys, head of medicine at the Royal Free and University College Medical School in London, designed to develop a treatment for a rare form of heart disease. Mr Vallance said he planned to sign 10 such deals this year. Under the agreement, Prof Pepys' company Pentraxin Therapeutics receives a small upfront fee allowing GSK to gain an exclusive licence for his experimental drug when it is launched. "It's a wonderful idea," said Prof Pepys. "This new partnership with GSK is very exciting."

1 **Look through the whole article. Is it about finding new drugs in:**

a) the Amazon jungle?

b) university laboratories?

c) drug companies' laboratories?

2 **Look through the whole article and find the names of:**

a) a pharmaceutical company.

b) someone who works for it.

c) his job title.

d) a university researcher.

e) his job title.

f) the university department that he works for.

g) a company that he has started.

3 **Find words in paragraph 1 that mean the following.**

a) a noun for someone who is very famous in their profession s _ _ _ _ _ _ _ _

b) an adjective that means 'over a long time' l _ _ _ - t _ _ _

c) a plural noun for people working together p _ _ _ _ _ _ _ _ _ _ _

d) an adverb to say that something is done in a good way e _ _ _ _ _ _ _ _ _ _

e) an adverb to say that something is done without spending a lot of money c _ _ _ _ _ _

f) an adverb to describe the way that people work together c _ _ _ _ _ _

g) a noun for the time when a new product is sold for the first time l _ _ _ _ _

h) a noun for a period of 10 years d _ _ _ _ _

i) a word ending in -ing that means 'giving' p _ _ _ _ _ _ _ _

j) an adjective to say that the result of something is good s _ _ _ _ _ _ _ _ _

4 **Read paragraph 2 and decide if these statements about expressions are true or false.**

If ...

a) a company *licenses* (line 17) ideas from a university, it pays the university to use them.

b) you *take full control* (lines 18–19) of something, you share control with others.

c) you prefer x *rather than* y (lines 21–23), you like y more.

d) you get a *reward* (line 31) for something, you get money, etc. for the work that you did on it.

e) a company *cuts back* (line 34) spending on something, it increases the amount that it spends.

f) work is *unproductive* (line 35), it gets good results.

g) you *attempt* (line 36) to do something, you try to do it.

5 **Complete the table with words from lines 19–52, in the form they are used in the article.**

verb	noun
control	....
discover	....
develop	....
treat	....
....	plan
agree	....
license	....

6 **Now match the nouns in Exercise 5 to their meanings.**

a) a way of curing a disease

b) when you pay for the right to use someone's ideas in a product

c) when two or more people decide to work together on something

d) the power to make someone or something do what you want

e) a series of actions, etc. to achieve a result

f) making or improving something

g) finding something new

Over to you 1

Should the purpose of universities be more for a) teaching, b) pure research, or c) research to develop new products? Give your reasons.

Over to you 2

Which possible new products could these university departments be involved with developing?

• Engineering

• Chemistry

• Linguistics

TEXT BANK

RETURNING UNWANTED PRODUCTS

Before you read

Returns are products that are sent back to the manufacturer or supplier because they don't work or because customers have changed their minds. How often do you return products a) to shops and b) to online retailers? Is it easy to do this?

Reading

Read this article from the *Financial Times* by Sarah Murray and answer the questions.

LEVEL OF DIFFICULTY ● ● ○

TEXT BANK

Hidden beauty of the 'uglies'

By Sarah Murray

With computers, transport managers can pack a truck so that only the minimum of space is left empty. They can work out exactly how to fill the vehicle with goods ready for market. But what about transporting the "uglies" – the boxes of different shapes and sizes containing broken and unwanted products – back to the manufacturer?

Martin Patten, manager of the technology programme for Europe at Cisco Systems, the computer equipment supplier, says, "You can't use space on trucks in the best way for returns because people might use different wrapping or put things in bigger boxes." Worse, products usually need to be collected from all sorts of different places. As a result, it can cost four times as much to take something back as to send it out.

One factor behind increasing return rates is the growth in online retailing. "With online shopping there's an attitude of 'I'll buy it and, if I don't like it, I'll send it back'," says Jonathan Wright, a senior executive in Accenture's global supply chain consultancy. "With Internet sales, up to one in five products gets sent back, which is huge."

Moreover, if that process is inconvenient, shoppers can go to other online retailers for their purchases. "If returning products is not customer-friendly, it's going to hurt the retailer's business," says Scott Harkins, vice-president of product marketing at FedEx.

However, an even bigger challenge is on the way. European Union law now requires manufacturers and importers of electronic goods to collect and recycle them at the end of their lives. "The transport of goods after the sale of the product is now as important as it is before the sale, and that's a huge change," says Mr Wright.

1 **Look at the headline and look quickly through the whole article. What are 'uglies'? Why do they have this name?**

2 **Complete these statements with expressions from paragraphs 1 and 2.**

a) If you p........................ a truck, you put goods on to it.

b) If you calculate how to do something, you w........................ o........................ how to do it.

c) In speaking and writing, you can introduce a new idea with 'w........................ a........................'.

d) Products that are sent back to the supplier or manufacturer are called r........................ .

e) Material used to protect and contain a product is its w........................ .

f) If you take something from a particular place, you c........................ it from there.

g) If companies transport goods for delivery, they s........................ them o........................ .

3 **Read paragraphs 3 and 4 and decide if these statements are true or false.**

a) Customers are sending more products back because of poor quality.

b) People shopping online buy things knowing that they can always send them back.

c) The percentage of goods bought online and returned is not very big.

d) Sending things back is always easy, so there is no competition between online retailers on this.

4 **Choose the alternative with the closest meaning to the expression in italic.**

a) *Moreover* (line 37), if that process is inconvenient, ...
   i) But
   ii) Then
   iii) In addition

b) ... shoppers can go to other online retailers for *their purchases*. (lines 39–40)
   i) the things that they buy
   ii) the things that they sell
   iii) the things that they return

c) "If returning products is not *customer-friendly* ... (line 41)
   i) easy for customers to use
   ii) hard for customers to use
   iii) difficult for customers to use

d) ... it's going to *hurt* (line 42) the retailer's business," says Scott Harkins, vice-president of product marketing at FedEx.
   i) help
   ii) support
   iii) damage

e) *However* (line 45), an even bigger challenge is on the way.
   i) And
   ii) But
   iii) Although

f) European Union law now *requires* (line 47) manufacturers and importers of electronic goods to collect and recycle them at the end of their lives.
   i) forces
   ii) needs
   iii) allows

g) "The transport of goods after the sale of the product is now as important as it is before *the sale* (lines 53–54), and that's a huge change," says Mr Wright.
   i) they sell
   ii) they are sold
   iii) they are selling

5 **Look through the whole article again. Which two of these things are not specifically mentioned in relation to returning goods?**

a) The cost of fuel for trucks.

b) The difficulty of packing returned goods on trucks.

c) Returning goods bought online.

d) The difficulty of arranging a convenient time to collect things.

e) New EU rules on recycling.

Over to you 1

With Internet sales, up to one in five products gets sent back, which is huge. Does this figure surprise you? Why? / Why not?

Over to you 2

Online shopping for clothes has grown very quickly in recent years. Will this growth continue, or will there be a natural limit to it? Think, for example, about:

- the difficulty of choosing the right clothes.
- problems in returning them when they are not suitable or the wrong size.

TEXT BANK

Unit 1

Overseas experience

1 1 e   2 c   3 d   4 b   5 a

2 1c: ii), iii), vi)   2a: iv), vii), viii)   3b: i), v)

3 a) True

  b) True

  c) False (You give it less importance than it really has.)

  d) False (You find it difficult.)

  e) True

4 To current and future employers

5 Because …

  a) they may have school-age children.

  b) their spouse's career must also be considered.

  c) this makes a stressful situation even more stressful.

  d) it is becoming more economically powerful.

  e) people think you have become a permanent expat.

Performance reviews

1 She is against them.

2–3

verb	noun
suggest	suggestion – f
improve	improvement – b
appraise	appraisal – d
replace	replacement – c
survive	survival – i
target	target – e
answer	answer – a
file	file – g
experience	experience – h

4 a) ii   b) i   c) ii   d) i   e) iii   f) iii

5 1 f   2 d   3 a   4 c   5 b   6 e

6 a) False (She has never learnt anything about herself.)

  b) True

  c) True

  d) False (Job appraisals don't answer this question.)

  e) False (She has only had to suffer one side of the process.)

  f) False (She thinks it's too tiring.)

Unit 2

Looking after employees

1 SAS

2 a) pioneer   e) actually

  b) gather   f) Expenses

  c) process   g) Revenue

  d) downturn   h) treat

3 c

4 a) It collects and analyses information.

  b) Because he wanted to keep employees happy.

  c) By reducing costs and working harder to bring in more money through sales.

  d) If you treat people well, they will make a difference to your business.

5 a) 35-hour week   d) sports centres

  b) medical care   e) hairdressers

  c) childcare   f) food

6 a) i   b) ii   c) ii   d) i   e) iii

Italian companies

1 a) Salvatore Ferragamo

  b) Ferruccio Ferragamo

  c) Salvatore Ferragamo

  d) Marilyn Monroe, Sophia Loren, Lauren Bacall and Judy Garland

2 a) ii   b) iii   c) i   d) ii   e) iii   f) ii   g) i

3 a) True

  b) True

  c) False (They are new.)

  d) True

  e) False (It is the amount that is sold, or that could be sold.)

4 furniture, textiles, rubber and plastic products, winemaking equipment

5 b

Unit 3

Business-to-business selling

1 b

2 Students' own answers

3 a) travel department in your company, your company's purchasing department

  b) the travel agency

  c) It is wasting money because of its unprofessional methods.

verb	noun
report	report
manage	management
compete	competition
solve	solution
negotiate	negotiation, negotiators

5 b, e, d, f, g, a, c

6 c

Closing the sale

1 c, b, d, a

2
1 business owner – e
2 sales management – f
3 sales people – c
4 sales cycle – b
5 qualification process – a
6 purchasing director – d

3
a) closing
b) unpleasant
c) threaten
d) solution
e) authorisation
f) big discounts

4
a) technique
b) summary
c) benefits
d) proposed
e) deal
f) disappeared
g) outcome
h) reasonable

5 b

Unit 4

Partnerships in innovation

1
a) Procter & Gamble
b) Bob McDonald
c) IRI
d) University of Lund
e) ConAgra and General Mills
f) Clorox
g) Los Alamos National Lab
h) Sederma

2
d) Tide Total Care
f) Glad brand plastic bags
g) a chemical used in babies' nappies
h) Olay Regenerist anti-ageing creams

3
a) the world's largest consumer goods company
b) global industry leader
c) consumer product innovation
d) annual awards event

4
a) False (It's when it works with other organisations.)
b) False (It's used here to refer to a series of new products.)
c) False (It's better and more expensive.)
d) True
e) False (It's usually a large one.)
f) True
g) True

5 c

Accepting new ideas

1 b, c, d, a

2 a) True

b) False (You talk about it so that people notice it.)
c) False (You see it.)
d) True
e) False (It is not accepted.)
f) True

3
a) chief executive
b) brought in
c) again and again
d) commissions
e) leadership
f) resisted
g) necessary

4 a) iii   b) i   c) ii   d) ii   e) iii   f) i

5 a

Unit 5

Techniques for dealing with stress

1 paragraph 1–c, paragraph 2–a
paragraph 3–b, paragraph 4–d

2–3

noun	adjective
organisation	organisational – f
psychology	psychological – h
health	healthy – c
stress	stressed – b, stressful – e
motivation	motivating – g
production	productive – a
ability	able – d

4
a) well-being
b) warning signs
c) irritable
d) lack
e) confidence
f) spot
g) workloads
h) massively
i) guilty

5 a) i   b) ii   c) i   d) i   e) iii

Stress in the public sector

1 1 d   2 g   3 a   4 c   5 b   6 e   7 f

2
1 b/c   Staff absence levels
2 d/e   public sector
3 d/e   private sector
4 b/c   stress levels
5 a   government's spending cuts
6 f   stress-related absence

3
a) True
b) False (More than a third of employers reported an increase this year.)
c) True
d) False (Only a fifth of organisations have increased their focus on this.)
e) False (Public sector workers take 9.6 days per year and private sector workers take only 6.6 days on average.)

f) False ('More than half' do.)

g) True

4 a) close the gap

b) challenging

c) deal with

d) emotionally difficult

5 b

Unit 6

Unusual entertainment

1 a) ii   b) i   c) iii   d) iii   e) ii   f) ii   g) i

2 a) Slovenia

b) No. He runs the class jointly with someone else.

c) Types of steak

d) A three-year degree in butchery in Ljubljana

e) He comes from a family of butchers.

f) Because companies want to offer a different kind of corporate entertainment.

g) Sometimes

3 a) in   d) on

b) of   e) up

c) off   f) out

4 a) challenged   d) count down

b) hold, up   e) equipped

c) colleagues   f) go about

5 a

Is hospitality a crime?

1 c

2–3

verb	noun
are reviewing	review – f
bribe	bribe – a, bribery – b
fear	fear – c
cancel	cancellation – e
entertain	entertaining – g
fly	flights – d

4 a) True

b) True

c) True

d) False ('People are very worried and they should be worried.')

5 a) legislation

b) break

c) risky

d) guidelines

e) lavish

f) commit an offence

6 a) no   d) yes

b) no   e) no

c) yes

Unit 7

Advertising new websites

1 a) Google, Skype, Amazon

b) Index Ventures

c) Saul Klein

d) Spotify, Lovefilm, Glasses Direct, Wonga, Just-Eat

e) Kevin Cornils (chief executive of Glasses Direct), Mat Braddy (marketing chief at Just-Eat)

2 television, word-of-mouth, billboards

3 a) in   d) from

b) with   e) by

c) on

4 a) total lifetime value

b) marketing channels

c) spectacles

d) loan provider

e) takeaways

f) analysis

g) awareness

5 a) Here, a *goal* is also an objective.

b) *Educate* here means 'inform'.

c) If you have an *alternative*, you have a choice.

d) *The high street* is the main street of a town, where there are a lot of shops. *The high street* does not refer to shopping malls.

e) *Do an ad online* means 'put an ad online'.

f) No, they want to reach them and communicate with them.

6 b

New entrepreneurs

1 d, b, c, a

2 a) In the 1980s.

b) ' ... the rules of the game have been totally rewritten.'

c) The way that entrepreneurs start successful companies is now completely different.

d) Because of the Internet.

e) No, some use the Internet, but they are not Internet companies.

f) 1,000

g) Because they think that a way of making money will come later.

3 a) i   b) iii   c) i   d) iii   e) ii
   f) i   g) ii   h) i   i) iii

4–5

verb	noun
understand	understanding – e
succeed	success – c
targeted	target – b
jump	jump – f
wasting	waste – d
create	creation – a

6 b

Unit 8

Marketing sports

1 a) basketball, American football, motor racing, football

b) LA Lakers, Minnesota Timberwolves (basketball)

c) San Francisco 49ers, Denver Broncos (American football)

d) National Basketball Association, National Football League, Formula One motor racing

e) Bernie Ecclestone, David Stern

f) Singapore, Bahrain, Malaysia, South Korea (motor racing)

g) India, China (football)

2 a) basketball

b) The marketer tries to sell it to them.

c) They make it bigger.

d) The US and Canada (It could also include Mexico, but probably not here.)

e) No, you are sure it will happen.

f) Yes

3 a) iii b) i c) iii d) i e) ii f) i g) ii

4–5

verb	noun
market	markets – h
created	creation – e
penetrate	penetration – b
reach	reach – d
bite	bite – g
bounce	bounce – c
kick	kick – f
grow	growth – a

Marketing machines

1 a) Nestlé

b) Nespresso

c) Eric Favre

d) Tpresso

e) Special T

f) Denner

g) L'Or Espresso, Sara Lee

2–3

1 hot drinks market – f

2 boiling point – c

3 tea-making system – g

4 legal action – a

5 court battle – b

6 rival product – d

7 profitable business – e

4 a) False (They will be assembled in China.)

b) False (The parts will be made in Europe.)

c) True

d) False (It was launched initially in France.)

e) True

f) False (It has launched its own capsules for Nespresso machines.)

g) False (Nespresso is protected by 1,700 patents.)

5 a) Nestlé

b) Because Denner was selling coffee capsules for Nestlé's Nespresso machine at half the Nestlé price.

c) i) Nestlé's 1,700 patents for the machine, and ii) its legal action against Sara Lee, when it launched its L'Or Espresso machine.

6 a

Unit 9

Business travel

1 d, b, c, a

2 a) True

b) True

c) False (A lot of people are doing it.)

d) True

e) False (Someone else drives you.)

f) False (You do useful work.)

g) False (It might be cheaper.)

h) True

3 d, b, e, c, a

4 1 carry-on luggage

2 jet lag

3 long-haul flight

4 lower quality time

5 administrative tasks

5 c

Business ideas that take off

1 a) ii b) iii c) ii d) iii e) i f) ii

2 a) founders
   b) venture capitalists
   c) network
   d) male-dominated
   e) venture capital firms
   f) bunch of guys
   g) pitch

3 a) The two founders (Alexis and Alexandra)
   b) The two founders, a short presentation
   c) venture capitalists
   d) Pitching an idea, male-dominated venture capital firms

4 a) True
   b) False (Websites are built.)
   c) False (It is very strong.)
   d) True
   e) True
   f) False (They are only available for a short time.)
   g) False (It's used to say that something has been bought very cheaply.)

5 b

Unit 10

Employees' opinions of managers

1 c

2 1 c 2 f 3 i 4 g 5 a 6 d 7 h 8 e 9 b

3–4

verb	noun
employ	employee – g
survey	survey – a
suggested	suggestion – f
developing	development – e
commit	commitment – d
increase	increases – c
stress	stress – b

5 a) office politics   f) feedback
   b) worried   g) coaches
   c) highlighted   h) critical
   d) fairly   i) consult
   e) discuss

6 1 c   2 a   3 d   4 b

People management in a crisis

1 d, c, a, b

2 a) ii b) i c) iii d) iii e) i f) ii

3 a) False (It decided not to do this.)
   b) False (It 'undertook a series of measures'.)
   c) True
   d) True
   e) False (It reduced the workday.)
   f) False (It only encouraged them to do this.)

4 a) committed   f) employee-oriented
   b) mission   g) development
   c) goal   h) immigrants
   d) achieve   i) maintain
   e) treat

5 a

Unit 11

Family businesses in Asia

1 a

2 a) Walter Kwok
   b) Sun Hung Kai Properties
   c) Mukesh and Anil Ambani
   d) Reliance Industries
   e) Shiva
   f) McKinsey
   g) Joseph Ngai
   h) Infosys Technologies

3 a) the man and woman on the street
   b) tycoons
   c) dispute
   d) stake
   e) settle

4 a) True
   b) False (A model is copied by others.)
   c) True
   d) False (It consists of people they know and trust best.)
   e) False (They are people that you know.)
   f) False (It's the person who started the company.)

5 a) No, they have been on an epic scale.
   b) Yes, he even went to seek the god Shiva's help.
   c) Because many different issues are mixed together.
   d) By separating family, ownership and business issues.
   e) The longer the business will last.

6–7

verb	noun
heads	head – b
separate	separation – a
change	change – e
dominated	domination – c
found	founders – f
ordered	order – d

Is conflict a good thing?

1 c

2 a) Robert McHenry, Richard Brown
   b) chief executive, managing partner
   c) OPP, Cognosis
   d) Oxford, London

3 a) True
   b) False (It is discussed.)
   c) False (There is not enough of it.)
   d) True
   e) True
   f) False (It is harmful.)

4 a) surveyed
   b) employees
   c) find out about
   d) on average
   e) dealing with
   f) kind
   g) resolve

5–6

1 bad news – f
2 new research – c
3 successfully managed conflict – b
4 effective corporate strategy – e
5 international businesses – d
6 better performance – a
7 c, e, b, a, d

Unit 12

Working with universities

1 b

2 a) GlaxoSmithKline
   b) Patrick Vallance
   c) Senior vice-president for drug discovery and development
   d) Professor Mark Pepys
   e) Head of medicine
   f) Royal Free and University College Medical School in London
   g) Pentraxin Therapeutics

3 a) superstar   f) closely
   b) long-term   g) launch
   c) partnerships   h) decade
   d) effectively   i) providing
   e) cheaply   j) successful

4 a) True
   b) False (You are the only one in control.)
   c) False (You like x more.)
   d) True
   e) False (It reduces the amount.)
   f) False (It gets few or no results.)
   g) True

5–6

verb	noun
control	control – d
discover	discovery – g
develop	development – f
treat	treatment – a
planned	plan – e
agree	agreement – c
license	licence – b

Returning unwanted products

1 Goods that are returned to the supplier or manufacturer because they are not wanted. They have this name because they are not easy to pack on trucks.

2 a) pack
   b) work out
   c) what about
   d) returns
   e) wrapping
   f) collect
   g) send, out

3 a) False (It's because of the growth of online shopping.)
   b) True
   c) False (It's huge – very big.)
   d) False (If it's inconvenient, people will buy things from other retailers.)

4 a) iii   b) i   c) i   d) iii   e) ii   f) i   g) ii

5 a, d

Resource bank

TEACHER'S NOTES

Introduction

These Resource bank activities are designed to extend and develop the material in the Course Book. The Resource bank contains exercises and activities relating to:

Speaking

Each speaking unit begins with a language exercise that takes up and extends the language points from the Course Book unit, then applies this language in one or more activities. The speaking units are best done in the classroom. You have permission to photocopy the Resource bank pages in this book. In some units, you will give each student a copy of the whole page. In others, there are role cards which need to be cut out and given to participants with particular roles. These activities are indicated in the unit-specific notes below.

Listening

Students listen again to the interviews from the Listening sections in the Course Book, and do further activities on comprehension and language development. These activities can be done in the classroom, but they have been designed in a way that makes it easy for students to do them on their own as homework. Make photocopies for the students. Follow up in the next lesson by getting students to talk about any difficulties that they had. You could play the recording again in the classroom to help resolve problems if necessary.

Writing

A model answer is given for the writing task at the end of each case study in the Course Book. There are then two extra writing activities. These can all be done as homework. Again, make photocopies for the students. After correcting the writing exercises in class, go over the key points that have been causing problems.

Resource bank: Speaking

General notes

The language exercise at the beginning of each Speaking unit in the Resource bank can be used to revise language from the main Course Book unit, especially if you did the Skills section in another lesson. In any case, point out the connection with the Course Book Skills material. These language exercises are designed to prepare students for the role plays that follow, and in many cases can be done in a few minutes as a way of focusing students on the activity that will follow.

A typical two-person role play might last five or 10 minutes, followed by five minutes of praise and correction. An animated group discussion might last longer, and longer than you planned: in this case, drop one of your other planned activities and do it another time, rather than try to cram it in before the end of the lesson. If you then have five or 10 minutes left over, you can always go over some language points from the lesson again, or, better still, get students to say what they were. One way of doing this is to ask them what they've written in their notebooks during the lesson.

Revising and revisiting

Feel free to do an activity more than once. After one run-through, praise strong points, then work on three or four things that need correcting or improving. Then you can get students to change roles and do the activity again, or the parts of the activity where these points come up. Obviously, there will come a time when interest wanes, but the usual tendency in language teaching is not to revisit things enough, rather than the reverse.

Fluency and accuracy

Concentrate on different things in different activities. In some role plays and discussions, you may want to focus on fluency, with students interacting as spontaneously as possible. In others, you will want to concentrate on accuracy, with students working on getting specific forms correct. Rather than expect students to get everything correct, you could pick out, say, three or four forms that you want them to get right, and focus on these.

Clear instructions

Be sure to give complete instructions before getting students to start. In role plays, be very clear about who has which role, and give students time to absorb the information they need. Sometimes there are role cards that you hand out. The activities where this happens are indicated below.

Parallel and public performances (PPP)

In pair work or small group situations, get all pairs to do the activity at the same time. Go round the class and listen. When they have finished, praise strong points, and deal with three or four problems that you have heard, especially problems that more than one pair has been having. Then get individual pairs to give public performances so that the whole class can listen. The performers should pay particular attention to these three or four points.

One-to-one

The pair activities can be done one-to-one, with the teacher taking one of the roles. The activity can be done a second time reversing the roles and getting the student to integrate your suggestions for improvement.

Unit 1 Careers
Telephoning: making contact

A

- Get students to look again at the telephoning language in the Useful language box on page 11 of the Course Book. Then get them to close their books.

- Get students to do the exercise in pairs or with the whole class.

- Go through the answers with the whole class. Explain any difficulties.

1	Could I speak <u>to</u> Ken Wu, please?
2	This <u>is</u> Pedro Casas in Buenos Aires.
3	I'm calling <u>about</u> our latest order.
4	Could you transfer <u>me</u> to the production department, please?
5	Could you ask him <u>to</u> call me back?
6	Can I leave <u>a</u> message, please?
7	Could you tell <u>me</u> what it's about?
8	I'll put <u>you</u> through.
9	Can I get him <u>to</u> call you?
10	I can transfer <u>you</u> to his voicemail.

B

- Before the class, make two copies of the activity for each pair. Cut up the 'turns' in one of the copies for each pair. (Be careful not to mix up the sets of turns as this will cause mayhem in the classroom!) Keep the other copy intact as a key to hand out to students after the activity.

- Divide the class into pairs, hand out the cut-up version and explain the task: they have to put the turns into a logical order.

- Circulate, monitor and assist if necessary, but don't interrupt the pairs if they are functioning acceptably.

- When most pairs have finished the task, hand out the complete copies so that students can check their answers.

- Work with the whole class on the intonation of groups of numbers (rising intonation on each group, except the last, which has falling intonation).

- Get pairs to read the conversation in parallel. Circulate, monitor and assist if necessary.

- Work on any remaining difficulties.

- Get one or two of the pairs to do a public performance for the whole class.

(This telephoning situation is continued in Unit 8.)

Unit 2 Companies
Presenting your company

A

- Get students to look again at the presentations language in the Useful language box on page 19 of the Course Book. Then get them to close their books.

- Get students to do the exercise in pairs or with the whole class.

- Go through the answers with the whole class. Explain any difficulties.

1 c	2 e	3 d	4 a	5 f	6 b

B

- Before the class, make as many photocopies as there are students in the class.

- With the whole class, explain the task. Divide the class into groups of three and hand out the photocopies. Each student in each group should choose a different company.

- Give students time to prepare their presentations individually. Then get students to work in their groups and take it in turns to give their presentations.

- Circulate and monitor. Note down language points for praise and correction afterwards, especially in relation to presentations language.

- When the groups have finished, bring the class to order. Praise strong language points and work on half a dozen points that need improving, getting students to say the correct forms.

- Get one or two students to give their presentation to the whole class.

Unit 3 Selling
Negotiating: reaching agreement

A

- Get students to look again at the negotiation language in the Useful language box on page 27 of the Course Book. Then get them to close their books.

- Get students to do the exercise in pairs or with the whole class.

- Go through the answers with the whole class. Explain any difficulties.

1   We're interested <u>in buying</u> five of your machines.

2   We'd <u>like</u> to get the first <u>delivery</u> in November.

3   We must <u>get</u> a better price <u>than</u> the one you are offering.

4   We could <u>possibly give</u> you a discount of five per cent.

5   We can do that, providing <u>you make</u> a down payment.

6   Unfortunately, we <u>can't</u> agree <u>to</u> that.

7   If it <u>works</u>, we'll <u>increase</u> the order later.

8   That <u>sounds</u> a <u>fair</u> price to me.

9   Good, I think <u>we've covered everything</u>.

10   Right, <u>we've got</u> a deal.

B

- Before the class, make as many photocopies of the role cards as there will be pairs, and cut them up.

- With the whole class, explain the task. Point out that they must negotiate a discount in relation to the number of robots sold. (They do not have to negotiate anything else.) Divide the class into pairs and hand out the role cards.

- Give students time to prepare for their roles and assist them if necessary.

- Start the role play in parallel pairs. Circulate and monitor. Note language points for praise and correction, especially in the area of negotiation.

- When pairs have finished, bring the class to order. Praise strong language points and work on half a dozen points that need improving, getting students to say the correct forms.

- Get one or two of the pairs to do a public performance for the whole class, incorporating your improvements.

Unit 4 Great ideas

Successful meetings

A

- Get students to look again at the meetings language in the Useful language box on page 41 of the Course Book. Then get them to close their books.

- Get students to do the exercise in pairs or with the whole class.

- Go through the answers with the whole class. Explain any difficulties.

1   Can we ~~go~~ start, please?

2   Right, let's ~~to~~ begin.

3   The main purpose of this ~~here~~ meeting is to …

4   What do you ~~to~~ think?

5   The next thing to ~~go~~ discuss is …

6   I'm in ~~the~~ favour of …

7   Perhaps we ~~will~~ should …

8   I totally ~~am~~ agree.

9   I don't know ~~round~~ about that.

10   Hold on ~~up~~ a moment.

B

- Before the class, make as many photocopies as there will be groups of four, and cut them up.

- With the whole class, explain the situation. Divide the class into groups of four and hand out the role cards. Ask the HR manager in each group to chair the meeting, as well as give their own opinions.

- Give students time to prepare for their roles and assist them if necessary.

- Start the role play in parallel groups. Circulate and monitor. Note down language points for praise and correction afterwards, especially in relation to meetings language.

- When the groups have finished, bring the class to order. Praise strong language points and work on half a dozen points that need improving, getting students to say the correct forms.

- Ask a representative of each group of four for the outcome of their meeting.

- Get one or two of the groups to do a public performance for the whole class, incorporating your improvements.

Unit 5 Stress

Participating in discussions

A

- Get students to look again at the discussion language in the Useful language box on page 49 of the Course Book. Then get them to close their books.

- Get students to do the exercise in pairs or with the whole class.

- Go through the answers with the whole class. Explain any difficulties.

1 c, e   2 d, h   3 a, g   4 b, f

B

- Before the class, make as many photocopies as there will be groups of three, and cut them up.

- With the whole class, explain the situation. Divide the class into groups of three and hand out the role cards. Tell the chief executive in each group that they will be chairing/leading the meeting.

- Give students time to prepare for their roles and assist them if necessary.

- Start the role play in parallel groups. Circulate and monitor. Note down language points for praise and correction afterwards, especially in relation to discussion language.

- When the groups have finished, bring the class to order. Praise strong language points and work on half a dozen points that need improving, getting students to say the correct forms.

- Ask a representative of each group of three for the outcome of their meeting.

- Get one or two of the groups to do a public performance of all or part of their role play, incorporating your improvements.

Unit 6 Entertaining

Socialising: greetings and small talk

A

- Get students to look again at the socialising language in the Useful language box on page 57 of the Course Book. Then get them to close their books.

- Get students to do the exercise in pairs or with the whole class.

- Go through the answers with the whole class. Explain any difficulties and work on intonation and pronunciation.

> **1** b **2** a **3** a **4** b **5** a **6** b **7** b

B

- Before the class, make two copies of the activity for each pair. Cut up the 'turns' in one of the copies for each pair. Keep the other copy intact as a key to hand out to students after the activity.

- Divide the class into pairs, hand out the cut-up version and explain the task: they have to put the turns into a logical order.

- Circulate, monitor and assist if necessary, but don't interrupt the pairs if they are functioning acceptably.

- When most pairs have finished the task, hand out the complete copies so that students can check their answers.

- Get pairs to read the conversation in parallel. Circulate, monitor and assist if necessary.

- Work on any remaining difficulties.

- Get one or two of the pairs to do a public performance for the whole class.

Unit 7 New business

Dealing with numbers

A

- This exercise revises and extends the numbers language on page 71 of the Course Book.

- Explain the exercise to the whole class and demonstrate the first exchange using the example given, with you taking part A and a student taking part B.

- Get students to do the rest of the exercise in pairs. They should alternate for each item, so that Student A reads item 1 and B responds, then B reads item 2 with A responding, and so on.

- Circulate, monitor and assist if necessary, but don't interrupt the pairs if they are functioning acceptably. (If necessary, explain that 'GNP' means 'gross national product' – the total value of all the goods and services produced in a country in a year.)

- When the pairs have finished, bring the class to order. Get different pairs to do the exchanges again to the whole class.

> **1** A: The population of Colombia is forty-five million, nine hundred and twenty-five thousand, three hundred and ninety-seven.
>
> B: So the population of Colombia is about forty-six million.
>
> **2** A: The GNP of Colombia last year was two hundred and forty-three point eight billion US dollars.
>
> B: So the GNP of Colombia is just under two hundred and forty-four billion US dollars.
>
> **3** A: There are two thousand and forty-four Colombian pesos to the US dollar.
>
> B: So there are just over two thousand pesos to the dollar.
>
> **4** A: Inflation over the last five years has been five point two per cent per year on average.
>
> B: So inflation over the last five years has been just over five per cent on average.
>
> **5** A: Thirty-eight per cent of Colombia's exports went to the US last year.
>
> B: So just under forty per cent of Colombia's exports went to the US last year.
>
> **6** A: There are eighty point seven televisions per (one) hundred households.
>
> B: So there are approximately eighty-one televisions per (one) hundred households.
>
> **7** A: There are ninety-one point nine mobile phones per (one) hundred people.
>
> B: So there are roughly ninety-two phones per (one) hundred people.

B

- Before the class, make as many photocopies as there are pairs.

- The idea here is for students to exchange information about the economies of two countries: China and the US.

- Tell your students to work in pairs. Hand out the information.

- Start the activity. Circulate, monitor and assist if necessary. Note down language points for praise and correction later, especially in relation to numbers.

- When the pairs have finished, bring the class to order. Praise strong language points and work on half a dozen points that need improving, getting students to say the correct forms.

- Then get one student to read out the information they obtained about China, and another the information they obtained about the US.

- Check the answers with the whole class.

	China	United States
Population	1.34 billion	308.8 million
Average age	34.2 years	36.6 years
GDP	$4,327 billion	$14,093 billion
GDP per head	$5,970	$46,350
Doctors per 1,000 population	1.5	2.7
Hospital beds per 1,000 population	2.2	3.1
TVs per 100 households	96.1	98.9
Computers per 100 people	5.7	80.3
Mobile phones per 100 people	48	86.8

Unit 8 Marketing

Telephoning: exchanging information

A

- This is a continuation of the situation in Unit 1, Exercise B.

- Before the class, make two copies of the activity for each pair. Cut up the 'turns' in one of the copies for each pair. Keep the other copy intact as a key to hand out to students after the activity.

- Before doing the activity, get students to look again at the telephoning language on page 79 of the Course Book, particularly the international spelling alphabet in Exercise C. Then get them to close their books.

- Divide the class into pairs, hand out the cut-up version and explain the task: they have to put the turns into a logical order.

- Circulate, monitor and assist if necessary, but don't interrupt the pairs if they are functioning acceptably.

- When most pairs have finished the task, hand out the complete copies so that students can check their answers.

- Work with the whole class on the intonation of the phone expressions and on the international spelling alphabet. Remind students, if they have forgotten, about rising intonation on groups of phone numbers, except the last group, which has falling intonation. Remind them also about 'double seven', 'double three', etc.

- Get pairs to read the conversation in parallel. Circulate, monitor and assist if necessary.

- Work on any remaining difficulties.

- Get one or two of the pairs to do a public performance for the whole class.

Unit 9 Planning

Meetings: interrupting and clarifying

A

- Get students to look again at the meetings language in the Useful language box on page 87 of the Course Book. Then get them to close their books.

- Get students to do the exercise in pairs or with the whole class.

- Go through the answers with the whole class. Explain any difficulties.

1 just	**2** Hold	**3** Sorry	**4** you'll	**5** may
6 mean	**7** exactly	**8** saying		

B

- Before the class, make as many photocopies as there will be groups of four and cut them up.

- With the whole class, explain the situation. Divide the class into groups of four and hand out the role cards. In each group, choose a self-confident student to be Sam Rogerson and chair/lead the meeting.

- Give students time to prepare for their roles and assist them if necessary.

- When they are ready, start the role play in parallel groups. The chair should open the meeting.

- Circulate and monitor. Note down language points for praise and correction afterwards.

- When the groups have finished, bring the class to order. Praise strong language points and work on half a dozen points that need improving, getting students to say the correct forms.

- Ask a representative of each group of four to say what happened in the role play and what the outcome was. Contrast the different outcomes and encourage discussion.

Unit 10 Managing people

Socialising and entertaining

A

- Get students to look again at the socialising language in the Useful language box on page 101 of the Course Book. Then get them to close their books.

- Do the exercise with the whole class as a quick-fire activity and work on any difficulties. Practise pronunciation and intonation of the expressions.

> **1** b, f   **2** d, h   **3** c, e   **4** a, g

B

- Before the class, make as many photocopies as there are students in the class. (A and B in each pair both get the complete structure of the conversation, not just their own part.)

- With the whole class, explain the task and any difficulties (e.g. *awkward silence*). Then demonstrate the task by doing the first few exchanges with a student.

- Divide the class into pairs and give each student a photocopy. Then get students in parallel pairs to construct the conversation.

- Circulate and monitor. Note down language points for praise and correction afterwards.

- When the pairs have finished, bring the class to order. Praise strong language points and work on half a dozen points that need improving, getting students to say the correct forms.

- Get two or three of the pairs to do a public performance for the whole class, incorporating your improvements.

Unit 11 Conflict

Negotiating: dealing with conflict

A

- Get students to look again at the negotiating language in the Useful language box on page 109 of the Course Book. Then get them to close their books.

- Do the exercise with the whole class as a quick-fire activity and work on any difficulties. Practise stress and intonation of the expressions.

1	I see <u>what</u> you mean.
2	Why don't we <u>come</u> back to that later?
3	Let's come back <u>with</u> some fresh ideas after the break.
4	I'd like to make <u>a</u> suggestion.
5	Let's look <u>at</u> this another way.
6	Another possibility <u>is</u> to rethink the specifications.
7	Let's see <u>what</u> we've got.
8	Can I go <u>over</u> what we've agreed?
9	Let's <u>go</u> over the main points again.
10	We've got <u>a</u> deal.

B

- Before the class, make as many photocopies of the role cards as there will be pairs, and cut them up.

- With the whole class, explain the situation. Point out that they will role-play the final part of the negotiation. Divide the class into pairs and hand out the role cards.

- Give students time to prepare for their roles and assist them if necessary.

- Start the role play in parallel pairs. Circulate and monitor. Note language points for praise and correction, especially in relation to negotiating language.

- When pairs have finished, bring the class to order. Praise strong language points and work on half a dozen points that need improving, getting students to say the correct forms.

- Then get one student from each pair to say what the outcome of their negotiation was.

Unit 12 Products

Presenting a product

A

- Get students to look again at the product language in the Useful language box on page 117 of the Course Book. Then get them to close their books.

- Do the exercise with the whole class as a quick-fire activity, resolving any problems and working on pronunciation where necessary. (At this Pre-intermediate level, you can treat *robust*/*sturdy* and *flexible*/*versatile* as meaning the same thing. However, you could get your more dictionary-minded students to look at the *Longman Active Study Dictionary*, for example.)

> **1** b   **2** c   **3** a   **4** e   **5** f   **6** d   **7** d   **8** b
> **9** g   **10** c

B

- Point out to students that this exercise extends the expressions in the Useful language box on page 117 of the Course Book.

- Get students to do the exercise in pairs and then check the answers with the whole class.

1 c   2 f   3 b   4 a   5 d   6 e

C

- Before the class, make one photocopy and cut up the panel with the products so that you have a product for each group of three students. (In large classes, you can make several copies – more than one group will give a presentation about each product.)

- With the whole class, explain that they are going to do a presentation like the one they did in Skills, Exercise C on page 117 of the Course Book. Divide the class into groups of three and give each group a different product.

- Circulate, monitor and assist if necessary, but don't interrupt the groups if they are functioning acceptably. Note down language points for praise and correction afterwards, especially in relation to presentation language.

- When the groups have finished, bring the class to order. Work on any language that has been causing problems, especially in the areas covered by Exercises A and B.

- Get one member of each group to give a presentation of their product.

Careers

TELEPHONING: MAKING CONTACT

A There is one word missing in each of the expressions below. Put the missing word into each expression.

1 Could I speak Ken Wu, please?
2 This Pedro Casas in Buenos Aires.
3 I'm calling our latest order.
4 Could you transfer to the production department, please?
5 Could you ask him call me back?
6 Can I leave message, please?
7 Could you tell what it's about?
8 I'll put through.
9 Can I get him call you?
10 I can transfer to his voicemail.

B Work in pairs. Rearrange the two parts of this phone conversation into a logical order.

A Hello.

B Hello. Is this Kiev Agro?

A Yes, that's right.

B Could I speak to Ludmila Sharapova, please?

A Who's calling, please?

B Anton Schmidt at EFG Chemicals in Dresden.

A Could you tell me what it's about?

B I'm a supplier and I'm calling about our contract.

A I'll put you through ... I'm afraid there's no answer. Can I get her to call you?

B Yes, please. She has my number, I think, but here it is just in case: 00 49 351 ...

A 00 49 351 ...

B 489 00 01.

A 00 49 351 489 00 01.

B That's it. Could you get her to call me back as soon as possible. It's very urgent.

A OK, no problem. I'll do that. Goodbye.

B Thanks. Goodbye.

Companies

PRESENTING YOUR COMPANY

A Match each of the headings (1–6) to one of the expressions (a–f).

1 Introducing yourself
2 Stating your aim
3 Outlining the presentation
4 Introducing new information
5 Changing to a new section of the talk
6 Ending the presentation

a) Here are some key figures on our amazing growth over the last five years.

b) That's it for today. Thank you very much.

c) My name's Katie Woo and I'm Head of Marketing here at Fragrant Perfumes.

d) My talk is divided into four parts.

e) I'm here to tell you about our exciting new products to be launched next year.

f) That's all I have time for on lipstick. I'll move on now to shampoo.

B Work in groups of three. The directors of three new Internet start-ups make presentations about their companies to possible investors. You are one of the directors. Use the notes to make a presentation about your company.

	Linkalot	Vidcall	Source-it
Based	Hoxton, London	Stockholm, Sweden	Riga, Latvia
Nature of site	Social networking	Video calls using the Internet	Putting suppliers and buyers in touch with each other
Users	Young professionals aged 25–40	Businesses and individual consumers	Businesses in cars, electronics and construction
Current source of investment	Friends and family	Loan from a Swedish bank	Grant from (=money given by) the European Union
Amount already invested	€200,000	€550,000	€1.1 million
Purpose of new investment	Employ 10 new programmers	Develop new video technologies	Move into a bigger building with the most up-to-date equipment
Amount required	€1 million	€1.5 million	€1.9 million

Selling

NEGOTIATING: REACHING AGREEMENT

A Correct these expressions, using the same number of words.

1 We're interested to buy five of your machines.
2 We'd liked to get the first deliver in November.
3 We must got a better price that the one you are offering.
4 We could possible gave you a discount of five per cent.
5 We can do that, providing to made a down payment.
6 Unfortunately, we aren't agree for that.
7 If it work, we'll increased the order later.
8 That sound a fairly price to me.
9 Good, I think we're cover all.
10 Right, we're get a deal.

B Work in pairs. Student A is the production manager at a car company and wants to buy some robots. Student B is the sales representative for a company that makes industrial robots. Role-play the negotiation.

The production manager wants at least 12 robots, but is open to the idea of buying more. The sales representative should try to persuade him/her to do this, talking about the benefits of robots in relation to human workers (cheaper, more accurate, they don't take time off, etc.).

Negotiate the number of robots to be bought and the discount to be given.

During the role play, try to use one expression relating to each of the types (1–6).

1 Stating aims
2 Making concessions
3 Rejecting suggestions
4 Bargaining
5 Getting agreement
6 Finishing the negotiation

RESOURCE BANK – Speaking

Student A: Production manager	Student B: Sales representative
Discount objectives:	Discounts you can offer:
10–15 robots: 15% discount	10–15 robots: 10% discount
16–20 robots: 20%	16–20 robots: 15%
20–29 robots: 25%	20–29 robots: 20%
30 robots or more: 30%	30 robots or more: 25%

SUCCESSFUL MEETINGS

RESOURCE BANK – Speaking

A Cross out the extra unnecessary word in each of these expressions.

Chair/lead

1 Can we go start, please?   (*Beginning the meeting*)
2 Right, let's to begin.   (*Beginning the meeting*)
3 The main purpose of this here meeting is to …   (*Stating the aim*)
4 What do you to think?   (*Asking for comments*)
5 The next thing to go discuss is …   (*Changing the subject*)

Participants

6 I'm in the favour of …   (*Giving opinions*)
7 Perhaps we will should …   (*Making suggestions*)
8 I totally am agree.   (*Agreeing*)
9 I don't know round about that.   (*Disagreeing*)
10 Hold on up a moment.   (*Interrupting*)

B Work in groups of four. A company's human resources (HR) manager holds a meeting with three employee representatives from different parts of the company: production workers, sales force and general admin staff.

The purpose of the meeting is to discuss improvements to employee facilities and benefits – see the list below. They have already agreed to spend a maximum of €70,000 for the year. Chair or participate in the meeting and try to persuade the others to agree to the repairs and improvements that you want. Use the expressions above and others you know.

> Company to pay more towards cost of meals in company restaurant – €20,000
>
> Build roof over cycle parking area and make it more secure against thieves – €5,000
>
> Company cars: Volvos to be used instead of current make – €150,000
>
> Build an in-house company gym – €35,000
>
> Improve furniture and lighting in offices – €10,000

HR manager

You lead the meeting.

You have no particular priorities for spending the budget, but you want as many employees as possible to benefit.

Production staff representative

Your colleagues are most interested in reductions to the cost of meals in the restaurant.

They are not keen on the other improvements, except those for the cycle parking area.

Sales force representative

The restaurant, gym and office improvements are not important for your colleagues, as they are out most of the time visiting clients. Likewise, the cycle area improvement is of no interest to them, as they go everywhere by car.

Your colleagues are very keen on better cars for company employees.

General admin staff representative

Your colleagues like the idea of making the restaurant cheaper, the cycle parking area and improved furniture and lighting.

None of them has a company car as they never travel on business, so this is of no interest to them.

PARTICIPATING IN DISCUSSIONS

A Three company executives are discussing the possibility of moving the company's production abroad to a cheaper location. Group the expressions they use (a–h) under the headings (1–4).

1 Making suggestions   2 Giving opinions   3 Agreeing   4 Disagreeing

a) Excellent idea – lower costs will mean higher profits.

b) I'm not sure it's a good idea – quality will suffer.

c) Why don't we move production somewhere cheaper?

d) It would lower costs in the short run, but what about the long run?

e) It might be a good idea to bring in consultants who specialise in this.

f) I can't agree with you there. No one understands our business as well as we do ourselves.

g) I agree with the idea of using consultants – I know of a consultancy that specialises in this.

h) We've got to do something to lower costs.

B Work in groups of three. You are one of the executives at the company in Exercise A above. Role-play the meeting and discuss the advantages and disadvantages of moving production abroad. Use appropriate expressions from above and others you know.

Chief Executive (Chair/lead)

You want to reduce costs, but you are worried about the possibility that quality, for which your company is famous, will not be as good if you move production abroad.

You are open to arguments from both your colleagues.

Tell the Production Manager that he will not be forced to leave the company if production moves abroad: he will move to a higher-paid job at company headquarters.

Finance Director

You want to reduce costs above all else – you are not worried that quality standards may fall.

You want to move production abroad as quickly as possible, without taking the time to use consultants. You are willing to get on a plane tomorrow to go and look at possible suitable locations!

Production Manager

You joined the company as a 17-year-old production worker and you have risen to become Production Manager.

You don't want production to move abroad as your production workers would lose their jobs.

You think you will lose your job if production moves abroad.

RESOURCE BANK – Speaking

Entertaining

SOCIALISING: GREETINGS AND SMALL TALK

A Choose the more suitable response, a or b, to each of the expressions (1–7).

1 Leonora, do you know Antonio?
 a) No way.
 b) No, I don't think we've met.

2 Nice to meet you.
 a) Pleased to meet you.
 b) Fine, thanks.

3 How's business?
 a) Not too bad, actually.
 b) It's none of your business.

4 Have you heard the news about our latest product?
 a) No, and I don't want to.
 b) No, tell me all about it.

5 Could I use one of your PCs to check my e-mail?
 a) Of course. You can use this one.
 b) If you insist, but don't be too long.

6 I'm afraid I missed the name of your company.
 a) I'll say it just once more. This time, pay attention.
 b) It's Zeta Industries. That's Z – E – T – A.

7 Would you like to have lunch somewhere?
 a) Why?
 b) Sounds good. I'll just get my coat.

B Work in pairs. This conversation takes place over a business lunch. Rearrange the two parts into a logical conversation.

A The menu looks interesting. What's the salmon like here?

B Pretty good. I had it last night.

A OK, I think I'll go for the salmon.

B And I'm going to have the steak.

A That's decided then – steak for you and salmon for me. Is this your first time in Ljubljana?

B I was here in Slovenia a couple of years ago on a family skiing holiday, but I can't really say that I know Ljubljana. What I've seen of it so far looks great.

A How's business?

B We're having a great spring. Spring is our busiest time of year, of course. How about you?

A Things are a bit slow at the moment – could be better. But we have some great new products coming through so it should pick up in the autumn.

New business

DEALING WITH NUMBERS

A   Work in pairs. Student A reads each expression (1–8) and Student B expresses the same information using the word(s) and number given.

Example   A: *The population of Colombia is forty-five million, nine hundred and twenty-five thousand, three hundred and ninety-seven.*

B: *So the population of Colombia is about forty-six million.*

Student A

1   The population of Colombia is 45,925,397.

2   The GNP of Colombia last year was USD243.8 billion.

3   There are 2,044 Colombian pesos to the US dollar.

4   Inflation over the last five years has been 5.2% per year on average.

5   38% of Colombia's exports went to the US last year.

6   There are 80.7 televisions per 100 households.

7   There are 91.9 mobile phones per 100 people.

Student B

about / million

just under / billion

just over / thousand

just over / five

just under / forty

approximately / eighty-one

roughly / ninety-two

B   Work in pairs. Student A has information about China. Student B has information about the US. Communicate this information to each other.

Student A

	China	United States
Population	1.34 billion	
Average age	34.2 years	
GDP	$4,327 billion	
GDP per head	$5,970	
Doctors per 1,000 population	1.5	
Hospital beds per 1,000 population	2.2	
TVs per 100 households	96.1	
Computers per 100 people	5.7	
Mobile phones per 100 people	48	

Student B

	China	United States
Population		308.8 million
Average age		36.6 years
GDP		$14,093 billion
GDP per head		$46,350
Doctors per 1,000 population		2.7
Hospital beds per 1,000 population		3.1
TVs per 100 households		98.9
Computers per 100 people		80.3
Mobile phones per 100 people		86.8

Marketing

TELEPHONING: EXCHANGING INFORMATION

A Work in pairs. Rearrange the two parts of this phone conversation into a logical order.

A Hello.

B Can I speak to Ludmila Sharapova, please?

A Speaking.

B This is Anton Schmidt at EFG Chemicals in Dresden.

A Hello Anton, how are you?

B Fine. Good to talk to you – I've been trying to get hold of you for nearly a week.

A I've been away at a conference in Tokyo.

B Oh, right. I'm phoning about our contract. We need to start thinking about renewal – it's due for renewal next January.

A You should really talk to one of our salespeople about that – I'm just on the technical side.

B Who do you suggest?

A There's a new sales guy responsible for Germany. His name is Mikael Vasiliyev.

B How do you spell that?

A Like Michael, but with a K; Vasiliyev – V – A – S – I – L – I – Y – E – V.

B Is the first letter B or V – is that B for Bravo or V for Victor?

A V for Victor. And his direct line, dialling from Germany, is 00 380 44 …

B 00 380 44 …

A 977 8933.

B 977 8933. Thanks, Ludmila. I'll give him a call. It was nice talking to you. See you soon at a conference, I hope.

A Me too. Bye for now.

B Bye.

MEETINGS: INTERRUPTING AND CLARIFYING

A Complete these expressions with the words from the box.

| you'll | Sorry | may | Hold | saying | just | mean | exactly |

1 Could I .... comment on that?   (*Interrupting*)
2 .... on a minute.   (*Interrupting*)
3 .... to interrupt, but ...   (*Interrupting*)
4 If .... just let me finish ...   (*Dealing with interruptions*)
5 I'd like to finish, if I ....   (*Dealing with interruptions*)
6 How do you .... exactly?   (*Clarifying*)
7 What .... do you mean by ...   (*Clarifying*)
8 So what you're .... is that ...   (*Clarifying*)

B Work in groups of four. Rogerson Piccolo Vorster (RPV) is an architecture firm named for the three directors who founded it after they left architecture school together 35 years ago. They now want to retire. They must decide whether to a) sell the firm to outsiders, b) sell the firm to younger colleagues (called 'associates') or c) close the firm completely. Role-play this meeting, using the expressions above and others you know.

Sam Rogerson

RPV has a record of designing great buildings and you want to sell the firm to outsiders, for example another architectural firm, or even an engineering company, who could continue this work.

You think that any buyer will want to maintain the high reputation of the firm for designing exciting buildings.

Renzo Piccolo

You want RPV to be sold to some of the current associates. You trust these associates to continue the high reputation of the firm.

Outside owners would destroy its reputation, or at least not maintain it, and you would have no control over what it does in the future.

Dietrich Vorster

You want to close the firm completely.

Your personal reputation as an architect will suffer if the firm continues under new ownership. You do not want to see your name used in connection with new buildings which you have not designed.

Representative of the associates

You want to buy RPV from the current directors and continue to run it under the same name, so as to continue to benefit from the reputation they have built.

You promise to maintain the firm's great reputation, and to continue to consult the current owners on issues that you know are important to them.

RESOURCE BANK – Speaking

Managing people

SOCIALISING AND ENTERTAINING

A   Group the expressions (a–h) under the headings (1–4).

1   Making excuses
2   Saying goodbye/thanking

3   Making conversation
4   Networking

a)   I think I know someone who might be able to help you.

b)   It's very kind of you, but I must get to the airport for my flight.

c)   Have you been on holiday this summer yet?

d)   It was very kind of you to take me to that great restaurant yesterday. It was fantastic!

e)   Do you have children?

f)   That was delicious, but I couldn't eat anything more, thanks.

g)   You could mention my name when you contact them.

h)   Nice seeing you. Hope to see you in Dallas some time.

B   Work in pairs. Student A, you are a supplier visiting a possible new customer. Student B, you are the customer. Student B has picked up Student A from the airport and is taking him/her to his/her hotel. Use the prompts to have a conversation.

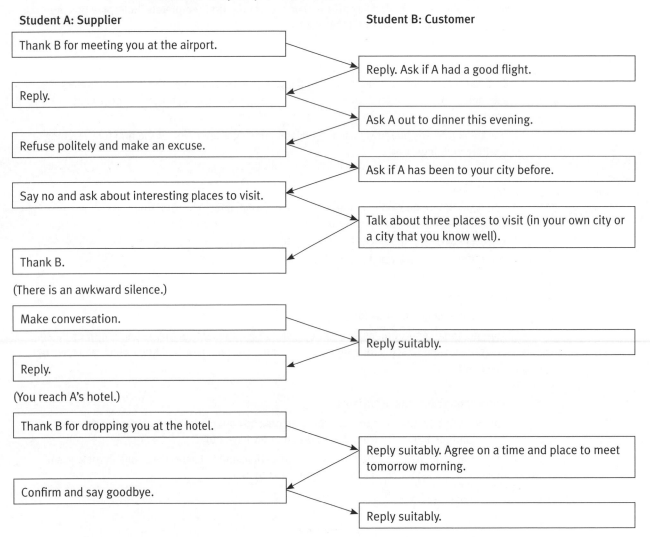

Student A: Supplier

Thank B for meeting you at the airport.

Reply.

Refuse politely and make an excuse.

Say no and ask about interesting places to visit.

Thank B.

(There is an awkward silence.)

Make conversation.

Reply.

(You reach A's hotel.)

Thank B for dropping you at the hotel.

Confirm and say goodbye.

Student B: Customer

Reply. Ask if A had a good flight.

Ask A out to dinner this evening.

Ask if A has been to your city before.

Talk about three places to visit (in your own city or a city that you know well).

Reply suitably.

Reply suitably. Agree on a time and place to meet tomorrow morning.

Reply suitably.

NEGOTIATING: DEALING WITH CONFLICT

A There is one word missing in each of the expressions below. Put the missing word into each expression.

Calming down

1 I see you mean.

2 Why don't we back to that later?

3 Let's come back some fresh ideas after the break.

Creating solutions

4 I'd like to make suggestion.

5 Let's look this another way.

6 Another possibility to rethink the specifications.

Closing a negotiation

7 Let's see we've got.

8 Can I go what we've agreed?

9 Let's over the main points again.

10 We've got deal.

B Work in pairs and role-play this negotiation. Student A is a Chinese supplier of woks (= large frying pans). Student B is a buyer for a chain of kitchen equipment stores in the US. After a day of negotiations, A and B have provisionally agreed the following. However, neither side is happy with this situation.

Price for the first batch of 1,000 woks	Discount for each batch of 1,000 woks thereafter	Delivery	Payment terms
5,100 yuan	1.5 per cent	6 weeks	20 per cent up front, the rest 60 days later

✂

Student A: Supplier

These were your objectives when you started the negotiation:

Price for the first batch of 1,000 woks	Discount for each batch of 1,000 woks thereafter	Delivery	Payment terms
5,500 yuan	1 per cent	10 weeks	30 per cent up front, the rest 30 days later

Before you agree to a final deal, you want to get two concessions from the buyer in the areas above.

First, outline what the current position is. Then negotiate two final concessions from the buyer so as to reach a deal that is closer to your original objectives.

✂

Student B: Buyer

These were your objectives when you started the negotiation:

Price for the first batch of 1,000 woks	Discount for each batch of 1,000 woks thereafter	Delivery	Payment terms
4,700 yuan	2 per cent	3 weeks	10 per cent up front, the rest 90 days later

After the supplier has outlined the current position, negotiate two final concessions from the supplier so as to reach a deal that is closer to your original objectives.

PRESENTING A PRODUCT

A Match the words (1–10) to their definitions (a–g) in the context of talking about products. Three of the definitions have two words each.

1	elegant	**a)**	a lot of people like it
2	flexible	**b)**	beautiful, attractive, graceful
3	popular	**c)**	can be used for many different purposes
4	practical	**d)**	strong, well-made and not easily broken
5	reliable	**e)**	easy to use, clean, maintain, etc.
6	robust	**f)**	always works well and does not break down easily
7	sturdy	**g)**	being the only one of its kind
8	stylish		
9	unique		
10	versatile		

B Match each of the headings (1–6) with one of the expressions (a–f).

1	Introducing the product	**a)**	Its unique selling point – its USP – is its extremely low price.
2	Describing the product	**b)**	You can use it in three different ways.
3	Stating the product's uses	**c)**	I'm going to tell you about an exciting new product.
4	Listing selling points	**d)**	Its three key benefits are speed, safety and economy.
5	Referring to benefits	**e)**	Questions, anyone?
6	Inviting questions	**f)**	It's 20 cm long, 12 cm wide and 1 cm thick.

C Work in groups of three. Prepare a mini-presentation about a product, using the expressions in Exercises A and B above and others you know.

tablet computer (e.g. iPad)	ergonomic chair (= one that's designed to prevent pain in your back, arms, etc.)	electric car
executive jet	smartphone (e.g. Blackberry)	business suit made of a new type of material

Careers

A 🔊 CD1.4 **Listen to part one and match the two parts of these expressions.**

1	finance	channels
2	television	channels
3	music	business
4	children's	business
5	movie	channels
6	chocolate-pudding	director

B **Now put the expressions from Exercise A into these groups.**

   a) TV programmes   **b)** jobs   **c)** types of company

C 🔊 CD1.4, 1.5 **Listen to parts one and two and replace the verbs in italic with infinitive forms of verbs that Melissa Foux actually uses. (One of the verbs she uses is a multiword verb.)**

1 *transfer* from sector to sector
2 *do* a subject at university
3 *perform* an internship
4 *gain* an understanding of something
5 *begin* as an auditor
6 *obtain* a job

D 🔊 CD1.6, 1.7 **Listen to parts three and four. Choose the correct alternative to replace the expression in italic so as to keep the closest meaning.**

1 … I think the thing that stands out is, really, not to *overcomplicate things*.
   a) make things easier   **b)** make things too difficult   **c)** keep things the same

2 Especially in the finance world, people can get *bogged down in* a lot of detail, …
   a) up to their ankles in   **b)** tiring out by   **c)** overloaded with

3 … and it's important to try and *maintain clarity* and always be able to see above all the numbers …
   a) keep things clear   **b)** keep things interesting   **c)** keep things difficult

4 What I found, in *coming across* people who have applied for positions in the companies I've worked in, …
   a) meeting   **b)** interviewing   **c)** employing

5 … is the key difference is, people who've done a lot of research on the companies that they've *applied to*.
   a) asked for more information about
   b) asked to join
   c) asked to leave

6 So I say, research is *the key*.
   a) the least important thing
   b) one of the most important things
   c) the most important thing

Companies

SUSAN BARRATT, CEO, NATURE'S WAY FOODS

A ◀)) CD1.18 **Listen to part one and find the following.**

1   an adjective meaning *cold* or *cooled*
2   a four-word expression meaning *most of which*
3   a word that means *different*
4   a word for what food is wrapped in
5   a two-word expression used for the chains in item 6 below
6   the names of three supermarket chains that sell food to consumers
7   a three-word expression that includes the chain in item 8 below
8   the name of a fast-food restaurant chain

B ◀)) CD1.19 **Listen to part two and complete the table with words that Susan Barratt uses.**

noun	adjective
	healthy
	convenient
	sustainable
	indulgent
efficiency	

C **Match the adjectives in Exercise B to their meanings in this context.**

a)   easy to prepare, use, etc.
b)   using the least possible amount of time, effort, money, etc.
c)   allowing someone to eat something that tastes good but may be unhealthy
d)   able to continue into the future
e)   good for your body

D ◀)) CD1.20 **Listen to part three. Which of these things does Susan Barratt mention?**

Someone who runs a company ...
1   should set strategy
2   should set clear goals
3   should be an expert in accountancy and finance
4   should get people to work together as a team
5   should socialise with their team at weekends
6   might suffer from the fact that they are continuously responsible for different things
7   might get lonely
8   must make some decisions on their own

Selling

A ◀)) CD1.28 **Listen to part one and match the three parts of these expressions.**

1	We sell products	to	... the television and online
2	... we sell	through	a wide variety of categories ...
3	... we sell both	across	consumers in Germany, Japan, USA, UK and Italy

B ◀)) CD1.29 **Complete these statements with appropriate forms of verbs from part two.**

If you ...

1 .... a product, you show how it is used, etc.

2 .... a sales presentation, you talk about a product or a number of products to an audience.

3 .... with your audience, you understand their needs and talk to them in ways they can relate to.

4 .... a sales pitch, you work on ways of talking about a product to possible customers in a way that will make them want to buy it.

5 .... a product inside and out, you know it very well.

C ◀)) CD1.30 **Listen to this extract from part three and replace the eight mistakes in the transcript below with what Sue Leeson actually says.**

We have many successful product areas. One of our most successful is beauty. Beauty works so well on TV for two reasons. First of all, each beauty brand has a terrific story behind it, and we can really bring life to the brand and to the sales pitch through telling that story in a very attractive way.

And secondly, each product is very easy to present. So if it's a skincare product, like a moisturiser, we can show how to apply it, the quantity to apply in order to give the best effects. Finally, we add another layer to our product presentation in that we always invite the expert behind that product to tell the story.

D ◀)) CD1.31 **Listen to part four and find words that mean the following.**

1	on the Internet	o _ _ _ _ _
2	changed	a _ _ _ _ _ _
3	terrific	f _ _ _ _ _ _ _ _
4	chance	o _ _ _ _ _ _ _ _ _ _
5	product	i _ _ _
6	picture	i _ _ _ _
7	catalogue	r _ _ _ _

Great ideas

DR KATE PITTS, RESEARCHER, E-RESEARCH CENTRE, UNIVERSITY OF OXFORD

A ◀)) CD1.39 **Listen to part one. Are these statements true or false?**

1   eBay is useful for large companies.
2   eBay provides a way to reach markets that is new.
3   Auctions are new.
4   Kate Pitts talks about USB sticks in relation to data and pictures.
5   She also mentions plug-and-play devices.
6   USB sticks have had no effect on other devices.
7   Digital cameras were certainly invented in the last 15 years.

B ◀)) CD1.39 **Listen to part one again and complete the table with words that Kate Pitts uses.**

verb (infinitive)	noun
boom	
turn over	
auction	
	transfer
demand	
	transport
benefit	
	satisfaction
invent	
	revolution

C ◀)) CD1.40 **Listen to part two. In which order do you hear these adverbs?**

a) actually
b) differently
c) nearly
d) slightly
e) strongly

D **Now match the adverbs above to their meanings.**

1   almost
2   really
3   a bit
4   firmly
5   in another way

Stress

JESSICA COLLING, DIRECTOR OF MARKETING AT VIELIFE

A ◀)) CD1.43 **Listen to part one and complete the transcript.**

There are lots of things that can make people feel ....[1] pressure
.... [2] work – for example, having too much to do, not feeling ....[3]
control, and also not having good relationships ....[4] the people that they work
........................[5]. All of these things can build ....[6], and when pressure gets too
much, it spills ....[7] ....[8] feelings of stress.

B ◀)) CD1.44 **Listen to part two. Are these statements true or false?**

1 The interviewer asks about levels of stress that can be considered normal.

2 Jessica Colling says that it's easy to say what a normal level of stress is.

3 What one person finds motivating, another person might find stressful.

4 Pressure and stress are the same thing.

5 Not everyone can manage high levels of stress over long periods.

6 If you manage stress well over a long period, you may start to suffer from it, but not badly.

C ◀)) CD1.45 **Listen to part three. Choose the correct alternative to replace the expression in italic so as to keep the closest meaning.**

1 How can companies help their staff to *achieve* a work–life balance?
   a) lose   **b)** search   **c)** find

2 Work–life balance is an interesting question, because ... everybody has a different *sense* of what works for them.
   a) idea   **b)** feel   **c)** sensation

3 However, companies can really help by being flexible in how they expect *staff* to work.
   a) directors   **b)** office workers   **c)** employees

4 ... if somebody doesn't like travelling in rush hour, you know, perhaps they could *come in* a little bit early ...
   a) enter work   **b)** get to work   **c)** return to work

5 And other examples might be, just *making sure* that people don't feel that they have to stay late, just because their boss is working late.
   a) assuring   **b)** ensuring   **c)** saving

D ◀)) CD1.46 **Complete these statements with appropriate forms of expressions from part four.**

If you ...

1 d........................ .... a problem, you think about it and try to solve it.

2 f........................ to do something, you often do it.

3 e........................ a feeling, you have it.

4 m........................ an activity, you are in charge of it.

5 l........................ .... children, you care for them.

6 r........................ a problem, you talk about it.

Entertaining

DR CHRIS BRUTON, CHIEF EXECUTIVE, CAVENDISH CONSULTANCY

A 🔊 CD1.51 **Listen to part one and replace the eight mistakes in the transcript below with what Chris Bruton actually says.**

The most popular events are still the major sports and the major events in those sports. Within sports it does vary. For example, those sports where the rules are fairly simple and obvious are more popular. Thus cricket, which is a personal, um, love of mine, is not actually one of the most popular, because the rules are fairly complex. Horse racing is a favourite, football – soccer as it's called in many countries around the world, but football in England – is very popular.

Car racing works well and then, moving onto the entertainment side, theatre, pop concerts, musicals – particularly, for many years, *Phantom of the Opera* has been very popular in New York and in London and in many other places around the world where it has showed.

B 🔊 CD1.52 **Complete these statements about what Chris Bruton says with appropriate forms of expressions from part two.**

1   Corporate entertainment is very different from what it was 30 years ago: it has
    c........................ e........................ .

2   Its quality is much, much better – it's v........................ s........................ .

3   The recent recession has had consequences for the financial sector – it has a........................
    the financial sector.

4   Financial firms have cut their budgets – they have r........................ them.

5   Financial firms have not g........................ f........................ cheaper events – they have
    just taken fewer people to the expensive ones.

6   The more expensive events have been less badly affected by the recession – they are
    h........................ u........................ better.

C 🔊 CD1.53 **Listen to part three. In what order does Chris Bruton mention these points?**

a) catering

b) umbrellas

c) aim

d) follow-up

e) planning

D 🔊 CD1.54 **Listen to part four. Are these statements true or false?**

1   Silverstone is 100 miles north-east of London.

2   Lewis Hamilton won the race.

3   Chris Bruton uses *helicopter* as a verb.

4   Heathrow is west of London.

5   Guests flew by small executive jet to Paris.

6   The plane that guests took did not fly faster than sound.

7   They stayed overnight in Paris.

New business

ABDIRASHID DUALE, CEO OF DAHABSHIILL

A ◄)) CD2.2, 2.3 **Listen to parts one and two and match the verbs with the expressions that follow them.**

1	transfer	that vision
2	send	their staff
3	have	money
4	reach	a vision
5	motivate	money
6	maintain	more profit
7	make	their relationship

B ◄)) CD2.3 **Complete these statements with appropriate forms of expressions from part two.**

1   If you have an idea about what something will be like in the future, you have a v _ _ _ _ _.

2   If your customers are l _ _ _ _ , they keep coming back to you.

3   I _ _ _ _ _ is the money you make from sales.

4   A customer's r _ _ _ _ _ _ _ _ _ _ are what he or she needs.

5   Satisfied customers are h _ _ _ _ customers.

6   A company's costs are its e _ _ _ _ _ _ _ _ _.

7   A b _ _ _ _ _ _ _ company is one that has gone out of business.

SUSAN BARRATT, CEO, NATURE'S WAY FOODS

C ◄)) CD2.4 **Listen to part three. Match the things that Susan Barratt mentions (1–6) with the quotations (a–f) from someone starting their own company.**

1	energy	a)	'I'm not going to give up easily.'
2	commitment	b)	'I never feel tired.'
3	making yourself different	c)	'We've carried out a big market survey.'
4	added value	d)	'We've got €100,000 in the bank in case there are any problems.'
5	understanding the market	e)	'We offer something that none of our competitors offer.'
6	cash	f)	'Our product will save customers €3,000 a year. Competing products only save customers about €1,000.'

D ◄)) CD2.4 **Listen to part three again and find adjectives that mean the following.**

1   not easy d _ _ _ _ _ _ _ _

2   not easy h _ _ _

3   very high s _ _ _ _ _ _ _ _ _ _

4   not the same d _ _ _ _ _ _ _

5   extremely important c _ _ _ _ _ _ _

6   enough s _ _ _ _ _ _ _ _

Marketing

RICHARD TURNER, EUROPEAN MARKETING MANAGER IN PHARMACEUTICALS

A 🔊 **CD2.16, 2.17** Listen to parts one and two and complete the table with words that Richard Turner uses.

noun	adjective
clinic	
reason	
tradition	
emotion	
regulation	
pharmaceuticals	
consistency	

B 🔊 **CD2.17** Complete the answers to these questions with expressions from part two.

In marketing pharmaceuticals, …

1 what is the biggest challenge? – It's the ....

2 are the laws weak? – No, they are quite ....

3 what is your main aim? – We want to help patients ....

4 how must you present your data? – In a ....

5 can you say that the product benefits are bigger than they really are? – No, we mustn't

   ....

6 do you use campaigns that say different things in different countries? – No, they are

   .... many different countries.

7 is it easy to know what to say in advertising? – No, it's a ....

C 🔊 **CD2.18** Listen to part three and replace the seven mistakes in the transcript below with what Richard Turner actually says.

Sadly, because of the regulatory laws that we need to obey, we're not able to promote directly to patients. We can only speak to the doctor, because the doctor makes the decision about the medicine. So, although we'd love to use all the advantages and opportunities that the Internet and the new communication methods offer, we're not able to use them as much as we'd like to do. That said, we are beginning … I think many companies are beginning to look at the possibilities that new technologies such as the iPhone may offer to present the data when we're face to face with the doctor, because it's a clearer and more involving way of presenting the data to the doctor than the traditional paper.

D 🔊 **CD2.19** Listen to part four. Are these statements about the words in italic that Richard Turner uses true or false?

1 Someone who works in science is a *scientific*.

2 Another word for 'doctor' is *physicist*.

3 Work to see if a drug is safe and effective is a *clinical trial*.

4 If you do a lot of work on something, you *spend a lot of effort* on it.

5 *Peak sales* is the time when a drug is just beginning to sell.

6 If there is a *patent* on a drug, other drug manufacturers cannot copy it.

Planning

A 🔊 CD2.30 **Listen to part one. Choose the correct alternative to replace the expression in italic so as to keep the closest meaning.**

1 If you're a business that has a commitment from a client for three years, you have a three-year contract, *it makes sense* to have a three-year plan, ...

   a) it's sensitive   **b)** it's sensational   **c)** it's sensible

2 ... because you can *project forward those revenues*, ...

   a) analyse sales   **b)** forecast sales   **c)** record sales

3 ... and you can *make some assumptions* about what you need to do as a business ...

   a) assume certain things   **b)** define certain things   **c)** respond to certain things

4 in order to deliver *the requirements of that contract.*

   a) what the contract writes   **b)** what the contract specifies   **c)** what that contract speaks

5 For a lot of smaller businesses, new businesses *entering* the market, ...

   a) continuing to sell in   **b)** starting to sell in   **c)** increasing their sales in

6 ... especially in technology for instance, when who knows what trends are going to *come into play* next month ...

   a) start playing the situation

   b) start influenced the situation

   c) start affecting the situation

B 🔊 CD2.30, 2.31 **Complete these statements with words from parts one and two that are related to the words in italic.**

If ...

1 you are *committed* to something, you have a .... to do it.

2 you have *contracted* to do something, you have a .... to do it.

3 you *relate* to someone in a particular way, you have a .... with them.

4 you can *manage* a task easily, it is ....

5 something has the characteristic of *simplicity*, it is ....

6 something has the characteristic of *flexibility*, it is ....

C 🔊 CD2.32 **Listen to part three. Are these statements true, false or is the information not given?**

1 Many business plans fail.

2 Entrepreneurs can forecast the future.

3 It's not necessarily bad if a business plan fails.

4 If a business idea doesn't work the first time, it should always be dropped.

5 The entrepreneur's successful business was completely unrelated to a previous version.

6 The business was based in Amsterdam.

7 When he was working on the first version, the entrepreneur saw the mistakes that would cause it to fail.

8 Failure can sometimes lead to success.

9 The entrepreneur is planning another new business.

Managing people

A ◀)) CD2.43 **Complete the table with appropriate forms of words from part one.**

verb (infinitive)	noun (singular)
.... [1]	influence [1]
manage	.... [2] (person) , ... [3] (thing)
pioneer	.... [4]
emphasise	.... [5]
control	.... [6]
profit	.... [7]
retail	.... [8]

B **Match the nouns above (1–8) to their meanings (a–h).**

a) a person or organisation that is the first to do something

b) selling to consumers rather than to other businesses

c) power to change other people's opinions, behaviour, etc.

d) the way organisations are structured, employees told what to do, etc.

e) the importance given to something in relation to something else

f) when you get more money from sales than you have spent

g) someone who tells employees what to do

h) the power to make decisions about how an organisation works

C ◀)) CD2.44 **Complete these statements with expressions from part two.**

1 The attitudes and beliefs that guide someone's behaviour together form their ph ....

2 Someone who starts a business is its f ....

3 Something that is real is g ....

4 Subjects, problems, etc. that are discussed are i ....

5 Moral ideas that guide your behaviour are your pr ....

6 Another word for 'help' is a ....

7 If you believe something strongly, you believe it f ....

8 Large amounts of money are s .... s ....

D ◀)) CD2.45 **Listen to part three. Match the issues (1–6) with the imaginary comments (a–f) made by employees working under one of the three managers mentioned.**

1	communication	a)	'He never shouts at people.'
2	involvement	b)	'When she says something, it's always so clear what she means!'
3	availability/visibility	c)	'He's a real hands-on type of manager.'
4	commitment	d)	'I think he will always do the best thing for all of us.'
5	respect/consideration	e)	'The door to her office is always open.'
6	trust	f)	'I want to do my best for the organisation.'

UNIT **11** Conflict

A ◀)) CD2.52 **Listen to part one and replace the seven mistakes in the transcript below with what Eileen Carroll actually says.**

Our organisation, the Centre for Effective Dispute Resolution, was funded 20 years ago. Its headquarters are in London, and its main activities are to teach business and make business more aware of more effective ways of dealing with disputes. And our two main areas of business are first, skills: so we've been active in training up to 40,000 mediators around the world. And we're also involved in supplying services. So we have mediators who mediate round the UK and round the world in business conflicts.

B ◀)) CD2.53 **Listen to part two. Match the issues (1–6) with imaginary comments (a–f) made by employees in an organisation.**

1 no communication
2 avoidance
3 sex discrimination
4 unfair work practices
5 clash of personalities
6 oppressive workloads

a) 'She's the best qualified person for the job, but they refuse to promote her.'
b) 'I just can't stand the sight of him – every discussion turns into an argument.'
c) 'Guillermo is doing exactly the same job as Alain, but as Alain was recruited a long time ago under a different contract, he gets paid twice as much.'
d) 'I get in at 7a.m. and I don't leave till 9 in the evening – day in, day out.'
e) 'Our manager communicates with us, but never about important issues.'
f) 'Our manager never says anything at all – he just sits in his office all day.'

C ◀)) CD2.54 **Listen to part three. Are these statements about the words in italic true or false?**

1 The interviewer could have used *solve* instead of 'resolve', with no change of meaning.
2 A *dialogue* occurs when people refuse to talk to each other.
3 *Typically* is an adverb related to 'typical'.
4 *Agenda* as used here means 'desk diary'.
5 *Format* as used here means 'dimensions'.
6 A *mediator* is always someone involved in one side of a dispute who tries to solve it.
7 A *debrief* happens when someone talks about their experience, in this case their experience of how a dispute was settled.
8 *Protagonist* is another word for 'mediator'.
9 *Constructive* activity is one that tries to achieve positive results.
10 If you have a *focus*, you work on a large number of things all at once.

RESOURCE BANK – Listening

JAMES WALLMAN, EDITOR OF LS:N

A ◀ CD2.62 **Listen to part one and complete the table with words that James Wallman uses.**

noun	adjective
intuition	1
simplicity	2
obviousness	3
essence	4
function	5
help	6

B **Complete these sentences with adjectives from Exercise A above, choosing the correct alternative. (The numbers in brackets refer to those in the table above.)**

1   It's not very pretty, but it really works – it's just very .... (3 or 5)

2   You can just start using it. You don't have to spend hours reading the manual – it's very .... (1 or 6)

3   It's so .... to use – just push the button. (2 or 4)

4   It's like having another pair of hands – it's so .... in the kitchen. (1 or 6)

5   When you see it, it's .... how to use it. (2 or 3)

6   Every home should have one – it's .... (4 or 6)

C ◀ CD2.63, 2.64 **Complete the answers to these questions with appropriate forms of expressions from parts two and three.**

1   Is the Tesla petrol-driven? – No, it's *e* ....

2   Is there a delay when you press the accelerator? – No, there is no *l* .... The response is *a* .... *i* ....

3   Do you have to press the brake for the car to slow down? – No, you just *r* .... your foot from the accelerator.

4   Does James Wallman like driving in cities? – No, he says it can be *b* ....

5   Have companies already invested in driverless cars? – Yes, he mentions three companies that have already *p* .... *m* .... into this.

6   Are some cars already driverless? – No, but some cars are *s* .... from being completely controlled by the driver to being partly controlled by computer.

7   What will driverless cars allow you to do? – In the future, you will be able to *h* .... *o* .... control of your car so the computer does all the driving.

D ◀ CD2.65 **Correct the mistake in each of these sentences, using forms from part four.**

1   The new iPad is really attractive – it looks well.

2   I'm writer and I need a computer for work – the iPad is ideal.

3   I read a lot – at the moment I read a novel by Paulo Coelho.

4   Every time I go to a Wi-fi café, it link me to e-mail.

5   I'm in constance contact with my friends around the world.

6   My iPad gives me access to a wealthy of information on the Internet.

7   It makes my life more connected and more funny.

RESOURCE BANK LISTENING KEY

Unit 1

A – B

1 finance director – b)
2 television business – c)
3 music channels – a)
4 children's channels – a)
5 movie channels – a)
6 chocolate-pudding business – c)

C

1 move 2 study 3 do 4 get 5 start off 6 get

D

1 b 2 c 3 a 4 a 5 b 6 c

Unit 2

A

1 chilled
2 the majority of which
3 various
4 packaging
5 major retailers
6 Tesco's, Morrison's, Waitrose
7 food-service companies
8 McDonald's

B – C

noun	adjective
health	healthy – e)
convenience	convenient – a)
sustainability	sustainable – d)
indulgence	indulgent – c)
efficiency	efficient – b)

D

She mentions 1, 2, 4, 6, 7 and 8

Unit 3

A

1 We sell products across a wide variety of categories …
2 … we sell to consumers in Germany, Japan, USA, UK and Italy
3 … we sell both through … the television and online

B

1 demonstrate 2 give 3 engage
4 develop 5 know

C

We have many successful product areas. One of our <u>strongest</u> is beauty. Beauty works so well on TV for two reasons. First of all, each beauty brand has a <u>fantastic</u> story behind it, and we can really bring life to the brand and to the <u>product presentation</u> through telling that story in a very <u>engaging</u> way.

And secondly, each product is very easy to <u>demonstrate</u>. So if it's a skincare product, like a moisturiser, we can show how to apply it, <u>how much</u> to apply in order to give the best effects. Finally, we add another layer to our <u>sales</u> presentation in that we <u>may</u> invite the expert behind that product to tell the story.

D

1 online 2 altered 3 fantastic 4 opportunity
5 item 6 image 7 range

Unit 4

A

1 False – 'It provides individuals and small businesses with a channel to market …'
2 True
3 False – 'It's not a new idea though – running an auction is almost as old as society.'
4 True
5 True
6 False – 'The technology itself also enabled a lot of other devices.'
7 False – 'I'm not sure it's – if it's strictly an invention of the last 15 years, …'

B

verb (infinitive)	noun
boom	boom
turn over	turnover
auction	auction
transfer	transfer
demand	demand
transport	transport
benefit	benefit
satisfy	satisfaction
invent	invention
revolutionise	revolution

C

c, e, a, d, b

D

1 c 2 a 3 d 4 e 5 b

Unit 5

A

1 under 2 at 3 in 4 with 5 with 6 up
7 over 8 into

B

1 True

2 False – 'It's difficult to say really what's a normal level of stress for somebody to feel at work.'

3 True

4 False – '… a high level of continued pressure can actually sometimes spill over into feelings of stress.'

5 True

6 False – '… actually if it [stress] continues without any break, then actually people sometimes tip over into feeling very stressed.'

C

1 c 2 a 3 c 4 b 5 b

D

1 deal with 2 tend 3 experience 4 manage
5 look after 6 report

Unit 6

A

The most popular events <u>remain</u> the major sports and the major events in those sports. Within sports it does vary. For example, those sports where the rules are fairly simple and <u>straightforward</u> are more popular. Thus cricket, which is a personal, um, <u>like</u> of mine, is not actually one of the most popular, because the rules are fairly <u>complicated</u>. Horse racing is <u>very successful</u>, football – soccer as it's called in many countries around the world, but football in England – is very popular.

<u>Motor</u> racing works well and then, moving onto the entertainment side, theatre, pop concerts, musicals – particularly, for <u>a number of</u> years, *Phantom of the Opera* has been very popular in New York and in London and in many other <u>cities</u> around the world where it has showed.

B

1 changed enormously 2 vastly superior 3 affected
4 reduced 5 gone for 6 holding up

C

c, e, b, a, d

D

1 False – It's 100 kilometres north-west of London.

2 False – Michael Schumacher won it.

3 True

4 True

5 False – They went by Concorde.

6 True

7 False – They flew back the same night.

Unit 7

A

1 transfer money 5 motivate their staff

2 send money 6 maintain their relationship

3 have a vision 7 make more profit

4 reach that vision

B

1 vision 2 loyal 3 Income 4 requirements
5 happy 6 expenditure 7 bankrupt

C

1 b 2 a 3 e 4 f 5 c 6 d

D

1 difficult 2 hard 3 significant 4 different
5 critical 6 sufficient

Unit 8

A

noun	adjective
clinic	clinical
reason	rational
tradition	traditional
emotion	emotional
regulation	regulatory
pharmaceuticals	pharmaceutical
consistency	consistent

B

1 regulatory environment 5 overstate the advantages

2 strict 6 consistent across

3 lead better lives 7 challenge

4 fair and balanced way

C

<u>Unfortunately</u>, because of the regulatory laws that we need to <u>follow</u>, we're not able to promote directly to patients. We can only <u>talk</u> to the doctor, because the doctor makes the decision about the medicine. So, although we'd love to use all the <u>benefits</u> and opportunities that the Internet and the new communication methods offer, we're not able to use them as much as we'd like to do. <u>Having said that</u>, we are beginning … I think many companies are beginning to look at the <u>opportunities</u> that new technologies such as the <u>iPad</u> may offer to present the data when we're face to face with the doctor, because it's a clearer and more involving way of presenting the data to the doctor than the traditional paper.

D

1 False – Someone who works in science is a *scientist*.

2 False – Another word for 'doctor' is *physician*.

3 True

4 True

5 False – *Peak sales* is the time when sales of a drug are at their highest.

6 True

Unit 9

A

1 c   2 b   3 a   4 b   5 b   6 c

B

1 commitment   2 contract   3 relationship

4 manageable   5 simple   6 flexible

C

1 True

2 False – Entrepreneurs cannot predict the future.

3 True

4 False – It can sometimes be adapted.

5 False – Lessons learned from the first version were used in planning the second version.

6 Information not given

7 False – He could not see them, because he was focused on something else.

8 True

9 Information not given

Unit 10

A – B

verb (infinitive)	noun (singular)
influence	1 influence – c)
manage	2 manager (person) – g), 3 management (thing) – d)
pioneer	4 pioneer – a)
emphasise	5 emphasis – e)
control	6 control – h)
profit	7 profit – f)
retail	8 retail – b)

C

1 philosophy   2 founder   3 genuine   4 issues

5 principles   6 aid   7 firmly   8 substantial sums

D

1 b   2 c   3 e   4 f   5 a   6 d

Unit 11

A

Our organisation, the Centre for Effective Dispute Resolution, was founded 20 years ago. Its base is in London, and its main outputs are to teach business and make business more aware of more effective ways of dealing with conflict. And our two primary areas of business are first, skills: so we've been involved in training up to 40,000 mediators around the world. And we're also involved in providing services. So we have mediators who mediate round the UK and round the world in business conflicts.

B

1 f   2 e   3 a   4 c   5 b   6 d

C

1 True

2 False – It occurs when two or more sides in a dispute communicate with each other.

3 True

4 False – It means the list of points that are discussed at a meeting, in this case a meeting to resolve a dispute.

5 False – Here it refers to the type of meeting, the participants, the place where it is held, etc.

6 False – A mediator is usually someone not actually involved in the dispute.

7 True

8 False – A protagonist is someone directly involved in the dispute.

9 True

10 False – You concentrate on one thing.

Unit 12

A

1 intuitive   2 simple   3 obvious   4 essential

5 functional   6 helpful

B

1 functional   2 intuitive   3 simple   4 helpful

5 obvious   6 essential

C

1 electric   2 lag, absolutely instant   3 release

4 boring   5 put money   6 shifting   7 hand over

D

1 The new iPad is really attractive – it looks good.

2 I'm a writer and I need a computer for work – the iPad is ideal.

3 I read a lot – at the moment I'm reading a novel by Paulo Coelho.

4 Every time I go to a Wi-fi café, it links me to e-mail.

5 I'm in constant contact with my friends around the world.

6 My iPad gives me access to a wealth of information on the Internet.

7 It makes my life more connected and more fun.

CASE STUDY WRITING TASK: MODEL ANSWER

To:	Regional Director
From:	Head, interviewing team
Subject:	Appointment of Sales and Marketing Director (Brazil, Argentina, Colombia)

Dear Claudia,

We recently interviewed three candidates for this position.

We have decided to appoint Chantal Lefevre.

I will briefly describe the candidate's strengths and explain the reasons for our decision.

Chantal has great personal qualities. She is a direct and honest person. She will have the respect of her sales teams, as she has a great sales record herself.

She is currently one of our sales representatives in Switzerland, but has worked in Spain and Portugal, so she will be able to adapt easily to Latin American markets. (She speaks Portuguese fluently. Her Spanish is only intermediate, but I'm sure she will improve quickly.)

It's not only a good salesperson that we need. Chantal has a marketing diploma. Her course included advanced statistical methods, and she will be able to work in technical areas in market research.

Please let me know when Chantal can start work at your office in São Paulo.

Looking forward to hearing from you,

Best regards,

Ricardo

(See the Writing file, Course Book page 126, for the format of e-mails.)

A **Write an e-mail reply from Claudia López.**

- Thank Ricardo for his e-mail.
- Say that Chantal Lefevre seems a very good choice for the job.
- Tell him when Chantal can start work, and say that Chantal should get in touch with you directly about arrangements for moving to São Paulo and starting work there.

End suitably.

B **Write a different e-mail reply from Claudia López.**

- You have met Chantal Lefevre at a sales conference.
- You are not sure that she is the right person for the job.
- Give two reasons (for example, she is not a leader – she may be a good salesperson, but this is not enough ...).
- However, you are willing to give her a trial period of three months to see if she can do the job.

End suitably.

Companies

CASE STUDY WRITING TASK: MODEL ANSWER

INVESTMENT PLAN

1 Objectives

To solve our current problems and enable Dino Conti to become a competitive international business, we propose an investment of $3 million.

2 Strategy and implementation

The Board of Directors has agreed the following investment plan.

Buy out our biggest competitor, Tutti Frutti Ice Cream. If you agree, I will contact California Investment Bank (CIB) as they have a lot of experience with buyouts. (I have a friend who works there.)

Increase our advertising budget. Following the buyout, we will advertise all our products in most markets under the Dino Conti brand. A big campaign will increase awareness of our products in parts of the US where we are not well-known. In Asia, we will sell under the Tutti Frutti brand, as consumers know this brand there. We agreed to drop our current advertising agency, as their campaigns have become 'tired'. Bill Kingsley will choose a new advertising agency in time for new campaigns to begin after the buyout is complete.

3 Benefits

After the buyout, we will be the biggest ice cream company in the Californian market, and number two in the US as a whole. With the buyout, we can enter the Chinese market. Tutti Frutti already manufactures in China. Its sales there are increasing by 20 per cent per year. We will move most of our production to Tutti Frutti's factories in the US and China. Their equipment is more modern than ours. This corresponds to our main objective: to become a competitive international business.

4 Cost

Buyout of Tutti Frutti Ice Cream	$2 million
Increase to advertising budget	$500,000

5 Timeline

We should try to complete the buyout within six months, by the end of March. If you agree, I will be the main contact with CIB, and will report to you regularly on progress.

Bill Kingsley will contact our existing advertising agency in order to end the contract. He will contact three other agencies in the US with offices in China and we will choose one by December 31st. New advertising campaigns in the US and China will start in spring of next year.

A Write an e-mail from Donna Martin, the director at Dino Conti who wrote the report above, to her friend Teresa Hall at CIB. (See the Writing file, Course Book page 126, for the format of e-mails.)

- It's a long time since you met. Ask her how she is.
- You want to arrange a meeting – say that the reason is too confidential to put in an e-mail.
- Suggest a day, time and place (your office or hers) – ask if this is suitable.
- You look forward to seeing her.

End suitably.

B Write a letter from Bill Kingsley to Anna Batista (account manager) at Dino Conti's advertising agency, Lomax and Associates. (See the Writing file, Course Book page 128, for the format of letters.)

- You have enjoyed working with Lomax and Associates over the years.
- Dino Conti has decided on a new strategy and it will need a new agency.
- You have decided to end your contract with Lomax at the end of this year.

End suitably.

CASE STUDY WRITING TASK: MODEL ANSWER

27 November

Dear Juan,

Below is a summary of the points we agreed at our recent meeting.

Length of contract
We agreed a period of 18 months to start with. If the contract is successful, we can arrange a longer period afterwards.

Suite/rooms
We will reserve the following numbers of rooms for your clients:
1 Platinum suite for 28 nights per year in all countries.
15 Gold Standard rooms for 65 nights per year in Europe and Asia, and 5 rooms in Latin America, but only for 50 nights, as we have fewer rooms of this type there.
18 Executive Standard rooms for 90 nights per year in all countries.

Services
Platinum: all facilities/services, bar and meals included.
Gold: all facilities/services included, except bar. Breakfast included, but all other meals and bar extra.
Executive: only breakfast included. All other meals, facilities and services extra.

Rates
Discount on advertised rates: Platinum 12%, Gold 9%, Executive 5%

Advertising
EPJS will include information about Megaluxe in all its advertising. We will pay 25% of advertising costs.

I hope you agree this is a fair summary of our negotiations. If you have any questions, please do not hesitate to contact me.

Yours sincerely,

Kristina Braun

Kristina Braun
Finance Director, Megaluxe hotels

(See the Writing file, Course Book page 128, for the format of letters.)

A Write a letter from a director of EPJS in reply to the letter from Megaluxe. This can be a reply a) to the letter that you wrote in the Writing task, or b) to the letter in the model answer above.

- You agree with the summary given by the Megaluxe director, except on one point, where you think they have made a mistake.
- Politely point out the mistake.
- If they agree to correct this mistake, you look forward to signing the contract and to working with Megaluxe.

End suitably.

NEW ATTRACTION – RECOMMENDATION FOR WINNING ENTRY

Introduction
This report outlines the key features of the new attraction that we feel should win the competition. It gives reasons why the project was selected and explains why the new attraction should be a commercial success.

Recommended project
Competitors from all continents have submitted a wide variety of projects, and the general standard is very high. It has been difficult to choose the one that we think should win, but we recommend the Barrier Reef Sea Aquarium in Queensland, Australia.

Key features
The aquarium will be in the sea itself. Visitors will walk underwater on the sea floor in glass tunnels to observe fish and sea life. They will be able to travel in a submarine with big glass windows to go further out to sea.

It will make money not only for the local community, but also for the protection of sea life and the sea environment of the Reef.

Australia is close to the booming economies of China and the rest of Asia. More and more people from that region have the money to travel abroad on holiday. People will come from all over the world to see the attraction, of course. We could market the attraction in magazines and on television all over the world.

The project's promoter says that they have plans for corporate sponsorship from multinational companies and Australian companies. (They say that many oil companies are interested, as it will help their image in relation to the environment.)

Recommendation
We should have discussions with the Aquarium attraction's project managers as soon as possible. We could ask them to come to your office in Mumbai to give a presentation and to discuss it in more detail.

A You are Karin Ali, a member of Dilip Singh's committee. Write an e-mail to John Warner, one of the Aquarium's project managers, and mention the points below.

- You represent Dilip Singh.
- You would like John Warner to come to Mumbai as soon as possible to meet Mr Singh and to present the Aquarium to him – suggest two or three possible dates.
- You look forward to meeting him.

End suitably.

B Write a reply e-mail from the Aquarium project manager to Karen Ali.

- Thank them for their e-mail.
- Thank them for their interest in your project.
- You would be happy to come to Mumbai to present it. Say which date would be suitable.
- You look forward to meeting Mr Singh and the other committee members.

End suitably.

RESOURCE BANK – Writing

Stress

CASE STUDY WRITING TASK: MODEL ANSWER

Recommendations

The management team met on July 5 to discuss ways of dealing with stress in the company. The following recommendations were made:

Anti-stress training

All staff members will go on a weekend course that gives ideas and techniques for reducing feelings of stress. All staff will go on this course together, to allow employees to discuss the things that cause stress. This will also be a good opportunity for team building. Dates to be announced.

Free gym membership

All employees will be able to go to a nearby gym to 'de-stress' at the end of the day. The agency will pay for this gym membership.

Work–life balance

This will be a new priority. We will encourage employees to go home on time at 6p.m. We will no longer expect staff to work at home in the evenings or at weekends.

Recruitment

Enough staff will be recruited to deal with the work that needs doing at any one time. If necessary, we will use more temporary staff.

Job evaluation

All jobs in the agency will be evaluated so that people are doing jobs for which they are qualified, but not over-qualified. (Some will be promoted, and no one will lose their job as a result of this!)

Positive work environment

We hope that the actions above will improve morale at the agency. We know that it's impossible to stop gossip, but we hope the gossip will be more positive in the future. There will also be a new rule: please do not interrupt colleagues when they are working, unless necessary.

A Write an e-mail from one of the people (2–4) on page 51 of the Course Book – Birgitte, Juliana or Jolanta – to a friend who works outside the agency.
(See the Writing file, Course Book page 126, for the format of e-mails.)

- Briefly outline two of the changes that will affect you.
- You think you will be less stressed as a result – give reasons.

End suitably.

B Write an e-mail from another of the people (2–4) on page 51 of the Course Book to a friend who works outside the agency.

- Briefly outline two of the changes that will affect you.
- You do *not* think you will feel less stressed as a result of the changes – give reasons.
- Tell your friend that you are looking for another job – give details.

End suitably.

Entertaining

CASE STUDY WRITING TASK: MODEL ANSWER

To:	All overseas managers
From:	Carly Forster, CEO
Subject:	This year's conference

I am writing to invite you to attend this year's conference. It will be held at the Bamboo Conference Centre, Macau, China, on July 14–16.

The location we have chosen is ideal for the conference events, and for networking and socialising. In the restaurant there will be wonderful Cantonese cuisine available. There will be a gala dinner on the Sunday evening in their private dining hall.

Macau is famous for its casinos, of course, and there are many casinos and night clubs close to the conference centre. There's also a shopping mall nearby.

This will be a great chance for us to discuss how the company can improve its products and services, to thank you for all your hard work for the year, and to give you all the chance to get to know each other better.

Looking forward to seeing you all there!

Carly Forster

(See the Writing file, Course Book page 126, for the format of e-mails.)

A   Write an e-mail from an overseas manager at GFDC to a colleague who works in another office.

- Ask if your colleague has received the e-mail from the CEO about the conference (either the one you wrote or the one above in the model answer).
- Give your opinion about the location, facilities, etc. (This can be positive or negative.) Give your reasons.
- Either a) say you will be there, or b) say you will not be there. Give your reasons.

End suitably.

B   A member of GFDC's marketing department writes a notice about the conference for the noticeboard in each department of the company. (The notice can relate to the conference location that you wrote about in the Writing task in the Course Book, or to another one.) (See the Writing file, Course Book page 131, for the format of notices.)

CASE STUDY WRITING TASK: MODEL ANSWER

To:	Susan Woo
From:	Kiyoshi Nagano
Subject:	Overseas expansion

Dear Ms Woo,

I'm writing from Taka Shimizu, a Japanese cycle company that is well-known in Japan and the US. We want to expand in Europe and South East Asia in order to become a truly global company. We also intend to train the workers that we recruit in our own training school. As part of this plan, we are looking for a new location abroad to build a new factory for bicycles. We have looked at several countries in Europe and Asia, and we are particularly interested in your country.

I would like to arrange a meeting with you so that we can discuss the proposal further. May I suggest one of the following dates: 30th September, 5th or 8th October.

I look forward to hearing from you,

Best regards,

Kiyoshi Nagano

(See the Writing file, Course Book page 126, for the format of e-mails.)

A   Write a short report briefly giving the reasons for choosing the country that you selected in the Case study. Also, say why you selected it, rather than a location in one of the other possible countries. (See the Writing file, Course Book page 129, for the format of reports.)

B   Write an e-mail from Susan Woo to Kiyoshi Nagano. (See the Case study writing task model answer above.)

- You have received his e-mail.
- Your country is very keen to work with overseas investors on projects like his.
- Accept one of the dates that he suggests for the meeting.
- Say that you look forward to meeting him.

End suitably.

CASE STUDY WRITING TASK: MODEL ANSWER

To:	CEO
From:	Marketing Director

At a meeting on 15 May, we discussed the changes we want to make when relaunching the Wincote XWS. They are as follows:

- **Product:** We need to change the material to make it cooler to wear when the lining is removed. We should use brighter colours, and we should improve the zip and the hood.

- **Price:** With the improvements above, the current price of $110 will be even more competitive, for example in comparison with Tundra, so I suggest that we do not change the price.

- **Promotion:** The slogan 'A jacket for all seasons' is good, but the advertising should be clearer. We should show not only the outside of the jacket, of course, but we should also show technical diagrams of the material used in the jacket, and of the lining.

- **Place:** There have been complaints about late delivery, so for orders on the Internet and by mail order, we must only work with reliable suppliers. We should keep using our current shop retailers, but we should also use supermarkets to sell the Wincote XWS.

I am sure that the XWS will be a successful product with these changes.

Steve Burton

A Write a sales leaflet for the new Wincote XWS jacket, based on the decisions you made in the Case study, or on the information in the model answer above.
(See the Writing file, Course Book page 131, for the format of sales leaflets.)

B The Marketing Director writes a notice for the noticeboard in the sales department at Wincote about Ayzee, a mail order company. Include the points below in the notice.
(See the Writing file, Course Book page 131, for the format of notices.)

- There have been many complaints from customers about Ayzee, especially about late delivery.
- We have decided to stop supplying Ayzee immediately. Do not accept any more orders from them.
- If there are any questions, contact the Marketing Director.

Planning

CASE STUDY WRITING TASK: MODEL ANSWER

Dear Brad,

I am writing to you as Editor of EPMC's exciting new health-and-fitness magazine. It's called *Healthy!* and it will give advice on health and fitness to people aged between 20 and 40. The first issue of the magazine will come out in September. (There will also be a website with the same articles, plus other useful information.)

In each issue, there will be an interview with a famous person, who will give readers their advice about health and fitness. You are well-known for your interest in this area. We think you would be the perfect choice for our first issue. (Of course, you do not have to provide diet and fitness plans yourself – we will provide these for you to approve.)

I am writing to ask if we can interview you in Los Angeles on a date that is convenient for you.

Yours sincerely,

Janet Peabody

Janet Peabody
Editor, *Healthy!*

(See the Writing file, Course Book page 128, for the format of letters.)

A You are the agent of the famous person that you wrote to in the Writing task. (Or you can choose to be Brad's agent – see the model answer above.) Write a letter replying to the magazine editor.

- Introduce yourself as the person's agent.
- Choose one of the following options:
  a) Agree to the magazine editor's request for an interview and suggest a date, time and location.
  b) Refuse the magazine editor's request and give a reason. (Invent one.)
  c) Say that your client needs more information before they can make a decision.

End suitably.

B Write an Internet advertisement for the magazine to be used just before its launch. Give information about:

- what the magazine and website contain
- the celebrity feature in the first issue (who it is, an example of their advice, etc.)
- how much a 12-month subscription costs
- a promotional offer, for example body lotions and eau de cologne, for those who subscribe to the magazine or the website within seven days

Recommendations

Following recent discussions about staff problems at ACSA, I would like to make these recommendations:

Salary / bonuses

Some consultants have complained that the current system is unfair, because the end-of-year bonus is decided by their manager. I recommend that the end-of-year bonus is based on the value of properties sold by the consultant: 0.2 per cent of the value of the properties he or she has sold. In this way, each consultant will be more motivated as they will know exactly the bonus that they will receive at the end of each year. This will cost more per consultant than the current system, but total costs will be lower – see the next section.

Redundancy

I recommend that we make Ahmed redundant. Last year, only 11 per cent of total sales were made by him – he should make more sales after two years here. He is not co-operative, he is not a team player, he doesn't come to many meetings and he hasn't added any names to the client database.

Database

All consultants must contribute to the client database. Each consultant must add at least 20 new possible clients per year.

Sales meetings

All consultants must attend the monthly sales meetings. Excuses will not be accepted. If a consultant does not come to two meetings in a row, he/she should be fired.

Teamwork

We will send all consultants on two team-building courses a year to improve consultants' teamwork and social skills. Consultants must go on these courses.

A Write an e-mail from one of the six consultants at ACSA to a friend who works in another company. This e-mail is in relation to a) the recommendations that you made in the Writing task, or b) those in the model answer above.

- Briefly give your opinion about each recommendation.
- Say how the recommendations will affect your work.
- Say if you want to continue to work at ACSA, or to leave.

End suitably.

B The HR director at ACSA writes a notice for the noticeboard about the next team-building course the consultants must go on. Include the points below in the notice.

- name of the course and name of the training organisation
- where the course will be held
- dates
- key benefits that consultants will get from the course

CASE STUDY WRITING TASK: MODEL ANSWER

Dear Shareholders,

The multinational drinks group Universal Cola Corporation has made an offer to purchase the company. Our reasons for not accepting their offer are as follows:

- If H&C is bought by UCC, we will lose our independence and our separate identity, despite all the advantages that UCC can offer (in production, selling, etc.).

- Our 'green' image would suffer. This image is one of our biggest assets and will become more and more important in the future.

- H&C would lose many customers when they discover that a large multinational has bought it. Many people feel better about buying from a family firm rather than from a big multinational.

- We do not know how many H&C employees and managers UCC would keep. (They have made some promises, but we have seen what has happened with promises like these in the past with other takeovers.)

- People who work at H&C like the family atmosphere and do not want it to change. They would feel less motivated under UCC's management.

- We have had an offer from another small, privately-owned company, FTC. FTC has the same values and principles (green production, etc.) as H&C. We could merge as equal partners. We must consider this offer instead.

Yours sincerely,

Beatrice Van Etten

Beatrice Van Etten, CEO

(See the Writing file, Course Book page 128, for the format of letters.)

A Universal Cola Corporation succeeds in buying Herman & Corrie. A manager at H&C writes an e-mail to a friend working in another company.

- Explain what has happened.
- You don't know if you will be made redundant.
- You will have an interview with someone from the HR department this afternoon.
- You will know by the end of next week if you will keep your job or not.
- You are not sure if you want to stay at H&C anyway.
- Say what you might do instead.
- You will let your friend know what happens.

End suitably.

George Marshall Awards

Product Report

Introduction

As a member of the Selection Committee, I have now seen all the entries for this year's award. As always, we are looking for innovation and creativity in developing, marketing and launching a new product. We are looking for products with lasting benefits. They should also be environmentally friendly.

Product description – Music keyboard with lighted keys

I was very impressed when this product was presented. It's an electronic keyboard that has keys that light up when tunes are played. The lights help you learn quickly which finger goes with which key. The keyboard plays 200 songs automatically, but you can also play tunes on your own. There are two speakers built into the keyboard. The planned price is US$280.

Marketing

The presenters said they will be using short adverts on television, especially during children's programmes. They will also be advertising in specialist music magazines and on the Internet, with adverts on music-related sites.

On the Internet, they have a very original approach. The adverts allow you to use a demonstration version of the product, where you press the keys on your computer keyboard and keys light up in the advert on the computer screen, and a tune comes out of your computer speakers. This will certainly make users want to buy the real product!

Environment

The presenters said that the product contains no dangerous chemicals and can be recycled safely.

Conclusion

This product will be of great benefit to children and adults learning keyboard instruments. It has a very good chance of winning this year's award.

(See the Writing file, Course Book page 129, for the format of reports.)

A The chair of the George Marshall Awards selection committee writes a letter to the Chief Executive of each company competing for this year's award. (See the Writing file, Course Book page 128, for the format of letters.)

- Introduce yourself.
- Invite the Chief Executive to the Best New Products Awards Ceremony in Melbourne where the winner will be announced. (Give a date, time and place.)
- They can bring up to three colleagues who have been involved with the product that is competing for the award.
- You look forward to seeing them at the ceremony.

End suitably.

Pearson Education Limited
Edinburgh Gate
Harlow
Essex CM20 2JE
England
and Associated Companies throughout the world.

www.pearsonelt.com
www.market-leader.net

First published 2001

Third edition 2012

ISBN: 978-1-4082-7922-9

Set in MetaPlus 9.5/12pt

Printed and bound by Neografia in Slovakia

Acknowledgements
We are grateful to the following for permission to reproduce copyright material:

Text
Extract 1. adapted from "Working abroad", *The Financial Times*, 24/10/2010 (Rigby, R.), copyright (c) Rhymer Rigby; Extract 5. adapted from "The careerist: Beating stress", *The Financial Times*, 10/01/2010 (Rigby, R.), copyright (c) Rhymer Rigby; Extract 7. adapted from "Rules of the game have been rewritten", *The Financial Times*, 08/02/2011 (Johnson, L.), copyright (c) Luke Johnson; Extract 9. adapted from "Business traveller: Using time efficiently", *The Financial Times*, 01/06/2010 (Rigby, R.), copyright (c) Rhymer Rigby; Extract 12. adapted from "Hidden beauty of the 'uglies'", *The Financial Times*, 17/05/2007 (Murray, S.), copyright (c) Sarah Murray

The Financial Times
Extract 3. adapted from "What to do at closing time", *The Financial Times*, 10/01/2011 (Southon, M.), copyright (c) The Financial Times Ltd; Extract 5. adapted from "Stress-related absence rises", *The Financial Times*, 25/10/2010 (Groom, B.), copyright (c) The Financial Times Ltd; Extract 6. adapted from "Bribery law threat to business hospitality", *The Financial Times*, 17/01/2011 (Sherwood, B.), copyright (c) The Financial Times Ltd; Extract 7. adapted from "Web start-ups buy more TV airtime", *The Financial Times*, 22/12/2010 (Bradshaw, T.), copyright (c) The Financial Times Ltd; Extract 8. adapted from "Nestlé defector stirs up tea market", *The Financial Times*, 12/01/2011 (Simonian, H.), copyright (c) The Financial Times Ltd; Extract 10. adapted from "Rise in level of job satisfaction", *The Financial Times*, 05/05/2009 (Groom, B.), copyright (c) The Financial Times Ltd; Extract 12. adapted from "GSK looks to academia for new drugs", *The Financial Times*, 14/02/2011 (Jack, A.), copyright (c) The Financial Times Ltd

In some instances we have been unable to trace the owners of copyright material, and we would appreciate any information that would enable us to do so.

Project managed by Chris Hartley